Understanding China

Understanding China

There is Reason for the Difference

Gary Moreau

This book is dedicated to the amazing people of China,
who have taught me more about myself than
I could ever teach them about anything.
And to my daughters, Leah and Ava,
who, more than they will ever know, define who I am.

FOREWORD

Many political and business pundits have predicted that this will be the China Century in the same way that the last century was the American Century. Being neither a pundit on much of anything nor a political handicapper, I offer no opinion on that prophecy.

However the historians ultimately label the coming century, nonetheless, the Chinese are certain to have a major role in the drama. China is already the number one or two economy in the world, depending on how you measure it. They are a growing military power and home to one-fifth of the world's population.

The rise of China has been dramatic and significant enough to cause the United States, the country behind the American Century, to "pivot to Asia." Both Hong Kong and Macau, former British and Portuguese colonies, respectively, were returned to its control in the last two decades, and China has increasingly engaged its neighbors in the many historical disputes over control of the South China Sea, through which one-third of the world's ocean freight currently passes.

Some of that freight is of low monetary and strategic value—toys, apparel, and consumer electronics produced by China's factory to the world, which has dominated the low end of the global supply chain for the last two decades, but which is moving quickly up that supply chain, a move that will have profound implications for global trade in the coming century. Much of the shipping that moves through the South China Sea, however, is energy and raw materials destined for countries in Southeast Asia other than China. According to globalsecurity.org, tanker traffic in the South

China Sea is three times that of the Suez Canal and well over five times that of the Panama Canal.

I have lived and worked in Beijing, China, since August 2007. And being an old but ardent student of life and people, I have observed a great deal about China and the Chinese and the growing impact of both on the rest of the world.

I am an American, now sixty years old, who came not as a diplomat or academic sinologist, but because I was in need of a job, and a US multinational company offered me a good one if I would accept relocation to Beijing. Until recently, I managed a company of more than 450 people, and I was the only foreigner in my company, as the Chinese refer to us.

I write primarily for my daughters. I want to leave them some permanent record of who I am and how I think—the person I was. I suppose, by definition, that means I'm attempting to leave them my legacy. What I really want, however, is for them to simply know me.

Which leads to the one irrefutable and overriding message I can convey about my experience in China. The Chinese have taught me more about myself than I could ever teach them about anything. That, ultimately, is their great charm and their great influence. You can't come here without developing a clearer understanding—good or bad—of the person you really are.

With time and patience I believe my extended time here in China has allowed me to figure a few things out. Many continue to befuddle me. But in almost all cases, I've at least learned which questions to ask.

The Chinese really are different. Their culture, the sum total of their beliefs and behaviors, is truly and fundamentally different from Western culture. It's obvious the minute you step off the plane, an observation that often turns to terror when you take your first hair-raising taxi ride to your hotel.

Many excellent books have been written that outline those cultural differences with great clarity and in great detail. Should you ever decide to visit China, even for a holiday, I strongly suggest you read one of them so you know what to expect.

This book is not one of them.

Before coming to China, I read many books about Chinese business etiquette and Chinese customs. They were helpful in preparing me for what I was to encounter. After a few months, however, I became frustrated at my inability to understand the why behind the what. I understood the custom or the behavior, but I didn't understand why it was what it was. That made the difference from my own customs often feel like irritations or frustrations. Something just didn't feel right. There was less joy to the experience than I felt there should have been in such an exotic and high-energy environment.

Even more important to my work as a businessman, I felt lost. I could avoid offending my colleagues or my customers, but I could not influence their behavior. And in the end, isn't that what business is all about—influencing behavior?

Eventually I realized that it was not enough to understand the differences between Chinese and Western culture. That merely allowed me to react to the Chinese in much the same way that a leaf floating down a fast-moving river reacts to the currents and the eddies.

To truly enjoy China and to know success in its commercial world, I had to learn to anticipate. And that, I knew, meant I had to understand the why behind the what. I had to understand not just how our cultures differed, but why they differed. What gave rise to these different beliefs and behaviors?

Only then could I find comfort in the chaos. Only then could I overlook the behaviors so many Westerners find offensive or uncivil. Only then could I be effective in my work. Only then would I really know China.

I looked far and wide to find books that could help me unravel this mystery. But while I found hundreds of insightful histories, how-to's, and anecdotes of personal experience, I found no book that addressed the fundamental question of why all these other books are even relevant or came to be. I found nothing that probed the question of why—why is Chinese culture so different from the culture of the West?

That gave rise to the idea for this book. It has been penned over the long journey of my personal discovery. To share, of course. But also to help me along the journey. I have a passion for writing, but more than anything else I have an obsession with thinking. And that is why I write. Writing is merely the symbolic expression of thought. And since the power of the alphabet will never equal the power of the mind, writing forces clarity of thought. It disciplines the mind.

So, who should read this book? Certainly anyone who has a diplomatic or commercial interest in China. Even if it merely validates what you already know, there is value in validation, and if you really do understand the insights forthcoming, you will recognize that value without hesitation.

What if you are merely visiting China on holiday or are part of a tour? Whether you read this book or not will depend on whether or not you want to enjoy the trip. Would you prefer to be enlightened or frustrated? Both come to Westerners in abundance when they visit China for the first time.

The real reason to read this book, however, is the point I made above. No single experience in my six decades of life has taught me more about myself than my time in China. It is an education, I say with confidence, I would not have received if fate—and the need for a job—had not brought me here to the Middle Kingdom.

The book is divided into several parts. The first is fundamental to the others. It is the core exploration of the why behind the what. Why have China and Chinese culture evolved in a way so distinct from that of the West?

The second relates more directly to the business climate within which foreign companies operate here. No X's and O's, however. I will spare you the normal jargon, business analytics, and dry strategic language of most business literature. I will look strictly through a personal lens, one full of a passion for understanding, a lot of irony, and hopefully a little humor. Which is why, I believe, this section will also interest those who have no interest in commerce or business.

The third section is an exploration of what it means to live in China. I have had the chance to see China during an amazing time in its long history from the ground level. I have worn its dirt on my hands, its soot in my eyes. I have seen the gleaming cities and the impoverished countryside. I have driven on its highways of insanity and ridden on its overcrowded buses and trains. Some of what I have seen is sad, some is downright funny, but it is all exhilarating and inspiring.

Lastly, I will look at the ins and outs of China's politics and what I believe to be its real geopolitical ambitions. I will make every attempt not to repeat what you've heard on the evening news or the Sunday morning talk shows. Most of that I disagree with anyway. Instead, I will attempt to give you a broader, more personal perspective.

Whatever your reason for picking up this book, and even if you had none originally, I strongly suggest you read all sections. You will ultimately see that each reinforces the other. Because that's the way it is in China. There is no beginning and no end. Everything exists in relation to everything else. Business, family, marriage, career are all intertwined. Not intermingled per se, but coexisting, hopefully, in harmonious balance.

To understand what I mean by that, however, you'll have to read the rest of the book.

Enjoy the journey!
Gary Moreau

CHAPTER 1

THE LOGIC BEHIND CULTURE

Culture is the collective behaviors and beliefs that define a common group of people, be they united by geography, shared history, ethnicity, or simple choice. But why are those behaviors and beliefs common? Why do people share them? And why do they differ between cultures?

After a lot of thought. I ultimately concluded that it all comes down to what psychologists call "precognitive conclusion," or what pollsters call "pre-biased conclusion." Essentially, we interpret reality as we expect it to be. Or, as is often the case, we interpret reality as we allow ourselves to.

It's a matter of efficiency. Scientists have shown that our brains process as little as one-billionth of the data that our senses make available. We process only enough data to reach a probable conclusion, and then we move on. That threshold is different for each of us, but we all do it. Otherwise we would never get anything done. We'd spend all our time processing and no time acting on our conclusions.

But what does this have to do with culture?

If culture is a common collection of behaviors and beliefs, then we must ask what creates that commonality. Is it genetic? Is it taught? And how is it that while cultures evolve, there is a consistency over time that survives despite the rapid and disruptive change that occurs as history unfolds?

If we interpret reality as we expect it to be, those expectations are ultimately based on past experience. We see what we expect to see because that is what happened before in similar circumstances. If history doesn't repeat itself, as the old saying goes, it certainly influences our expectations of the future, whether a decade out or by lunch today.

We might say, therefore, that expectations define culture. But that would only be symptomatically true. That would be like saying that breathing defines life.

What ultimately defines culture is the way in which we interpret reality.

Westerners are inclined to believe that interpreting reality is an oxymoron. There is only one reality, and our quest is not to interpret it but to decipher it.

That, however, is the great Western myth. And precognitive conclusion is the culprit. While Western science is considered objective and conclusive, the truth is that a great many scientific discoveries are ultimately proven to be wrong.

Science is not a body of knowledge. It is a method for interpreting reality. And while it is perhaps the best method for minimizing the potentially harmful impact of precognitive conclusion, it can never eliminate it.

In general, precognitive conclusion is a good thing. It makes us much more efficient in day-to-day living, and it even enables magicians to entertain us with their sleight of hand (and authors to entertain us with surprise endings). Without it we'd never get out of bed in the morning.

But it has one important vulnerability. We don't always reach the right conclusion. We sometimes make snap judgments or rely on the wrong data, and that can get us into trouble. In the extreme, pre-biased conclusion can lead to racism and bigotry, sexism, and all kinds of other inappropriate behavior.

———

Another word for how we interpret reality is reason, or logic. The philosophical definition of reason, according to *Webster's College Dictionary* (Random House, 1991) is, "The faculty or power of acquiring intellectual knowledge…"

There are two primary forms of reason—deductive reasoning, in which our logic moves from left to right, starting with cause and finishing with effect—and inductive reasoning, in which our logic moves from right to left, starting with effect or result and speculating backward to explain the cause.

And these two forms of reasoning, in the end, explain the difference between Western and Chinese culture. The Chinese world view—their collective body of expectations—is built on a foundation of inductive reason, whereas the Western world view is built on a foundation of deductive reason.

It is the difference between the circle, the best physical representation of the Chinese world view, and the straight line, the defining geometry of Western religion, Western science, and ultimately, Western culture.

In short, we as Westerners and the Chinese confuse and exasperate each other because we interpret reality through a completely different lens, resulting in behaviors that either appear completely random or boringly predictable, but either way, exasperatingly irrational.

There are, however, many layers between reason or world view and behavior. It is those layers—the path to the middle from opposite directions—that we must explore in an effort to eliminate the misunderstanding and irritation that often follow.

CHAPTER 2

THE LINEAR WEST

It is an oversimplification, of course, to attribute an entire culture to one individual. When it comes to Western culture, however, I think Aristotle comes pretty close to being the architect of it all, consciously or not.

Aristotle was an ancient Greek philosopher (c. 384 BCE–c. 322 BCE) who, together with Socrates and Plato, laid much of the groundwork for western philosophy. In his case, however, the main focus of much of his philosophy was the systematic concept of logic that he pursued in an effort to define a universal process of reasoning that would support the explanation of every element of reality.

In essence, Aristotle gave us deductive logic. A deduction, as he defined it, was a reasonable argument that "when certain things are laid down, something else follows out of necessity in virtue of their being so." This theory of deduction is what philosophers now call a syllogism: a deductively logical argument.

The implications of deductive logic are enormous and far-reaching. It suggests, for example, that for every cause there is an effect that is consistent and thus predictable. The process of determining that relationship is what is now commonly referred to as the scientific method.

Science, contrary to popular perception, is not a body of knowledge per se. It is nothing more or less than a process for interpreting reality. Which is precisely why new "scientific" discoveries often obsolete previously documented science.

Albert Einstein himself, in what he later referred to as the biggest blunder of his career, advocated that the size of the universe is fixed and static.

The static universe, in fact, was also known as Einstein's universe due to his faith in the scientific theory behind it.

Alas, Edwin Hubble's discovery that the color of heavenly bodies changes as they move away from us, now known as the red shift, "proved" that the universe was, indeed, expanding, and Einstein, along with most prominent scientists, abandoned the static universe theory.

As late as the latter half of the twentieth century, the medical profession generally believed that peptic ulcers were caused by the stress of modern life and prescribed antacids and lifestyle modification to address them. In the 1980s, however, Barry Marshal, who would ultimately win the Nobel Prize, discovered that the bacterium *H. pylori* was the true root cause of peptic ulcer disease.

Since 1950, twenty-one new elements have been discovered and added to the periodic table: five from the year 2000 alone. In 2006 the International Astronomical Union declassified Pluto as a planet. Scientists discover approximately 18,000 new species of plants and animals *every* year, and they estimate that there are another five million yet to be discovered.

Dark meat chicken, margarine, and peanut butter are no longer considered taboo by most nutritionists. Sushi, granola, and bran muffins, on the other hand, once considered healthy by most Americans, are now considered unhealthy or potentially unsafe by most dietary experts.

While some of these discoveries may reflect an evolution in thinking rather than a new scientific discovery, they do reinforce the idea that science is not a fixed body of either knowledge or truth. It is no more nor less than a protocol—a deductive one ideally suited to Western culture—for interpreting reality. Which is exactly why Richard Smith, former editor of the *British Medical Journal*, infamously noted that, "Most scientific studies are wrong…"

"Wrong," however, may be the wrong conclusion. I prefer "incomplete." And I will use the horrendously divisive issue of evolution versus creationism or intelligent design to explain my point.

Georges Seurat (1859–1891) was a French post-impressionist painter and draftsman. He is famous for his development of the painting techniques known as chromo-luminarism or pointillism, using dots of multicolored paint rather than physically blending the colors on the canvas. Viewed collectively, the eye blends the colors optically, and a picture emerges.

Seurat's most famous work was *A Sunday Afternoon on the Island of La Grande Jatte,* a beautiful picture that every eye can easily understand largely because of the enormous number of dots of paint employed. It took him two years to paint it.

If you were to remove half of the dots of pigment, however, depending on how the remaining dots were juxtaposed, you would undoubtedly experience far more difficulty in comprehending the picture and its representation. You would be forced to conjecture.

Which is how I feel about the evolution versus creationism argument. Both leave too many unanswered questions for my inquisitive mind. While I believe evolution is a reality, it has never been replicated in the laboratory, and I cannot bring myself to look into the eyes of a child or enjoy the splendor of a mountaintop vista and accept in my heart that it all "just happened."

My conclusion, therefore, is not that either side is right or wrong, but that we have not uncovered all the pigments of color yet. We are forced to conjecture the real painting, and as a result, there is naturally room for differences of opinion, often defined in the context of other religious, scientific, or social beliefs.

Such an interpretation, however, requires a certain comfort with ambiguity, something that deductive thinkers often have difficulty with. After all, if there is a cause to every effect, and an effect flows from every cause, ambiguity is, by definition, ignorance, and who wants that?

The Chinese, on the other hand, are perfectly at home with ambiguity. In some ways ambiguity is the ultimate piety of inductive reasoning. Taoism, after all, teaches that reality, or The Way, is much too complex for any human to ever understand, science or not.

Perhaps that is why I have yet to hear any two Chinese even discussing the origin of life. I have yet to see any talk show or documentary devoted to it. No magazine to my knowledge has ever investigated it, and few Chinese, I suspect, ever give it a thought.

It is a non-argument to the inductive thinker. We are where we are. What matter does it make how we got here? We live in the present, and since the present and past, as are the living and dead, are simply different dimensions of a reality we can't comprehend, the past and present aren't really distinct anyway. Why treat them so?

———

But reality is the stuff of life, so the deductive process of interpretation gives the Western people who accept it a certain lens through which they interpret the world. Interpretation, of course, subsequently defines expectation, and it is expectation that drives much of human behavior, the DNA of culture.

These behaviors inevitably exhibit certain common characteristics that ultimately define the most critical parts of Western culture. I'll explore just a few of them here.

Predictability

The whole premise of the linear connection of cause and effect that is at the heart of the scientific method precludes randomness and brings order to chaos. Outcomes, once the root cause has been determined, are universally consistent. This, of course, leads to a high level of predictability.

Conversely, Westerners are often uncomfortable with unpredictability. We like to know what to expect. While uncertainty can bring us excitement, such as the contents of a wrapped gift, we generally prefer to know what lies around the next corner. We prefer to know that if we do A, the result will be B.

This explains why the US insurance industry took in more than $1.1 trillion in premiums in 2014, an amount many times the amount of money earned by the Chinese insurance industry as recently as ten years ago, when it took in less than $34 billion. Simply put, the Chinese have far more tolerance for risk.

Risk management, the business "science" of optimizing predictability, now is on the agenda of every board of directors in America, and entire departments of highly paid professionals now fill their days developing risk management strategies and assessing often intangible and often undefinable risks that were once considered a reality of doing business and the collective responsibility of the entire organization.

Universal Explainability

One of the basic premises of the scientific method is that everything can be explained. We may not have discovered the explanation, but there is a universal assumption that an explanation exists.

I see this personified in many forms. When tourists first arrive in China, they are often flabbergasted if they don't get the answers they are looking for from service personnel in the prompt fashion they have come to expect. Part of the reason is bureaucratic perplexity and the general lack of a modern data system that a modern American hotel may employ, for example.

However, I'm convinced that part of the reason is that the Chinese often fail to see the relevance of the question. As inductive thinkers they simply don't see the need to know or the rationale for explaining something you won't be able to change anyway. Why waste your time?

As a result, the Chinese are seldom as curious as Americans or other Westerners. I have often asked my colleagues what they think a new construction site might be along a road we both take to work, only to be told they had not noticed any new construction site.

This can initially be a challenge in the workplace. If a machine operator sees a pool of oil on the floor, it is not enough for him to clean it up, which he will do diligently. He must also find out where it came from and take steps to both assess the immediate impact and to prevent it from happening again. However, these are often taught behaviors.

Digital Morality

Cause and effect is a linear notion. Deductive logic moves from left to right in a linear pattern, which in turn leads to linear notions of morality. There is right and there is wrong, and they cannot occupy the same place on the deductive line of morality. Morality, as a result, is digital, not relative.

Many Chinese struggle with this concept, not because of any lack of spiritual values but because they are inductive and holistic in their world view. Morals are incremental. Relationships and the obligation that flows from them, however, are holistic and the cornerstone of Chinese culture. To betray one's family, for whatever reason, is holistically immoral, while to steal a loaf of bread is incrementally immoral.

To the deductive Westerner wrong is wrong for the simple reason that in a linear world view, right and wrong cannot occupy the same space. Which is why two wrongs never make a right.

Two, however, is incremental. One. Two. To betray a family member or friend, however, is holistic and has potential repercussions for the extended family, past and present.

The Chinese grasp the notion of digital morality and will generally accept and abide by it in the multinational workplace. Your risk, as a foreign business, is not that they won't understand, but that they will consider it naïve and uninformed and will override it not for personal gain but to protect you and the company.

Personal Values

Because we reason from left to right, Westerners put great stock in individual values: the right to free expression, the equality of all people, and the right to personal freedoms. These values are the bedrock of our society. Without them, we believe, civil society cannot exist.

As I will discuss later, however, these are individual, incremental, and isolated concepts. What good is free expression if no one is listening? What good is paper equality if that is not what happens in the streets each day?

What good is personal freedom if its boundaries are enforced so tightly that there is little room for judgment and common sense?

As one highly educated Chinese friend noted, "I live in the freest country in the world. I can ignore traffic signals. I can go up the exit ramp if there are too many cars trying to enter the highway. I can do whatever I want to do whenever I want to do it so long as I don't threaten the peace and security of the state. What a small price to pay for such freedom."

What would your local police do if you tried to enter the highway by going up the exit ramp? What would they do if there was an accident on a divided highway and you turned around and drove back to the previous exit on the wrong side of the median? What would they do if you stood by the side of the road selling the fish you had just cost without either a fishing license or the right to sell your catch? (In China, and I have seen it with my own eyes, they might well buy the fish and take it home for dinner.)

The Love of Process

Process and cause and effect go hand in hand, particularly in business. Western corporations spend massive amounts of time and effort codifying and enforcing processes in an effort to achieve a desired result with consistency and certainty. At times, as any Western corporate worker can attest, these processes take on a life of their own, rising to the level of near-spirituality.

The Chinese put little stock in process. It is a linear concept that only wastes time and money since the process itself is inevitably designed for the extremes, and extremes are, by definition, extreme. Most of the time the business process, if you will, is a waste of time, money, and flexibility. Which is exactly why American corporations are spending billions of dollars each year attempting to dismantle the costly and inflexible processes that their companies—in the name of progress and risk management— have developed and installed over the years.

Few companies are successful. Once a process is in place, there are vested interests involved. Someone's livelihood undoubtedly depends on the continuation, fruitful or not, of that process.

11

This is one of the reasons that Chinese companies are generally so much quicker and faster than their Western counterparts. One example follows.

A few years back my company had to rebuild—from the ground up—a very expensive and complicated piece of infrastructure that was in no way proprietary in its technology. It's a project that normally takes at least two to three months and costs millions of dollars, and we dutifully—due to our love of process—solicited quotes and project plans from a number of Chinese and foreign companies. Not surprisingly, the foreign companies, including those with offices in China, were twice as expensive and would take twice as long.

We were familiar with one of the Chinese companies and knew they had done this same work many times per year all over China. And we convinced our corporate engineers, given the cost and the lead time, to give them a try.

When they showed up to begin the job, our corporate engineers, of course, were on hand. And the first question they asked was, "Where is your equipment?" They were essentially carrying crowbars and simple saws and other equipment. The demolition and lifting, the foreman explained, would be done by hand.

The American engineer in charge of the project—an experienced, capable, and nice guy, I might add—then asked to see the timeline and milestones for the project.

"What timeline?"

"The one with the key milestones of the projects and the dates you will achieve them. We need to monitor progress so we know when we have to make adjustments to the work plan. Every day this goes beyond schedule puts us way over budget."

"Oh, we don't need that. It's a waste of time. We do this every day. My men know what to do and when to do it."

After a bit of continued tussle, during which the contractor made it clear he had no intention of complying, considering it a waste of time and money, the American project leader relented. "OK, but I have seven milestones that I know are critical to the projects, and at the very least I need a completion date for each one."

To which the Chinese supervisor sighed, took the sheet of paper with the list of the seven milestones, took a pencil from behind his ear, put the start date at the top of the page, the promised completion date at the bottom, divided the difference by seven, and handed the dated paper back to the project engineer.

In the end, the contractor did an excellent job, finished several days early and well under budget, at a fraction of what the foreign contractors had quoted.

The Win-Win Negotiation

If cause and effect run along a linear path, multiple paths may be parallel. In essence, they operate independently, creating the opportunity for the most Western of all concepts—the win-win. Negotiators are taught that this is the sweet spot of any negotiation and the surest path to a productive and successful negotiation.

The concept requires a firm belief in both cause and effect and digital morality. These are the root elements of what Westerners call fairness: the ideal that by looking out for the best interests of the other party, you will promote your own.

It's a fantasy. The win-win negotiation is really a strategy whereby you convince your adversary that he is winning when, in fact, you're fleecing him for all you can get.

And sometimes it works. Words are mere symbols designed to foster more efficient communication. They are totally artificial and in the end not particularly efficient. If, however, you learn how to manipulate them in a certain way, you can convince people of things that simply aren't true—like you're virtually saving their life by taking $300 for a vitamin supplement, even though there is no hard evidence of its effectiveness.

A wise old lawyer once told me that the best settlement is the one that everyone is unhappy with. I agree with that. But that's hardly an issue of fairness. That's a tapestry of largely negative results and emotions such as fear that we believe is the best we're going to get, or the most we're willing to risk losing by trying for more.

Sigmund Freud essentially said that all life is personal. We are the hero in all of our dreams and the villain in all of our nightmares. And I believe he was right.

But it is essentially an inductive view. If we view our lives linearly, as Western culture teaches us, we cannot find fairness along the same path. Like truth and falsity, two of us cannot occupy the same spot along a single line of fairness. The best we can hope for is to reach a relatively comparable point along our individual paths. Even that, however, is pretty rare.

The key to overcoming the inevitable disparity, as every inductive thinker will tell you, is obligation. It is the sense of relationship and obligation that bridges the individuality that Freud refers to. It doesn't eliminate the inequity, but it does make it irrelevant. Which, in the end, is the same thing.

Universal Obligation

While Westerners pay special attention to friends and family, our deductively linear-based codes of civility and morality are universal in their application. We naturally stand in line even if we know nothing about the people who precede us. We hold the door for perfect strangers and routinely make room for a car attempting to enter a crowded street.

As the logic of deductive reasoning influences our collective behavior, so too does it define our culture. There is, of course, no single Western culture. There are numerous regional and ethnic cultures that collectively define the Western world. Without exception, however, the behaviors that define them are the result of linear reasoning—the supremacy of cause and effect.

CHAPTER 3

THE CIRCULAR EAST

If Aristotle was ultimately the father of Western culture, Chinese culture is built on a tapestry of behaviors influenced by Taoism, Confucianism, and Chinese folk religion. All, however, share one common trait. They are all inductive in their foundational reasoning.

Confucius, a Chinese philosopher, educator, political figure, and founder of the Ru School of Chinese thought, lived about 200 years before Aristotle (551 BC–479 BC). While compiled by his disciples, not Confucius himself, the most reliable information about his life is found in the *Analects*, followed by the *Zuozhuan*, written long after his death, and a narrative history called the *Mengzi*, a compilation of the well-known fourth-century follower of Confucius's thought.

From these accounts Confucius was born in the walled city of Lu, in what is now known as Shandong Province in southeast China. Politics were contentious in Lu at the time, as they were in most of China, due to the challenge to the leader of the three Huan families who held ancestral rights to the most important ministerial positions.

To learn and act as political advisor, among other reasons, Confucius ultimately went to neighboring Qi, and later he and his disciples went into exile before ultimately returning to Lu.

It was a time of great upheaval, but also great creativity in China. It was a time of consolidation when the many fiefs into which the earlier Zhou dynasty kings had divided their realm began to consolidate through war and annexation into larger political states. Having gained in power these states paid less deference to the Zhou king and began to appoint a political bureaucracy, or civil class, appointed for loyalty and ability rather than noble birth.

These states developed well-organized armies and sophisticated tax systems, and a flourishing merchant class began to evolve. Metal currency was introduced, and long before the West, China developed cast iron, a technological breakthrough of far-reaching proportions in everything from weapons to tools and building materials.

It was during these tumultuous but creative times that Confucius, in stark contrast to the deductive reason of Aristotle, formulated his ideas for a complex system of philosophy, morality, politics, and social structure. Many parts might be thought of as religious in their nature, which is where I believe Taoism and Chinese folk religion left their mark on Confucius, allowing us to safely refer to Confucianism as the underlying system of Chinese culture to this day.

Confucius saw the bloodshed of his times and reasoned there had to be a better way. Even if you could stop someone from doing something immoral, he reasoned, if he felt no shame, he would just do it again when the opportunity presented itself and there would be no social and political development for the general population.

Essentially, Confucius wanted to internalize morality through rites and rituals and patterns of behavior that set a standard now known as "face."

It was the perfect moral system for China because it was built on the individual, not the institution that is represented by an absolute moral code. It was at that point, therefore, that Western and Asian culture took diametrically divergent paths to the establishment of social order.

Europe externalized the codes of social order through the rule of law—an institution. China internalized the codes of social order through the emphasis on "face" and obligation—inherently personal and relationship-oriented notions.

The most apt geometric symbol of Chinese culture, therefore, as noted earlier, is the circle rather than the straight line that best symbolizes the foundation of Western culture. The circle is holistic in its perspective. As Confucius once famously quoted, "Wherever you go, there you are."

These behaviors inevitably exhibit certain common characteristics that are quite distinct from those of Western culture. Let's explore the same characteristics attributed to Western culture from the Chinese perspective:

Predictability

Rather than believing in the supremacy of cause and effect, the Chinese believe that reality is defined by the balance, or lack thereof, of opposing forces, commonly referred to as yin and yang and represented by the intertwined black and white symbol universally associated with Chinese culture. (In actuality, yin and yang are not opposing forces per se. One cannot exist without the other. But to understand them in that context, you must have an inductive mindset.)

As a result, the Chinese are far less likely to hold to absolutes. They put great stock in concepts like luck and good fortune and are far more prone to superstition and ritual. Reality is far less predefined and much more open to shifting forces that greatly reduce the predictability of reality and life.

Which is why the Chinese, in addition to being renowned gamblers, are generally less curious than their Western counterparts and show less interest in understanding how inanimate machines work or in explaining cause and effect. Things are as they are. Knowing why, simply for the sake of knowing, is not considered a productive use of time and energy by most.

Most Chinese generally keep track of the news—it might affect them—but it is not the obsession here that it is for many Americans. Retail stock investors, who often know little about how the markets work or the fundamentals of the companies they invest in, generally invest for the very short term on the basis of rumors or the advice of their family and social network. Even then they are often just acting out their collective roots, honoring personal obligation (think of it as the respect of going along without challenge as opposed to a sense of servitude) or helping to rebalance the opposing forces of good and bad fortune in the group's favor.

Seldom do they perform the kind of exhaustive research a Western institutional investor would perform. Many have no idea how to read a profit and loss statement or balance sheet. To them the invisible forces of good luck and market timing are far more important than the cause and effect Westerners believe they can glean from the financial ratios they study with such vigor. (Prior studies of the random walk theory of investing, or even the popularity of index fund investing, would tend to support the Chinese perspective.)

This also helps to explain why there are few companies in China more than a decade or two old. Some last only one or two years at most, not because they disappear but because their private owner pivots into another industry, perhaps completely unrelated, in which he or she senses more short-term profit opportunity. As at a blackjack table in a Macau casino, if you find no luck at the table you're at, switch tables. Perhaps your fortunes will change.

A humorous facet of this proclivity is that I have yet to hear a single Chinese individual criticize the ability of meteorologists to predict the weather, a national sport in the United States and elsewhere. When I ask my colleagues what the weather forecast is, they often pull out their smartphones to check, apparently for the first time. The implication being, of course, that the weather will be what it will be, and no human, even armed with the most sophisticated technology, can predict that. Why waste time listening to their inevitably inaccurate procrastinations?

Universal Explainability

One of the basic premises of the scientific method is that everything can be explained. Of course, many things have yet to be explained by Western scientists. The universal assumption, however, is that it is only a matter of time and technological advances in scientific equipment before they are.

No such belief exists among the Chinese. They naturally accept that some things simply defy explanation, such as the behavior of foreigners. Besides, what value is there in knowing if you can't use the knowledge to make money, vanquish enemies, or improve health?

This sword cuts both ways, however. While they waste little time contemplating or even exploring the inexplicable, they are at times lacking in the natural curiosity that drives many successful businesses and institutions and is a key source of innovation, an inherent element of the modern economy.

An argument goes on today as to whether or not the Chinese are capable of the innovation that drives much of modern business. They can copy, but can they create?

A lot of young Chinese entrepreneurs are working hard to prove the doubters wrong. And with some success. The Chinese are clever, have a strong work ethic, and as inductive thinkers are far less risk averse than their Western counterparts. And it is this latter trait, as history has proven again and again, that has proven to be the key to innovation.

Did you know that the ATM has been around since the 1960s? It never got put to use, however, because the risk-averse banks that studied its possible application could not get outside the mental box that suggested that based on past paradigms, customers would never conduct financial transactions with a machine. One day, however, someone had the courage to say, "Let's do it anyway," and the rest is history.

Thomas Watson, the president of IBM, infamously noted that he thought the world market for computers would eventually total five at most.

When Steve Jobs purchased the Mac Operating System from the Palo Alto Labs, a subsidiary of Xerox that saw no commercial application for the product, do you think he built an elaborate business case based on projections of future cash flows and net present values? I don't know, of course, but I would be surprised to learn that he even doodled on a cocktail napkin. He just did it.

In the end, however, I believe a willingness to take risks will not be enough to win in the future tech-driven market, where previously unknown disrupters will make entire industries obsolete within a single career. To have the chance to take risk, you must be either incredibly lucky or, for most of us, insanely curious.

And this is where I believe the Chinese face their most formidable challenge. They will have to make some fundamental cultural and institutional changes that will not be easy, and a powerful vested interest group will fight each change to the death.

First and foremost, I believe China will have to dramatically reform its education system. Today it is largely a system of rote learning where teachers lecture and students listen quietly. It excels at creating students who are wizards with computers and mathematics but leaves most students unprepared to defend their ideas or to work collaboratively.

The second change must be access to reasonably priced credit for small businesses and start-ups, a segment shunned by the large state-owned banks that control the majority of the lending in China, instead focusing their effort on the huge state-owned enterprises (SOEs) that, with the backing of the Chinese government, are sure to repay their loans.

There must also be reform in the bureaucratic red tape currently required to start a business. It can be mind-boggling, and few entrepreneurs have the patience, the knowledge, or the funds to endure the process. The government's current crackdown on corruption will help immensely in this matter.

The vast repository of regulations that theoretically govern the economy must also be simplified, and enforcement must be consistent among cities and provinces. Today your place of business and the relationship you have with local regulators can artificially distort the competitive playing field, making it sometimes impossible for more nimble and efficient competitors to gain the scale to compete effectively with competitors in other municipalities who enjoy more "support" from their local government and regulators, however achieved.

Lastly, while I fully understand the necessity to control population growth in a country of this size, I believe this will be another incentive for the government to continue to relax China's one-child policy. The economy of the future will be an ecosystem of collaboration, and in no other arena do we learn to compromise, collaborate, and develop our sensibilities to the wants and desires of other people than within the family unit.

Single children of single parents (thus no aunts, uncles, or cousins) will be disadvantaged in acquiring the skills of cooperative innovation and creativity. (Creativity, I believe, is stimulated, not genetically bequeathed. There must be some genetic enablers present, but most creative people, I believe, become so through an advanced ability to observe, listen, and apply that knowledge along pathways distinct from historical momentum.)

Digital Morality

In the world of holistic and circular reasoning, morality is always relative, circumstantial, and colored in varying shades of gray. What is proper in one set of circumstances may be unthinkable in another. On the opposite sides of a circle, right and wrong can easily occupy the same latitude or longitude.

In China there is no cheating as we know it in the West. The Chinese start with results and work back. If a shopkeeper can convince you to pay five times what an item is worth, that is his good luck and your loss of face.

It doesn't have to be an issue of good and bad, virtue and evil. When I first arrived here, I needed to get a Chinese driver's license to legally drive my children to the hospital or to a school event. But the city where my resident visa was registered did not offer the hundred-question multiple choice driving test in English—only Mandarin. In an effort to help, a friend of mine introduced me to a "consultant" who made his living helping people like me. He spoke English, but when I noted that I still needed to know the answers to the questions, he laughed and said, "Don't worry, I know them. I will answer on your behalf."

The schools are overcrowded and the teachers underpaid, so virtually all Chinese parents, even of the noblest spirit, offer gifts to the teachers of their children so that even if they are not provided special treatment, they are at least not ignored. Can we really blame either the parent or the teacher who, after all, must eat and have a place to sleep?

The same is true in hospitals, which are notoriously overcrowded, with the doctors and nurses paid state wages while no longer provided the housing and other benefits of the socialist economy.

I take great pride in my personal integrity, and I have never participated in these typically Chinese activities. I could say that I do so because
I am a man of character and hold high values. And I would like to think
there is an element of truth to that. In reality, however, I do it because this
was the world view in which I was raised and upon my father's death at a
young age, I promised him I would abide by it. (A wise advisor I now count
as a friend often says, "People say that soldiers die for their country. That's
not true. They die for their buddies.")

And one has to wonder if bribery is really a less efficient way to determine the hierarchy of power than the false meritocracy we comfort ourselves with in the West. Much of the government bribery that exists in
China is internal—a subordinate providing gifts to his superior to improve
his chances for a promotion. But can't a capitalist case be made that whoever has the most capital to invest must be the most capable? And is the
United States truly a meritocracy? Is it not a pipe dream that the ability
to perform a job can be objectively measured by another individual with
inevitable biases and a personal world view and career agenda?

If that were possible, few people would ever get fired for performance,
and every corporate team would be the high performance team that all
corporations seek. But that is clearly not the reality. How can we blindly
defend the contradiction?

Personal Values

Westerners are universally befuddled that the Chinese willingly accept the
control the government exerts over their daily lives. But the Chinese care
little about personal freedoms and ideals such as the freedom of expression. To the deductive thinker, the principle of expression stands on its
own. To the inductive thinker, on the other hand, what good is the freedom of expression if no one is listening or willing to act on what you
express?

They start at the right—at society and the economy—and work back
from there. If the Communist Party of China (CPC) continues to deliver

jobs and prosperity, there will be no threat to its power. All political unrest in China is economic, not ideological.

The Chinese, in fact, are far more pragmatic than ideological. I have met with dozens of Chinese officials over the years and always found them to be pragmatic in their solution to problems and holistic in the solutions they seek.

In the immediate run up to the Summer Olympics of 2008, the Security Bureau of the municipality in which the plant I ran at the time was located—less than fifty kilometers from the Forbidden City—announced that eighty factories (mine was one of them) would have to shut down for thirty days in the interest of security. All employed potentially dangerous materials in their production processes, an acceptable risk in nearly every municipality in the world, but this was the Olympics and China's grand entrance onto the world stage. "But," the official went on, "you have two weeks to convince us that the measure is not necessary in your case."

The general managers of each of these facilities were assembled in a large meeting hall to hear the news. As you can imagine, there was a collective gasp in the room as the GMs recognized the economic impact this would have on their companies and the potential damage this might do to their bonuses and their relationship with the home office.

One foreign GM immediately stood up in anger and went on a tirade about how security is the government's responsibility and we pay a lot of taxes for that protection. It was completely unacceptable, in his view, to expect the companies who provided economic sustenance to the area to do the government's work.

His plant, of course, was shut down.

A couple of days later, I received a phone call from another foreign GM who said that a group of GMs had gotten together and thought we should hire a lawyer to fight the restriction. I laughed out loud and said I thought that was the absolutely worst thing we could do and they could count my company out.

Instead, I asked my staff to contact the Security Bureau and set up a meeting with the head of the bureau and his senior staff, committing that I too would be there with all my own senior staff.

At the start of the meeting, I expressed empathy for the enormity of the task the bureau was facing and pledged my complete cooperation. After all, I noted, we live in the community as well and want to see the games be as much of a success as the government did. I asked them to explain their specific security concerns relative to our factory in the hope that we could work out some mutually acceptable plan of action that would preclude the kind of financial hardship a total shutdown would create.

His answer was concise, clear, and totally transparent. And within thirty minutes we had worked out a plan that was acceptable to me and would address their primary concerns. Our plant, as a result, was allowed to run at full production throughout the Olympics with minor inconvenience and little incremental cost.

The Love of Process

In an inductive world, outcome is all that matters. The path to a successful outcome is of little value since it is assumed to be both variable and potentially circular. To the Westerner, A leads to B leads to C. To an inductive reasoner, the path through Q may, in fact, be the quickest and most effective way to achieve the desired result.

In the inductive world, process and morality intersect in very different ways than they do in the West. In the process-centric West, both morality and process are absolute. There is a right way and a wrong way. And the wrong way, morally speaking, is always the wrong way, no matter what the circumstances.

Not so to the inductive thinker. Corruption is not corruption in the Western sense, if it is both normal and efficient. It is merely an alternative path to selection, which is inevitably required in both government and business.

To believe that corruption is wrong, you must essentially accept the infallibility of cause and effect. You must believe that all decisions can be made efficiently and objectively and will lead to the desired result. Westerners generally do. The Chinese have no such confidence.

As I will discuss in a later chapter, this is creating a conundrum for the Chinese government at the moment as President Xi Jingping pursues a relentless crackdown on government corruption. One of the unintended consequences has been government paralysis. While Westerners might assume that better decisions are getting made in the absence of corruption, the reality is that no decisions are getting made, a result some would argue is more damaging to China's development than the corruption itself.

While some business processes are developed with an eye toward tighter control, most are developed in the interest of efficiency and predictability. The standard operating procedure (SOP) is the backbone of most Western management systems.

At the same time, most American corporations are spending millions of dollars attempting to become more flexible, to get closer to the consumer, to be more reactive to employees, and generally to become faster in making decisions and acting on them.

There is an obvious connection and contradiction here. The near-spiritual belief in process is at the heart of the competitive and financial challenges faced by many large, traditional US companies today. And, again, this is a reality that is extremely difficult to change. Pride of authorship, fear of job loss, and sheer momentum stand in the way. By virtue of deduction, deductive thinkers are generally risk averse.

Not so the Chinese, and this created many conflicts when we first opened operations here. We essentially imported our American business processes into China, and there was trouble from the beginning.

The Chinese truly do live and work to a different standard of time. Their clock is exponentially faster than that of most Western business. They fully expect that if they request a quotation on a new product in the morning, they will have it by the end of the day. New products, even if engineering, new tools, and fixtures are required, should be ready to ship in two to three weeks at most.

I won't tell you what the standards for these processes were at my own company. We were middling compared to most American companies, but we weren't even close when it came to the Chinese standard, and we lost business as a result.

We eventually got close to the local standard, but we had to throw out a lot of processes to make it happen. And this, as you can imagine, sounded ear-piercing alarm bells for many of the staffers at our corporate offices in the United States.

It wasn't always an easy win, of course. Our unscheduled machine downtime was incredibly low, even for a new plant, but our mechanics, in a rush to get a machine running again, often ran into the parts warehouse and took parts without filling out the proper paperwork, particularly on the off shifts when the warehouse manager wasn't there. As a result, at some point in time, a mechanic went to the warehouse to retrieve a part only to discover that there weren't any because the buyer had no idea we were out of them.

We eventually worked it out, however, and process no longer gets in the way to the extent it once did.

The Win-Win Negotiation

The Chinese are powerful negotiators, as any tourist who has shopped at a local market can attest. (If you think you got a good deal on your last holiday in China, I assure you that a Chinese person would have gotten a much better one. I'm hoping you enjoyed the experience).

As a general rule, I discourage Westerners from even trying to negotiate a major business deal with a Chinese counterpart. You won't win. Because, as noted in the last chapter, you are looking for a win-win settlement. They, on the other hand, are looking to extract every last pound of flesh they can. There is no win-win to them. There is only win-lose. And they will do everything they can, deductively logical, truthful, or not, to make sure you are on the losing end.

As I will discuss in more depth in a later chapter, negotiations in China, despite the calming tea and peaceful beginning atmosphere, are always conducted with a knife at the opponent's throat. Otherwise the children could work out the big deals and you could all play golf.

If you are negotiating a business deal and the settlement emerges relatively peacefully, you probably got a bad deal, unless, of course, they have previously established respect for your negotiating skills. At some point in either process, a little fur has to fly; someone has to storm out; someone has to draw weapons—figuratively speaking, of course (the negotiation to end a legal dispute, as I have discovered firsthand, can be particularly dramatic).

Additionally, foreigners negotiating in China are often frustrated at the circular logic behind many negotiations. "How is that relevant to this negotiation?" is a common frustration often uttered, or at least thought, by Westerners in the heat of an effort to reach a deal. But the question itself is irrelevant to the Chinese. They care little about process and what is deductively logical. They care only about the outcome.

This can be a huge challenge for Westerners negotiating business deals in China. In order to move the negotiation toward our desired win-win solution, our natural tendency in a negotiation is to attempt to show empathy and good intent. Unfortunately, that often gets interpreted as weakness or, at the very least, confuses the opposing party.

A Chinese negotiator will not stop pushing until the person is convinced you have reached your bottom line and that line is no longer negotiable. Civility, unfortunately, sometimes gets misinterpreted as not having gotten there yet.

There are several ways to clarify your position with a Chinese negotiator. One, of course, is to pound the table and storm out of the room. However, that does not come naturally to most Westerners, and your competing negotiator may not believe your sincerity. And, in some cases, it is interpreted as a lack of character or sophistication and can ultimately work against you.

I prefer silence. I am not gifted at confrontation anyway, so if I have reached my bottom line, I will often just sit silently for an extended period of time, even if no one else is talking. To the Chinese silence can be interpreted as a sign of deference or of strength, depending on your position.

At the very least, when a lead negotiator shows an innate comfort with silence, it suggests that person will not likely be swayed from the current position, and the opposing side will conclude that this is your bottom line.

After sufficient silence has been endured, I apologize for the loss of everyone's valuable time and suggest there is no further reason to continue the discussion.

Seldom will they simply cave in to your demands, however. If they do, you probably could have gone further. The best outcome for you is for them to ask to meet again the next day to resume the discussion. This gives their lead negotiator the opportunity to save face and avoid showing any sign of weakness.

Universal Obligation

The Chinese divide people into two groups—those they have an obligation to and those they don't. If they have no personal relationship with you, then you don't exist, which is why most Chinese refuse to line up and why Chinese drivers refuse to acknowledge any rules of right-of-way or simple etiquette of the road.

If, however, there is obligation between two people, it can be unlimited. Adult children would never even consider sending their parents to a nursing home, and even the most undeserving brother-in-law is given a good job or money to live on if you are in a position to do so.

On the other hand, the Chinese can't comprehend why a foreigner would hold the door open for a perfect stranger or voluntarily defer to a fellow patron who has arrived at the checkout counter at the same time. Such actions are motivated by universal, impersonal values that the Chinese simply don't share.

The family is sacred. To treat everyone the same is to somehow defy the natural order of things. It's almost selfish in a way. It denies the disciplinary and selfless beauty of collectivism and heritage at the heart of Chinese culture.

In the business world the obligation that flows from relationship is often loosely referred to as Guanxi. In reality, however, it is a complex basis for business relationships, and as a rule I advise foreigners not to use the term. It is a uniquely Chinese concept that can take years to develop and fully comprehend.

Many Westerners view it simply as a process of making friends or showing respect. A bottle of wine here, a dinner there, and you're *guan xi* buddies. This, however, is a gross oversimplification, and if you think of it in this way, it is possible to insult your Chinese "friend," or, at the very least, convince him you are a barbarian.

The most important aspect of *guan xi* is trust, so I encourage foreigners doing business here to focus on that one issue instead. There is one theory that the handshake originated because ancient warriors typically carried their protective shields in their right hand. In order to shake hands, therefore, they had to lower their shield, the ultimate sign of trust when the warrior opposite you is holding a lethal sword or spear.

Remember, however, that words carry little weight in inductive society. Results are all that matter. Which means that when it comes to trust, behavior is the true measure of sincerity. Forget the reassurances of faithfulness and goodwill. They mean nothing. Cooperate instead. Nothing demonstrates trust more than cooperation.

I never buy expensive gifts or offer bottles of liquor to the government officials I work with. In the midst of today's anti-corruption crusade, they would never accept them anyway. Instead, I offer my cooperation.

When Beijing hosted the APEC conference in October 2014, the local Environmental Bureau closed down all the factories in my area in an effort to ensure "APEC blue" skies. Many companies, of course, strongly resisted. However, I made the conscious effort to promptly agree, asking only that we be allowed to maintain 40 percent of our production so that we could continue to service important customers. The officer quickly agreed, and to this day I know we fared much better than our more combative neighbors.

Circular versus Linear

Everything I have discussed in the last two chapters boils down, once again, to the difference between the circle and the straight line.

Absolute values such as liberty, democracy, and freedom of expression are all linear in form. There are degrees and there is a strictly hierarchical methodology for calibrating their existence.

Relationships, on the other hand, are circular in nature. They ebb and flow. They don't just exist; they take work. And they are much more difficult to cultivate and understand. They are multidimensional.

Both, however, are the foundation of the Western and Chinese sense of obligation, respectively. And that is the key to the differences in the two cultures. Expectation defines the acceptability of options of behavior. It is obligation, however, that makes the final choice. And it is thus obligation, and the foundation on which it is built, that ultimately defines the core distinctions between two cultures.

CHAPTER 4

TAOISM & CONFUCIANISM

Taoism, or Daoism, is a belief system or religion based on a short manu-script of teachings called the *Tao Te Ching*, written in China in the sixth century BC. It is most commonly known by the black and white symbol—the Great Polarity—and the concept of yin and yang.

The concept is fairly straightforward, but very far-reaching. Essentially, reality is defined by the interplay of concurrent but opposing forces—yin and yang. Each is universal and each is defined only by the other. They cannot exist independently.

Yin is considered passive and generally associated with femininity, darkness, and water, while Yang is considered active and associated with masculinity, light, and air. To be clear, however, the associations each stand independently. Light and darkness are not gender-related.

Unlike the forces of good and evil that define most monotheistic reli-gions, there is no vertical relationship between yin and yang. They exist lat-erally, on an equal plane from any moral or judgmental perspective. They are essentially unassuming of each other.

At the heart of Taoism, Chinese folk religion, traditional Chinese medicine, the Chinese art of the placement and arrangement of physical surroundings called fêng shui, the Chinese martial arts, and a good part of Chinese culture is the concept of *qi*, the energy flow or life force that pervades the natural world (think Yoda in *Star Wars*).

I think of *qi* as another dimension of yin and yang. As I think of it, it is yin and yang in motion. *Qi* is all about flow, and flow only occurs when the innate components of that which is flowing are in balance.

The imagery of balance is everywhere in Chinese culture; it's architecture, it's art, and it's even entertainment—Chinese acrobatics, for example. This, of course, gives Chinese culture a relative nature quite distinct from the absolute beliefs of Western civilization.

In fact, the ultimate reality in Taoism, referred to as the tao, or Way, is virtually unknowable. It is indescribable and cannot even be given a name, much less understood. It merely is, preceding life and the earth itself.

The tao encompasses yin and yang, and while unknowable, it is not void of content. It is, in fact, everything.

It is not surprising, therefore, that the Chinese are not consumed with explaining all reality in the way that Western science is. The Chinese are quite at home with ambiguity and uncertainty, which has implications for everything from how they negotiate to how well they do or don't plan.

Reinforcing the validity of ambiguity is the fact that the tao encompasses both life and death. They are merely two dimensions of the same reality, and therefore death is not to be feared or desired. It just is, which is a common Chinese perspective on many things.

If you are the kind of person who likes hard and fast answers, you will be frustrated in China. For the first two or three years of my time here, I would leave meetings with government officials, shaking my head as to what just happened. I didn't have a clue what we talked about or what we concluded.

But my Chinese colleagues could quickly and easily set me straight. Two hours of often circular discussion could be boiled down to one or two sentences that I understood.

They are equally baffled by us—the foreigners. When I first arrived here, I thought it appropriate to visit the mayor of a poor village next to my plant to offer my support and share the goodwill of neighbors. So my staff set it up, and the mayor eagerly received us and gave us a tour of the school and the surrounding village.

When I later made a passing reference to the visit to the head of the development zone that my company is part of, the woman's jaw visibly dropped, as if I had just uttered the most absurd thing she had ever heard.

She wasn't angry. She was simply befuddled. "The villagers are my responsibility. If you have any problems with the villagers, you come to see me and I will take care of it."

Now I get it. And I understand the point of her confusion. More than anything else, Confucianism defines a complex system of social, political, and familial roles: "Do not worry about holding high position; worry rather about playing your proper role." My role is to run a business, create jobs, and pay taxes. Her role is to govern the villagers.

CHAPTER 5

THE INDIVIDUAL VERSUS THE GROUP

Most Western social, political, and economic systems are based on the foundation of the individual. As deductive thinkers we start with the building blocks and build from there. We have an objective. We have an end-game. But we don't start there and work backward. The individual is the building block. Society is the end game.

In the United States the public debate, to the extent there is one, always centers on the individual. The right to bear arms; the right to free speech and to gather and protest; the right to marry regardless of sexual identity or preference; the right to end an unwanted pregnancy; the right to succeed to the maximum of your potential. These are all individual rights. "All men are created equal…"

We believe these things because we believe in cause and effect. We believe that if we are uncompromising in our commitment to individual rights and ideals, this will lead to a more advanced economy and enlightened society.

That may be true if you likewise believe in the supremacy of process, which comes naturally to the deductive thinker. Individual rights without process is anarchy, and most Westerners would reject this as an unsustainable social and economic model.

It is the lack of supremacy of process in inductive reason, where you start with the result and conjecture back, that causes the Chinese to be far more collectivist in their approach to business and politics than their Western counterparts.

They are no less individualistic. In some ways they are more so. In the absence of the personal obligation that flows from personal relationship, they care little about your opinion or your convenience. They park their cars wherever it is most convenient for them. They will reach over you at the order counter to place their order ahead of yours. They will, without hesitation, cut you off at an intersection, and it would not occur to them to make room for you to enter a crowded street from a driveway or parking lot. If anything, you are more likely to get a blast of the horn than a friendly gesture of deference. There are many, many exceptions, of course, and the number is growing by the day.

Inductive reason pays no homage to process. Chinese drivers routinely ignore traffic signals. Without exception they violate the prohibition against using your mobile phone while driving. Speed limits are merely suggestions in the absence of a speed camera, and if a camera is present, the police inevitably extend the courtesy of notifying you before you reach it.

At the same time, I have yet to hear a single Chinese person complain about the inability to own a gun. And the government is judged almost solely by the economy and the economic opportunity it provides, rather than the political source of its legitimacy or its commitment to free speech and political dissent.

That's not to say that the Chinese people are not critical of their government. They are openly so. It is common for Chinese people to air their grievances with the government openly and publicly. And if they get no satisfaction at the local level, they frequently come to Beijing for redress. Most provinces have offices in Beijing to handle such traveling protesters, and it is not uncommon to see elderly couples parading around crowded public venues in Beijing wearing sandwich boards that detail their complaint.

They are inevitably led away by the police, but from my firsthand experience, it is always in a gentle, if not deferential, manner. There are no shields, batons, or water cannons.

There is, however, a stark line between proclaiming an individual grievance—they almost always have to do with compensation from the government—and disrupting the civil order. In part, it's a matter of practicality. It's a country of 1.4 million people, after all, and until recent decades, all resources have been scarce.

Such emphasis on social and political order is often misinterpreted in the West as symbols of oppression and a lack of personal freedom. That, however, is a deductive conclusion.

In a 2014 survey published by the Harvard Kennedy School's Ash Center for Democratic Governance and Innovation—covering thirty countries, from the United States to Kenya—President Xi Jinping, chairman of China's Communist Party, ranked highest among both the Chinese (95 percent approval) *and* among respondents worldwide. This feat is even more remarkable given that he was only the fourth most recognized name among world leaders, behind Barack Obama, Vladimir Putin, and David Cameron.

And despite constant friction between China and the United States on the international front, a remarkable 51 percent of Americans polled rated Xi favorably on his handling of international affairs.

Of note relative to the US "pivot to Asia," Xi ranked high in Asian and African countries, with the exception of Japan, a key US ally that increasingly finds itself isolated in the region.

One other interesting note. Of the ten global leaders rated—Xi, Putin, Obama, Cameron, Hollande, Merkel, Abe, Rousseff, Modi, and Zuma—all oversee vastly different political systems and paths to economic development.

The top three in terms of domestic support, however, were Xi Jinping of China, Prime Minister Narendra Modi of India, and Vladimir Putin of Russia, who lead both the world's largest democracy and the world's largest Communist states.

How can that be?

In early February 2015 I was browsing my MSN homepage when I came across an article entitled "The 15 Least Free Countries in the World." It was written by *Business Insider* and based on a study by an organization called Freedom House.

Included were many countries one would expect, including Somalia, Equatorial Guinea, South Sudan, and Chad; a few of the "stans" that wouldn't have come to mind, including Uzbekistan and Turkmenistan; and a country I have never heard of called Eritrea.

And there it was, just above North Korea on the list—China, number two of the least free.

Curiously, the article began with this perplexing paragraph:

China's President Xi Jinping launched an aggressive anti-graft campaign in 2013, promising to crack down on corrupt officials and business leaders both at home and abroad.

Huh? What am I missing? How does that get you on the list of "least free" countries? I say, "Good for him!"

So I looked at this Freedom House report the article was based on, and it was quickly obvious that when they say "freedom," they mean "political freedom," or, more to the point, a freedom of speech that puts more importance on Pufacts over context. Can I detain dissidents who may ruin the livelihood of millions of inncocent people? Some would say no; some would say yes. The Difference is context, not fact.

The report noted that 190 "activists" were detained in China in 2014 alone. That's out of a population of 1.4 billion, of course, and there was no indication what these 190 people were doing. The word *activist* is meant to suggest they were doing something noble, but I suspect there are 190 people arrested per day in the "free" countries for doing something they felt they should be allowed to do—like ignoring traffic signals and talking on their mobile phones while driving.

Again, the frustration, the misunderstanding.

Despite their radically individualistic behavior, the Chinese put society first, the individual second—*if society allows it.* Because they are inductive.

That is exactly why you hear the word *harmonious* so much in the Public relations and the speeches coming out of Beijing. It is propaganda in the literal sense, of course, but it isn't. Harmony is the ultimate objective in all aspects of the Chinese world view—the harmony of yin and yang, the harmony of individual rights and the optimal balance for the overall society, the harmony of your rights and the rights of the group.

There is no willingness to sacrifice or die for individual rights or outcomes. There is no pretense that principles overcome outcomes. There just is.

I have yet to meet the Chinese person—and I will say this often, I'm sorry, but it's true—who was more proud of anything other than being Chinese. Said differently, there will never be a bond stronger among people of Chinese descent than the bond of their common Chinese heritage.

That's true of many cultures, of course. But here it usurps everything, such as prejudice, racism, bias, wealth, and political opportunity. The Chinese themselves will criticize what it means to be Chinese; they will criticize how Chinese tourists behave when they leave the country; they will criticize government corruption and the lack of political freedom; they will criticize the inherent flaws in the *hukou* system (to be discussed later). But they will never, ever—with few exceptions—give up the concept of their being Chinese.

In *pinyin*, which is the Chinese language expressed using the Roman alphabet, and which I shall discuss in a later chapter, the literal translation of the name of China in Chinese, *Zhong Guo*, is the Middle Kingdom. And that's because China has historically seen itself as the center of the earthly universe. And not without reason.

CHAPTER 6

THE CHINESE FAMILY

Everybody loves children. Every culture embraces them. As so many songwriters and poets have reminded us, they are the future itself.

Nowhere, however, have I seen children quite so revered as they are here in China. They are universally adored, coddled, and the focal point of every family's life. There are many reasons for this, not the least of which is the fact that Chinese culture turns on personal relationship and obligation, and no relationship is more deep-rooted and binding than family. Confucius, in fact, made filial piety (*xiào*) the cornerstone of much of his philosophy of rights and obligations.

As a result, or perhaps because of it, the government historically provided limited financial support for the elderly. That is considered a family obligation. Because of the dissolution of the family unit due to migration and urbanization, greatly increasing life expectancy, and what is referred to as the "4-2-1 problem," however, it is an obligation increasingly difficult to satisfy, and the government is stepping in to help. (Due to the one-child policy, one child may face the financial burden of caring for 4 grandparents and two parents – while each generation is living longer.)

The 4-2-1 problem arises as a direct result of China's one-child policy, officially known as the family planning policy, implemented in 1979 in an effort to control population growth. In practical terms it means that in the typical three-generation family, two generations of which are retired, one child is responsible for supporting six of his or her elders (two parents and four grandparents), an obligation that doubles when the third-generation member is widowed or whose spouse does not or cannot work. (There are almost no spouses who choose not to work here. It's just not an option for all but the richest of Chinese. And if the spouse does work, the couple would be supporting four parents and eight grandparents.)

Now imagine that this one child is lost due to natural disaster (eg, earthquake) or otherwise fails to succeed due to poor study habits or an inability to compete successfully in the workplace. While this greatly enhances the propensity to overprotect and coddle children, it likewise puts them under tremendous pressure to perform, particularly in school, where standardized exams largely determine the career path that will be open to them. Neither—overprotection or undue pressure—is likely to be helpful to the child's proper development.

Now extrapolate the one-child policy laterally. In addition to having no siblings and being raised by parents who themselves had no siblings, many only children have no aunts, uncles, or cousins either. They have, in other words, not a single familial peer with whom they must compete on an equal footing.

Needless to say, this can have profound implications in terms of how adult Chinese express themselves, work through problems, share, or otherwise compete throughout their lives. I see the impact every day. It's not that people are arrogant or self-centered as those terms are normally used. They simply struggle to collaborate or compromise. They never had to.

This, of course, can also lead to an inability to embrace diversity, generally reinforcing the cultural tendency that inhibits ethnic and cultural assimilation, a tendency likely to be reinforced by the gender imbalance indirectly caused by the one-child policy.

While the male/female imbalance has shown signs of improving recently, it has been running at 117 to 100 in recent years, well above the global average of 103 to 100 through 107 to 100 that is considered biologically normal. This, of course, is due primarily to the practice of gender-selective abortions, although it is technically illegal for doctors or other health-care providers to disclose the sex of an unborn fetus to the parents. In practice, it is quite easy to find out, and every soon-to-be-parent that I've discussed the question with has.

In reality, the one-child policy has never been universally applied. There have always been exceptions for people living in rural areas (parents were allowed a second child if the first was a daughter or physically or mentally challenged); ethnic minorities, of which there are fifty-five, have generally been excluded from the restriction; and some cities have allowed parents to have a second child if both parents were themselves only children.

Like almost all national policies in China, the family planning policy is administered provincially and provincial and local authorities have been given wide latitude as to its application and enforcement. Sichuan Province, for example, site of the devastating 2008 earthquake, immediately made an exception for parents who lost their only child in the quake.

And of course, the central government did, as has been widely reported abroad, relax the family planning policy even further during the Third Plenum of the Communist Party of China's Eighteenth Central Committee in October 2013, allowing married couples, only one of which is an only child, to have a second child.

The reason for further relaxing the policy remains a little unclear since the government concurrently announced it will not abandon the policy altogether, as some had predicted. I believe, however, and it is strictly my guess, that part of the rationale had to do with the simple principle of fairness and the desire to address the growing gulf between the rich and everyone else.

You see, while I have no doubt that there have been cases of overzealous local officials forcing women to abort a nonexempt second child (I, myself, am unaware of any such case), the primary penalty for violation of the family planning policy is financial. In addition to paying a fine, which is undoubtedly negotiable, depending on your relationship with the local government, the offending couple has to pay the educational and medical costs of the second child—which, for the wealthy, isn't a deterrent at all.

I suspect, therefore, that the net impact of the new policy on Chinese birthrates will be quite small. Those who want and can afford a second child already have or will have one. And those who can't—well, they can't afford it.

Living in China can be inexpensive if you're willing to do without modern conveniences and live in a confined space. Raising a child under any circumstances is not inexpensive. To get the kind of education you will need to be anything other than a manual laborer, someone will need to pay. And universal health care, even under the best of circumstances, has its limitations. Most people will need money when serious illness strikes.

And then there are those, of course, who are so consumed with getting ahead that they don't have time for marriage, much less children.

All that said, however, the Chinese do universally adore children. With few exceptions young children traveling with their parents on the subway are offered seats in otherwise jammed subway cars that would not be sacrificed for their parents. In a country in which today's hard work is universally considered a sure path to tomorrow's grand aspirations, children are the hope of a comfortable future. This can be, of course, a source of great pressure. But it also puts them in a position to be the recipients of a great deal of excessive coddling by parents and grandparents, creating what is sometimes referred to as the generation of "little emperors."

CHAPTER 7

COMMUNICATION

One of the questions I am frequently asked by visiting Westerners is how I can live and work among people I cannot communicate with—the implication being, of course, that language is essential to communication (my Chinese is admittedly limited).

In reality I often find that I communicate more effectively here than I do when among fellow native English speakers. I have to work a little harder, but it is that extra effort that makes the difference.

Words, of course, are not natural to the universe, like oxygen or meteors. They are a human invention designed to facilitate communication through the use of commonly accepted symbols and sounds. In English we call them the letters of the alphabet. In Mandarin they are called, quite appropriately, characters, or ideograms.

Problems arise in lingual communication, however, for the simple reason that symbolism is limited in its effectiveness. It is, in the end, merely symbolic. Symbols, by definition, are mere representations of an object, a thought, or an emotion. They aren't the real McCoy.

In the end, all language is a translation, no matter how fluently spoken. Which is precisely why we need poets and authors. Try as we might, it is difficult, nay impossible, to precisely communicate complex human emotions such as love and sorrow.

Mastering an expansive vocabulary can help. The more symbols you know, the better your chances of using the right one to express your thought. That assumes, however, that the listener's vocabulary is equally expansive. Otherwise you might as well be speaking a different language. Which, essentially, you are.

In the end, the effectiveness of your communication has relatively little to do with the size of your vocabulary. The effectiveness of your communication, in fact, has more to do with how well you listen than how well you speak.

Americans, in particular, are what linguists call "transmitter oriented" in our communication. To our way of thinking the speaker has the burden of getting his point across. "I like people who say what they mean," is akin to citing the Pledge of Allegiance in asserting your American-ness. "Give it to me straight." "Say that to my face, buddy." Or, my mother's favorite, "If you've got nothing good to say, don't say anything."

Which is why Americans who are trying to communicate with someone who does not speak English are naturally inclined to speak loudly, as if shouting will somehow impose a state of fluency. But alas, "Nope, even when you say it louder, I don't understand a word you're saying. Maybe if you get really frustrated, that will help."

By contrast, the Chinese, like most Asian cultures, are receiver oriented in their communication. It's the linguistic version of *caveat emptor*, or "buyer beware." From their linguistic perspective, the onus is on the listener rather than the speaker to communicate effectively.

Which puts an entirely different twist on one of the more infuriating group of Chinese most Westerners will encounter in China—the hawkers, shopkeepers, and promoters who make up the mobilized and relentless army of people who want to sell you something. They are both tenacious and aggressive and to many Westerners, irritating.

Walk anywhere near the entrance to the Forbidden City, and you will be deluged with people trying to sell you their souvenirs or their guide services. Walk into the modern tourist trap posing as a traditional Chinese market, and you will be immediately assaulted by shopkeepers pulling you into their shops while promising you, their friend, of course, a very special price.

And whatever you do, never venture into a grocery store or hypermarket on a Sunday afternoon. Even the Western chains that have been lured by the siren of Chinese commerce are no exception. You will be drowned by a cacophony of unnervingly high-pitched voices distorted into sheer tonal agony by the tinny microphones and sound boxes inevitably employed in even the smallest of spaces.

While all this aggressive yelling and shouting and invasion of personal space initially seems quite rude to the average Westerner, you have to view it through their cultural lens. Their communication is receiver, rather than transmitted, oriented. Which simply means that while it is perfectly polite to be aggressive in attempting to sell something to the innocent passerby, it is equally polite for you to ignore them. Trust me, you won't hurt their feelings.

But whatever you do, don't confuse them. Ignore means ignore. Pretend they don't even exist. Do not look at them or say anything. The case could be made, in fact, that it is downright rude to say, "No, thank you," as that will surely cause them to linger and perhaps miss the more lucrative selling opportunity walking behind you.

By becoming more receiver-centric, I have learned to communicate more effectively in any language. Because I've become a better listener.

And what do I mean by that? The next time someone is speaking to you, ask yourself a simple question. Are you listening to respond or to understand? Transmitter-oriented people are inclined toward the former. But if that's the case, there's really no sense in having the conversation to begin with. It's just wasting everyone's time and sucking the air out of the room for nothing.

If you're truly listening to learn, on the other hand, you just might get some value out of the conversation. And if you're getting value, you just might try a little harder.

The problem is that most of us aren't very good listeners. For starters, listening simply takes more work than talking. Windbags are the laziest people on the face of the earth. Really, how much effort does it take to just babble on and on about nothing?

Albert Mehrabian, a UCLA researcher, performed several studies in the late 1960s that ultimately gave rise to what is commonly referred to as the 7/38/55 rule, which holds that words themselves account for only 7 percent of the effectiveness of communication, while tone and body language account for 38 percent and 55 percent, respectively.

Like most rules, this one is often misrepresented and almost always oversimplified. Nonetheless, there is an important truth buried therein. We listen as much with our eyes as we do with our ears. And how something is said, or more to the point, how something is perceived, is as important as the words (or symbols) used.

Context is likewise important and often influences how we interpret both body language and tone. If you're sitting in the doctor's office waiting to hear the results of your lab tests, you can be reasonably assured that the doctor isn't going to come in and start waxing eloquent about the bouquet of the 1982 Lafite Rothschild.

I worked in a factory one summer while in college and had a crusty old supervisor named Newt. Well, I did something I wasn't supposed to, and Newt called me into the office and told me to sit in the hard wooden chair in front of his utilitarian gray metal desk. He proceeded to walk around the desk, lean over until his nose was almost touching mine, place his hands on the armrests of my chair just in case I might get the crazy notion that I could just walk away, and speak. Actually, yell would be the more appropriate symbol, since his decibel level was on a par with an angry American in Paris who just couldn't get his point across.

It didn't really matter what Newt was saying. I knew he wasn't happy. He was the boss, and I had screwed up. In fact, the words got cut short when his dentures popped out from all the exertion. But I got his meaning nonetheless.

Mandarin, the official language of China, is the ultimate symbolic language. The Chinese characters that are the written form of the language are symbolic pictures in the most literal sense. Knowing Latin is no help. The only way to learn to read Chinese is through rote memorization. It's generally believed, in fact, that you need to recognize roughly 2,000 characters in order to be considered fluent. That takes more than thirty days with the foreign language DVDs you bought at the airport.

In the case of Mandarin, moreover, you're dealing with more than a foreign language. You've also got to add a foreign culture and a different communication style (receiver versus transmitter) into the mix—a culture so different from our own that it can have a profound impact on the most important of communication tools: tone and body language.

Learning to read Mandarin is a difficult challenge even for the most ardent student. I have met few foreigners who can. And those few have been here for years and probably grew up here.

Unfortunately, English and Chinese share no common etymology. They are completely different from the ground up and have absolutely nothing in common. To learn to speak one or the other, you have to learn to shape your mouth and position your tongue in ways you're probably not accustomed to.

As a truly symbolic language, traditional or simplified Chinese in the written form, called *zhang guo zi*, can only be learned through years of rote learning. You must memorize the characters or ideograms, although I'm told there are common elements to the characters that do assist in the process.

Recognizing the complexity of learning Chinese in this fashion, Mao Zedong came up with the brilliant and practical idea of creating a form of Chinese called pinyin, first introduced in the early 1960s, which Romanizes the Chinese characters, the idea being that foreigners could thus more quickly and easily learn to speak the language.

However, the Roman alphabet doesn't quite lend itself to the tonal complexities of Chinese, forcing the creators of pinyin to employ diacritics, or little graphical symbols above certain letters, to indicate which of the four tones apply in that usage.

This makes Chinese a musical language. Pronunciation is everything. To the Chinese ear, each of these tones is distinct in its sound and, unfortunately, its meaning. Unfortunate because, to the Western ear, the tones are almost indistinguishable. This, I'm told, is why foreigners with musical talent can learn Chinese more easily than those without such natural skills. And I, alas, cannot carry a tune in the bucket, so it is but another reminder of just how hopeless it is for me to ever become truly fluent in Chinese.

In essence, each word, pretones, has four different meanings. And the meanings can seemingly bear no relation to one another. Buy and sell, for example, although conceptually related, are the same word, altered only by the use of different, almost indistinguishable, tones.

And, unfortunately, there is more than just your financial condition at stake. For example, you might truly insult someone when you meant to say something complimentary, but for a slip of a tone.

Even the Chinese struggle at times with this tonal challenge. Relatively simple questions can often turn into lengthy exchanges between two native Chinese speakers who are attempting to use context to clarify meaning. While foreigners are often frustrated by the fact that when they attempt to communicate through a translator, the translator may carry on with the Chinese speaker for what seems like an eternity, only to give you a two-word answer to your original question. It is not that they shared a good laugh at your expense. They were simply clarifying the question and/or answer.

Perhaps the most infuriating aspect of learning Chinese for foreigners, however, is that you can say something in what to your ear is perfect Chinese, and your Chinese audience may look at you as if you spoke a third language that they didn't know existed. And to add insult to injury, when they finally comprehend and repeat what you should have said, it sounds virtually identical to what you were sure you did say.

A former boss who traveled all over the world and who was both interested in language and sensitive to culture, attempted for years to order a Coca-Cola in a restaurant. This, it would seem, should have been an easy task since Coca-Cola, the brand, is well-known throughout the world and the Chinese word for the drink is *keula*, which sounds similar to the way a native English speaker with a slight accent might pronounce it. Inevitably, however, his request was met with blank stares until one of our Chinese colleagues said what sounded like the exact same word, and a flash of recognition and a smile crossed the perplexed server's face.

"That's exactly what I said," he would say, and to my ears he was right. But alas, not once in the years that I worked with him did I ever see him get his request across. And he was certainly not alone.

I frequently want to say to my closest colleagues, who have listened to my accent for years now, "Look, you speak very good English, but I cut you a lot of slack. Your enunciation is far from perfect, and you often use the wrong word, but as long as I understand what you mean, I let it ride and just go on. Why can't you extend me the same courtesy? If I mistakenly use the fourth tone when I should be using the first tone, you should be able to figure out what I mean."

But they can't. And it has little to do with their willingness to be sympathetic with the lingual plight of foreigners. They just don't get it.

Here's why. If you are a native English speaker and conversing with someone who has a different native tongue but who speaks English, even very fluently, the chances are that person speaks with an accent, however slight. Nonetheless, you can understand the conversation, although you might have to try a little harder.

Now imagine that you could not understand virtually any English speaker with even the slightest accent. Without a doubt that would greatly reduce the number of English-speaking foreigners you could communicate with.

And that is how it is for the Chinese. There is no accent of any kind in spoken Chinese. There can't be simply because the language is tonal, and accents, by definition, offer their own tonality.

Contrary to common Western belief, there is no such thing as the Chinese language. There are between seven and thirteen of what the Chinese refer to as the primary dialects, depending on how you classify them, and numerous secondary dialects. But dialects are not accents because most are mutually unintelligible. To the linguist, they are not dialects at all, but distinct languages.

And then there are the truly distinct languages of the ethnic minorities and isolated or otherwise outlying regions of China. All told, in fact, it is estimated that 250 distinct languages are spoken in China. Your attempt to speak with imperfect tones only increases that number. Is it any surprise, therefore, that if you speak with less than perfect tones, you are unlikely to be understood?

I learned this lesson early in my time here, when I was in a meeting in which I was the only native English speaker. Knowing that one of my colleagues was not entirely comfortable speaking English, I suggested he speak to the group in Chinese. One of his own colleagues, however, suggested that his native dialect was different from their own so that when he spoke Mandarin, he was often difficult for them to understand. Far better for them, she noted, if he spoke English, despite his lack of fluency.

The colleague in question was the first to agree. He was, in fact, relieved, as I'm sure the reverse was true for him as well. I wasn't, in other words, from a lingual perspective, the only foreign tongue in the room.

Thankfully, English is pretty common in the urban areas of China. The children all study it in school, and chances are anyone you come in contact with under the age of thirty will speak at least a few phrases. Get stuck at a retail store trying to figure out a label, ask the nearest teenager, and he or she will be happy to help you out.

One thing you will quickly learn, however, is that fluency is relative. Every airline attendant working for a major Chinese airline speaks English, many with a limited accent. With a little probing, however, you will quickly find that their vocabulary is limited to the vocabulary of airline travel. Wander beyond that border and you've lost them.

But beware, that doesn't mean you won't get an answer. They are unlikely to tell you they don't understand, particularly in that setting, where you are the customer and they are the service provider, and as soon as they finish with you, they can move on to their other duties.

Be particularly diligent around popular tourist sites. If you are a foreigner, it is likely that a well-dressed young person will approach you to ask if you might spend a few minutes helping that person practice his or her English. Without any exception I am aware of, it's a con. That person will ultimately try to sell you something, the most common version of the con being to take you into a nearby building to show you some of the artwork he or she created at the university.

The most challenging fluency issues arise in business settings when you are speaking with a Chinese person who appears to speak fluent English.

That person has a large vocabulary and speaks with little accent. There is virtually no hesitation in the responses.

Beware. That doesn't mean for a minute that you're actually communicating. It only means that you sound like you are.

When I go into a new business situation where I know communication is going to be critical, the first thing I do is ask the Chinese person with whom I am speaking where that person went to school. If he or she went to school outside of China, then I assume I'm OK, not because foreign schools are better at teaching English than Chinese schools, but because there is something to be said for immersion. (Unfortunately, that seems to be changing, much to the chagrin of Chinese parents. There are so many Chinese students studying abroad today that it is often possible for them to live in a Chinese world abroad. And many of them do, socializing and living only with fellow Chinese expats and thus losing the benefit of cultural and lingual immersion.)

Even when speaking with the most fluent members of my staff, therefore, I typically try to communicate my point from several different angles, ask a lot of follow-up questions, and generally come back to the topic in a day or two to ensure understanding.

The main trick is to use a limited vocabulary and to use the same one all the time. And by all means avoid American sports metaphors and business jargon that may not have made it past Silicon Valley yet. And, of course, speak slowly and deliberately—not like you're speaking to a child but like you are speaking to someone for whom English is not his or her mother tongue.

Outside of the major cities, life gets a little more complicated. The factory I manage is in a rural area, and many of the business owners and executives I deal with do not speak English at any level. I always provide someone to translate, but I know that they will always bring someone who, in their eyes, can also translate.

Here's the problem. That translator may not say a word during the meeting. So there is no chance to clarify understanding or ask follow-up questions. And while the translator's English fluency may be sufficient to travel abroad or pass the fluency certification exam, that person may not have a clue as to what is being said in a business environment.

But their boss, who is relying on their fluency to make an important decision, may not know that. And the translator is not going to tell him. That would be a loss of face.

Therefore, when we break for lunch or a break, my translators, usually fellow executives, particularly in important meetings, know enough to casually approach the presumed translator to learn where that person went to school, how long he or she has been working with this company, and so forth. (Remember, translators normally aren't identified. But if you look across the table and there are four men in their forties and fifties, and there's a young woman who can be no older than twenty-two, it's a safe bet. Also remember it would be truly embarrassing to them to just come right out and start talking to them in English.)

The point is, be careful.

My biggest challenge, however, was not communicating with the Chinese but in communicating with my fellow Americans back at headquarters. Of course, most Americans don't speak a foreign language. Unlike the Europeans, we have no need to and relatively little opportunity to practice.

As a result, Americans have acquired, and I'm as guilty as anyone, a world view that equates the ability to speak multiple languages with intelligence. If a European who fluently speaks five languages announces that the situation is X and the solution is Y, we're inclined to believe them.

Similarly, when a fluent Chinese person makes an observation about our Chinese business, my colleagues at headquarters are inclined to accept it as gospel even though the Chinese person may have little experience and even less idea what is being talked about. It's a classic case of form over function.

At times, of course, you may face the opposite challenge. Instead of trying to decipher how much an apparently fluent English speaker has truly received the communication you are attempting to share, you will be faced with an individual who is apparently speaking some type of hybrid between English and Chinese. It's called Chinglish.

More often than not, Chinglish is merely the literal translation of words that cannot be literally translated. It can be very confusing. And it can be downright comical.

I am actually fluent in Chinglish. When my colleagues visit from headquarters, I sometimes translate what my colleagues are saying in their personal version of English. I can do this, of course, because my ear has become accustomed to their enunciation and I generally know the vocabulary they use, even incorrectly. (It sounds, in actuality, like a takeoff of the scene in the old Woody Allen movie where the translator is standing at the bottom of the loading stairs to the airplane translating the South American dictator's broken English.)

The most comical forms of Chinglish appear on bilingual signs posted throughout China. There are numerous books devoted to documenting them, and I'm sure if you Google Chinglish, you find page after page of hilarious examples.

Verbal Chinglish can be the most comical, however, in part because it often catches you off guard.

As an example, at lunch one day a female colleague and executive who is one of our most fluent English speakers was telling us about her recent holiday to Kenya, where she went on a photographic safari with her husband, who was working for China Petroleum, the world's largest oil company, in South Sudan at the time. She had truly enjoyed the experience and told many fascinating stories about the Kenyans she saw: "truly wonderful people, very gentle, living in their little houses made from the shit of cow," forming a helpful little house with her hands as she spoke.

No translation necessary.

Which brings me to my final point on the topic of communicating in China. Of course, knowing the language is a great asset. The reality is, however, that most Westerners visiting China will not.

And that's OK. Because it is far more important that you understand the culture than the language and that you can learn in a relatively short period of time. If you want to be able to communicate in China, first and foremost, learn to be a good listener. Be sensitive to both body language and tone. But most of all, be aware of context, both physical and cultural.

Both, in fact, can be used to your advantage. I have often convinced Chinese business clients or vendors who speak no English that I speak far more Mandarin than I really do. It's like the airline English of flight attendants. There are seldom more than a few threads of conversation that could be occurring in a typical business meeting. And by following the speaker's body language, it can be easier than you think to understand which thread is being pursued. And knowing the simple Mandarin of "yes," "no," "too expensive," or "don't want," I can often respond without having any idea what was really said, but before any translation is offered.

If I make a mistake, my translator/colleague will save me. But if I am right, my negotiating counterpart is sure to be genuinely flustered and to assume that I have hidden my fluency and understand everything that has been said. He or she, at that point, is suddenly in a possibly defensive position and my negotiation position has improved greatly.

CHAPTER 8

RELIGION IN CHINA

While the Communist Party of China is officially irreligious, the Chinese government officially recognizes and accepts five religions: Protestantism, Catholicism, Islam, Taoism, and Buddhism. And all are openly practiced here.

Buddhism and Taoism, along with Chinese folk religion, are the most common. And while I admittedly know little about the core doctrine of any of them, my experiential sense is that all are practiced with "Chinese characteristics," meaning only that there appears to be a wide spectrum of beliefs and practices among those who consider themselves to be practitioners of these religions.

"Practitioner" may not fit in most cases. It strikes me as a digital, deductive word as commonly used. And few Chinese live their lives in that way except when it comes to superstition and tradition. Inductive thinkers, as previously noted, find it difficult to internalize institutions in the way Westerners do, so any of the largest organized religions, while visibly present, may face a very different type of worshiper here.

Islam is visible here, particularly in the western provinces, and these practitioners, I suspect, are the most doctrinaire of the major religions. Protestants and Catholics, on the other hand, while members of churches who follow all the appropriate religious protocols, appear—strictly in my observation-formed opinion—to be less dogmatic and believe in and follow the core theological doctrine of these religions "with Chinese characteristics."

Judaism, for its part, is here, but not at all visible. I have yet to meet a Chinese national who identifies their religious affiliation as Jewish. And part of that, of course, is due to the Jewish doctrine itself, which discourages non-Jews from converting to Judaism for purely theological reasons. If that sounds like an accusation of discrimination—which it is clearly not meant to be—let's just say that Judaism is not a religion of proselytization in the sense that Christianity and Islam are.

In the end, however, the challenge that the monotheistic religions face in China is not the government. It is the fact that all are largely deductive in their theology. The Ten Commandments, for example, are about as digital as it gets. There is no balance of *qi* in "Thou shalt not…"

However, as has been widely reported by the Western media, the government is focused on suppressing Falun Gong, a form of qiqong practice that involves meditation and a moral philosophy with Buddhist roots. It was first introduced by Li Hongzhi in Northeast China in 1992.

At first the government supported the movement through the state-run Qiqong Association and other government offices. But the movement grew fast, perhaps too fast, and included many members of the military—the PLA—and the Communist Party of China. By some estimates, at the height of its popularity, there were more practitioners of Falun Gong than members of the CPC.

This ultimately alarmed party elders, and in 1995 the government required all Qiqong groups to establish Communist Party branches. The Falun Gong, however, chose secession from membership in the Qiqong Association altogether and by 1999, with its membership growing and beginning to stage political, albeit peaceful demonstrations, the government decided to ban the organization and actively disorganize it.

There are many Western theories for the decision, many overshadowed with implications of religious persecution and the denial of human rights. In the end, however, I believe the CPC was merely alarmed at the number of party affiliates and the group's size and ability to organize. While there was never any stated threat to the security of the state or the party, I suspect certain members of the CPC leadership concluded that the risk of that changing were simply too great. As I have noted repeatedly, the protection of the state and the party are the overriding priorities of the party leadership. (They obviously view, based on history, that the state cannot be protected except by a unified party.)

Religion and spirituality, however, remain an integral part of Chinese culture and daily life. Many common Chinese cultural beliefs and practices, including fêng shui, traditional Chinese medicine, and the Chinese martial arts, are intertwined with the tenets of Taoism. I don't think it's a stretch to say, therefore, that the Chinese are overwhelmingly "spiritual" in their thinking compared to many Western countries even if they don't adhere to prescribed behaviors of any broadly organized religion.

However, statistics are hard to come by and frequently disputed, as is almost anything having to do with the topic of religion anywhere in the world today. Nonetheless, a 2010 study by the Pew Research Center found that 40 percent of Chinese identify with Buddhism or Chinese folk religion, a categorization that I assume includes Taoism. And while 52 percent didn't consciously affiliate with any defined religious belief system, that is not to say they are all atheists or irreligious. While some undoubtedly are, a good many, I suspect, are both situational and varied in their beliefs and may not make the distinction between faith and religion. (Personally I don't believe Chinese culture is conducive to any kind of Western polling, but that is another matter for another time.)

Christianity, of course, gets the most attention by the Western media. While noting again that any statistic on the topic appears to be disputed, another 2010 survey by Dr. Yang Fenggang of Purdue University's Center on Religion and Chinese Society identified thirty million Protestants and three million Catholics living and worshiping in China.

But, China's critics will quickly point out, such Christians live under the yoke of government regulation, and by implication, various forms of government restriction, if not oppression. While the regulatory part is technically true, however, the presumed implication of oppression does not align with my own experience in China.

Christianity has been in China since the seventh century, and Western Christian missionaries have been operating here since the sixteenth century. Both Sun Yat-Sen and Chiang Kai-Shek, the first and second presidents of the Republic of China (post-dynasty China), were Christians. Even the Vatican recognizes the sacraments performed by Chinese Catholic clergy as licit.

Since their arrival centuries ago, however, the work of foreign missionaries and foreign governments and their commercial support base have been intertwined. And since those Western powers at times seemed intent on enabling and profiting from China's opium addiction or carving up and colonizing the country for their own economic and political gain, it is not surprising that missionaries ultimately became the face of everything evil about foreign intervention in China, ultimately leading to the Boxer Revolution of 1899, in which foreigners in general and missionaries in particular were targeted for retribution.

Given that history it's no surprise, therefore, that when Mao Zedong and the Communists came to power in 1949, they took a dim view of Western Christianity and viewed the missionaries who were its face as puppets of Western oppression and exploitation. And threw them all out. Or at least made them feel unwelcome.

Mao, however, did not ban Christianity and ultimately reached a harmonious state of mutual accommodation with Chinese Christians leaders. In 1951 Y.T. Wu (1893–1979), a prominent Chinese Christian leader, initiated the Three-Self Patriotic Movement, which promoted a strategy of "self-governance, self-support, and self-propagation" in order to remove foreign influences from the Chinese churches and to assure the government that the churches would be patriotic to the newly established People's Republic of China and not some foreign power.

Within these parameters Christianity continued to operate openly in China until the Cultural Revolution of 1966–1976, during which all religious expression was effectively banned. While the Cultural Revolution did not eradicate Christianity in China, it did force it underground, resulting in the creation of "house churches" that many Westerners, largely incorrectly, associate with Chinese Christianity even today.

In 1979 the government lifted the ban on religious expression and officially restored the Three-Self Patriotic Movement, joined the following year by the China Christian Council (CCC). Together these two organizations, along with the Chinese Patriotic Catholic Association (CPCA), are collectively responsible for the oversight of Christianity in China.

But what does that mean, exactly?

I'm sure you would get a myriad of answers to that question depending on whom you ask. And I'm sure there are those who would vehemently assert that the concepts of Christianity and government oversight are inherent contradictions.

Tell that to the ancient monarchs of Spain, France, England, and Russia. Religion and politics have always been intertwined in ways both good and bad. Even in America today, religious leaders wield enormous legislative, electoral, and foreign policy power. Politicians court them. The courts protect them. The tax system subsidizes them. No president would dare to impose onerous regulations on them.

But here's what I've seen in China.

The churches must stay out of politics. Any attempt to stir up political debate would, I'm sure, be met with swift "regulation." And the churches, I am confident, cannot officially promote or endorse any religious allegiance that supersedes or compromises allegiance to the state—Jesus himself implored his followers to pay their taxes and obey their political leaders.

Beyond that, however, government regulation appears to have had little or no impact on the liturgical beliefs and practices of any Christian church. Chinese Christians, from my experience, hold beliefs and follow practices very much in line with Christians the world over.

There is one further caveat, however. Proselytization, particularly by foreigners and unregistered religious groups, is forbidden. And even registered groups are only allowed to proselytize within state-approved venues and private settings.

If you're visiting China, you will have no trouble finding Christian churches catering to Western tourists and expatriates openly operating in all the major cities of China. These churches conduct their services in English, and the look and feel is very much in line with what you're accustomed to, I'm sure.

These Western churches, however, are only open to foreign passport holders. Chinese nationals are not allowed to attend, even as guests. And I can tell you from experience that passports are mandatory and they are checked.

My own family attended one such church off and on for several years—there was a bit too much worship music for our tastes—and never found the program or the sermons to be visibly censored in any way. Government officials would attend from time to time and sit quietly and respectfully in the back, but there was no sense of ill will or intimidation. One sensed that like the rest of the working world, these officials had a to-do list and were merely checking it off.

It is true that for the six months leading up to the 2008 Olympics, the church was denied use of its meeting place, but I honestly believe that was a function of security concerns rather than political ones. If the government were truly concerned about political appearances, one has to assume that it would have encouraged the churchgoers to meet and would have paraded Western journalists through the services.

Beijing was genuinely and legitimately concerned that one of their critics—and every country has them—might try to use the games as a political soapbox, and I can say that meetings of any kind were carefully monitored and generally discouraged. Fair enough, in my book, as the games went off without a hitch and were the kind of positive spectacle they are designed to be.

And the fact is that Western missionaries are here in abundance. They operate Non-Governmental Organisations (NGOs) such as orphanages and disaster-relief organizations, but they're here nonetheless, very visible and making a difference. They don't proselytize, having adopted an accommodating strategy of "see what I do for people and ask me why," but within those parameters they appear to have, in most cases, earned the sincere gratitude and support of the government.

There are still house churches here, and they are still technically illegal. As is often the case, however, the issue is more complicated than it superficially appears. Many of these "Christian" churches have adopted religious doctrine and beliefs that would never be condoned by any respected theologian or member of the clergy in the Christian West.

What has surprised me the most, however, is how much the average Chinese who has never left the country and was surely born after the 1949 revolution knows about the monotheistic religions. While they may have never set foot in a formal church before, they know the stories of Noah and Job and are at least informed about the teachings of Jesus and Mohammed.

I have concluded that if there is religious conflict in China, it is not a conflict between the government and the monotheistic religions. The more important conflict is the conflict to reconcile the monotheistic religions with the fundamentally distinct teachings of Buddhism, Taoism, and Chinese folk religion.

And it all comes back to the conflict between inductive and deductive reason. Christianity, Judaism, and Islam are deductive to the core. They rely entirely on an acceptance of absolutes and incremental individualism. Confucianism and the Taoism and Chinese folk religion that are embedded in it, however, are fundamentally inductive systems of thought and faith that don't isolate the individual in a linear hierarchy but envelop the individual in a holistic system of life force, time, and the universe around them.

CHAPTER 9

SUPERSTITION

Prior to the arrival of the Year of the Sheep on February 19, 2015, it was widely predicted that the birthrate would fall for the remainder of the year and that some Chinese mothers on the verge of giving birth would choose cesarean sections if their baby didn't arrive naturally before the new year began.

Several Western friends noted that this "superstition" is all a bit illogical since the birth would not be natural and whoever or whatever creates the bad luck associated with being born in the Year of the Sheep would know. (Sheep are considered followers, although there are many historical exceptions.)

That, however, is deductive logic. Cause and effect. You can't "cheat" the natural order of things.

But that's not how the Chinese look at the issue. They are inductive logicians and, to them, there is no bowing to or "cheating" the natural order, since no one can really understand the natural order to begin with (The Way in Taoism), which is why there is only what is and what isn't. To the expectant mother, it matters little why the child was born in the Year of the Horse (positive) or the Year of the Sheep (not so good). It only matters in which year the child was born. Results are all that matter.

"Superstition" is not a word you can use accurately when referring to the Chinese. The word implies illogical thinking. To the inductively minded Chinese, however, there is nothing illogical whatsoever in what they believe. And technically speaking, they're right. Within the realm of inductive logic, there is no such thing as superstition. There is, what Yoda of *Star Wars* fame would say, only do or don't.

In a similar vein, you may have heard that the Chinese put a lot of stock in numbers. This flows from the dual reality that they are inductive in their thinking and that the spoken Chinese language offers so many homonyms—words that sound similar but mean different things.

That is why you will often hear the word *dui* (pronounced *do-aye*) so frequently in a conversation. It means "correct" and is used so frequently because when you are carrying on a conversation in Chinese, you must ask a lot of questions to determine the context in which words are being used.

Because of this, homonyms can exist beyond a single word, creating the opportunity for good or bad luck to be associated with a sequence of numbers, making the rules of numerical superstition difficult for the un-initiated to grasp.

The Chinese are typically tetra phobic, given that the word for four sounds a lot like the word for death. Fourteen is possibly the worst possible number as it is a homonym with "will die," and the number 514 is a homonym with the phrase "I will die." Who wants that?

The number eight is the Big Kahuna of good luck as its spoken variant is a homonym with the words for prosperity, wealth, and fortune. The number six can also be lucky since its spoken variant is a homonym with the words for flowing or smooth, although it's a notch below eight because it is better to be rich than flowing. The number 6 can have bad connotations when used in combination with certain other numbers.

As always, the Chinese have figured out a way to commercialize the superstition. When you buy a mobile phone or a license plate, you get to choose your number, but the cost of the number will be based upon the perceived or market value of the numbers you choose. A mobile phone number ending in 4444 would cost virtually nothing—if it even exists. A number ending in 8888 would cost a king's ransom since the number of occurrences simply multiplies the good luck associated with the number.

Again, I have often been asked, "Don't people staying on the fifth floor of a hotel know that they're really staying on the fourth floor?" Of course they do. But they're not. To the inductive logician, they are staying on the fifth floor, even though it is four floors above ground level. (Don't Americans staying on the fourteenth floor of a hotel know that they are really on the thirteenth floor if the hotel does not have a thirteenth floor stop on the elevator?)

Do you remember the Summer Olympics held in Beijing? They began at 8:08 p.m. on 8/8/2008. I assure you that was not a coincidence.

And as one who flies frequently between China and the United States, I noticed on one flight that the normally full flight I take was almost empty and there were no more than a handful of Chinese on board. And then it hit me: I was flying on 4/14/14. Few Chinese would take the chance of flying on an airplane on such an unlucky date. (Obviously the flight was uneventful.)

So what are we to make of all this as Westerners? In the end I've decided that there is nothing to make. There is no superstition in China. There is only truth. The "truth," however, is inductively defined, meaning that only the result matters. The Way, what we call "the natural order of things," is unknowable to the historically Taoist Chinese.

This is a hard concept for most Westerners to understand. But that's because they approach the issue deductively.

At times I've wondered if inductive logic isn't a bit like fatalism. Ultimately, however, I've concluded that they are very different concepts. Fatalism implies abdication. The Chinese abdicate nothing.

Personal accountability is higher on their list of priorities than it is for most Westerners. But "trying" means little. Achieving the desired result is all that matters. That's pretty "accountable" in my book.

The whole fascination with numbers is beyond my mental capacity to truly understand, having been raised as a deductive thinker. However, I am convinced that there is no more or less real support or detraction for it than there is for the Western concept that we determine our own destiny through our personal behavior and actions.

The thing I do like about superstition in China is that good luck is both collective and can be passed on. When we first arrived in China, my youngest daughter was four years old, and with the shape of her face and the light color of her hair, she was an immediately recognizable foreigner.

During our first Spring Festival, or Chinese New Year, as it's known in the West, we went to one of Beijing's popular temple fairs, which have become more like street fairs than the temple fairs of old. There's plenty of food, some entertainment, some traditional dancing—the Dragon Dance being the most recognized by Westerners—and plenty of arcade games.

My daughters, of course, wanted to participate in the latter rather than watch the traditional dancers, so we approached a crowded arcade game that involved throwing a strongly inflated—and thus bouncy—large plastic ball onto a table of very small bowls, some of which were sprayed in color. If you were to throw the ball and have it settle in one of the colored bowls (an ending, as in most arcade games, that is statistically unlikely), you win a prize commensurate with that color.

In the middle of the table, however, was a lone red bowl. (Red is the ultimate celebratory color in China. If you follow the stock market, a red arrow means the stock has gone up in price. A green arrow means it has gone down.) If, in the highly unlikely chance that the ball ended up in the lone red bowl, you won the largest prize of all—an incredibly large prize in the end—an event as statistically unlikely as my defeating Ronda Rousey in a UFC ring.

Most Americans would view such a game as a mere form of entertainment since surely no one possesses the skill to steer the ball into the bowl of their choice. Skill was of no concern to the Chinese lined up four deep on all four sides of the game, however. This is a game of luck, and luck is very much "real" to the inductive thinker, whether you have personal control over it or not.

My youngest daughter finally made her way to the front of the line—with a little Chinese elbowing on my part to help—and I handed the attendant the requisite number of coins for four attempts. As the Chinese adore children and have an innate sense of fairness they are seldom given credit for, the attendant insisted that my young, petite daughter stand up on the ledge surrounding the game to give her the chance to at least get the ball to the table. (I suspect he also recognized that if she were to throw the ball from such a flat angle, the ball was unlikely to ever stay on the table.)

So, with dozens of Chinese watching the little fair-haired foreign girl, my daughter hurled the first ball high into the air without even looking where she had thrown it. My first inclination was that she had thrown the ball much too high to have any chance of staying on the table, but when it came down, it bounced vertically enough to come down a second time, a third time, and what seemed like an infinite number of additional times.

Until it finally came to rest—snuggled securely in the red bowl in the middle of the table.

At first there was dead silence as the rapt crowd of Chinese processed what they had just witnessed. Then there was a spontaneous eruption of joy—cheering and dancing, shouts of ecstasy, and even hugging. They had been there. They had been there to witness the four-year-old light-haired foreign girl with blue eyes enjoy luck beyond comprehension.

Surely it would rub off on them. They too would surely enjoy good fortune in the coming year. Many lined up simply to touch her in the hope that this would enhance their unbelievably good fortune. Here, to their way of thinking, was clearly a moment that was truly special, made all the more special by the fact that it all flowed from a cute little foreign girl in their China.

And the most excited of all was the attendant himself. He had, in fairness, chosen the ball, completely at random but surely with good luck on his shoulder, the ball that had done the impossible. Surely he would soon be lucky in his own way.

I wonder, in comparison, how a Western crowd might have reacted to the event. Some would certainly have cheered—particularly the mothers and grandmothers in the crowd. However, I sense that some would have walked away, disappointed that it had not been them who had enjoyed the good fortune to throw the ball into the red bowl.

My older daughter, then six, faced a different, but related, series of circumstances. She was cute, with a mane of thick golden hair that you could pick out 500 meters away in a crowded subway station or park in Beijing.

If we visited a popular tourist attraction, such as the Summer Palace in Beijng, it was not uncommon for thirty to fifty people per day to ask me if they could have their pictures taken with my daughters, who reluctantly, but agreeably, went along. I was always lecturing them that we were guests in a foreign country and had to behave like good ambassadors of our own country.

Most were young Chinese women who found the girls to be cute and who inevitably posed with their faces next to my daughters' while flashing the two-finger V sign that all young Chinese girls seem to employ when having their picture taken. (I have asked dozens of colleagues as to the meaning of this gesture and inevitably receive the answer that there is no meaning. They only do it because they once saw a popular movie star from Hong Kong employ the gesture.)

There were, however, a surprising number of elderly men, always with family, who asked to have their picture taken with my older daughter, and the pose was always the same—they would rest their hand gently on the top of her head. I was never concerned about her safety because there was always family present and they always asked permission first. (Actually, it was normally the youngest of the clan who asked because they were the most likely to speak English.)

Nonetheless, I became obsessed with curiosity as to why the pose was always the same. And when I finally asked a colleague who I knew would know, she immediately responded that, "Her hair is the color of gold, and they believe that if they touch it, they will enjoy great monetary fortune in the coming year. If your hair were the color of hers, they would make the same request. After all, there is no gold hair among the ethnic Chinese."

CHAPTER 10

DEATH

It's not the most pleasant topic, to be sure, but what do you do with the dead in a country with the landmass roughly the size of the United States and 1.4 billion inhabitants? Like virtually everything else in China, the answer is changing.

The Chinese traditionally buried their dead in coffins and organized cemeteries that look pretty much like their counterparts the world over, although in the rural areas, the coffins are buried under grouped but seemingly random cone-shaped piles of dirt scattered among the wooded stands surrounding the local villages.

In the major urban areas, however, traditional coffin burial has been outlawed for some time, a ban now spreading to other cities interested in preserving precious land for economic and residential development. Just last year, it was widely reported that several elderly Chinese in the city of Anqing, in the province of Anhui, committed suicide to beat a June 1 deadline for the cessation of all coffin burials in the area (the local government disputes the connection).

And while cremation has been the norm in the larger cities for many years, several urban governments are now looking to the sea as a way to further reduce funerary land usage. "He Qingxun, head of the burial and funeral management division at the Ministry of Civil Affairs, said on Tuesday that more urban residents are choosing sea burials through the encouragement of local governments" (*China Daily*, April 4, 2014). In some cities, the article went on to note, local governments are even offering free sea burial services or cash subsidies to families to promote the practice.

And what do the Chinese think about death? Well, like the rest of the world, they mourn it. It is customary for friends to pay respects to the family of the deceased in much the same way they do in the West, although usually without the religious ritual or overtones.

Beyond that simple generalization, however, individual notions about the end of life are as broad and varied here as they are elsewhere, there being no scientific way to prove or disprove any of the many theories that have been offered on the topic.

Buddhists, from what I've learned, generally accept the Hindu concepts of karma and reincarnation. While the body is impermanent, the spirit lives on in one of six realms—heaven, human beings, Asura, hungry ghost, animal, and hell—depending on the accumulated karma, or cause and effect of one's positive and negative actions.

These subsequent lives are themselves impermanent as one continues to move through the six levels of existence until one potentially reaches the ultimate goal of Nirvana, escaping the limitations of existence and achieving ultimate peace through the extinction of desire.

The Chinese, including those who do not identify themselves as Buddhists, seem to share many of these same beliefs, albeit in varied forms, but with one important distinction. As in life, Chinese notions of death turn more on family and ancestral heritage than on the supremacy of a spiritual deity or force, or the more individualistic orientation of most organized religion. (Of course, nearly all organized religions promote collective identity and responsibility, but it is a collectivism defined by a spirituality external to self rather than an identity defined by self and our biological relationships.)

The Chinese perspective on death, as a result, appears to lack the clear line of demarcation between life and death found in most organized religion. The living and their ancestors, it appears, continue to interact between death and life in much the same way that the living still do. In this view the Chinese soul has a yin-yang flavor to it, the yin (*po*) soul being more material in nature (ie, the living), and the yang (*hun*) soul being more ethereal (ie, the departed).

From the Chinese I've talked to, however, the world in which the departed soul lives is rather ill defined. While I have heard references to both good places and bad places, these destinations appear more in line with the Buddhist notions of levels than the bipolar extremes of heaven and hell. What is fairly consistent among the Chinese I've spoken with, however, is the belief that whatever the afterworld looks like, the departed struggle with the same everyday challenges faced by the living. They continue to strive to achieve a better life—in the process struggling with the same bureaucratic impediments and need for money that the living do.

This is why it is common practice on the national holiday known as Qingming Festival, or Tomb Sweeping Day, for family members to leave money, food, and drink at the gravesite of their ancestors. In some cases the money is burned as a kind of offering. It's not legal tender, of course. It may be a picture of a new home or some other symbol of comfort and prosperity. In other cases, it is simply placed on top of the burial mound with a rock to keep it from blowing away—always pragmatic, the Chinese.

But I believe that the real objective of the holiday and the everyday honor and respect universally paid by the Chinese to their ancestors comes back to the desire to seek balance and harmony in the interplay of yin and yang. It is generally believed that due to the yin-yang connection between the living and the departed, one's ancestors have an ongoing influence over the life and well-being of the family left behind.

It is the same notion of reciprocity that drives all yin-yang relationships. If you honor, respect, and provide for your ancestors, they in turn will help you along in this world. Somehow disrespect or dishonor your deceased extended family, and you can expect they will place roadblocks in your path to happiness and success.

All of this serves to reinforce the gravity of obligation on which much of Chinese cultural tradition is built. For the Chinese, in fact, such obligation extends back thousands of years.

If that sounds a bit overwhelming, we must remember that important benefits come with obligation. You can certainly see how an only child setting out in life in a megacity of twenty million people, far away from friends and family, might feel a little less alone knowing that a long line of ancestors is behind him or her. You're never entirely alone in life, and you're never entirely on your own. The family is looking out for you—assuming, of course, you have fulfilled your familial obligations.

It also explains an observation I made almost upon arrival but never completely understood—the Chinese emphasis on the place of birth, which for older generations of Chinese was more likely than not to have been a village or small town. "What is your hometown?" is a standard question posed when two people meet for the first time, and in job interviews, and it is standard information in any proclamation of your identity (eg, letters of introduction, the Chinese equivalent of Facebook pages).

Your hometown, in fact, is just as much a part of your identity as your age or gender. And, to a degree, just as neutral. People appear to inquire about hometowns not so much because there are good ones and bad ones, although the Chinese, like people everywhere, are often quick to make generalizations about people based solely on where they are from. (For example, Fujian people have a good head for business. The girls from Suzhou are pretty). In general, it appears that the question has a deeper, almost spiritual purpose. As in "Where is your family anchored?"

Why? There is the practical explanation that the hukou system, the national registry system designed to control internal migration and limit the pace of urbanization, and which has a significant impact on the health care and education you have access to, is generally linked to your place of birth.

It is clear to me now, however, that your hometown, being the base of your extensive and tall ancestral tree, must provide a very comforting sense of permanence to an otherwise impermanent life. If Westerners believe that "You can never go home again," the Chinese, it appears, believe that you never really leave it.

Which, perhaps, is why so many Chinese endure the hardship of migration for the sake of work. The Chinese registry system known as the hukou system, in an effort to limit the pace of migration and avoid overwhelming the prosperous urban areas, makes it difficult for families to migrate as a family unit. If a mother or father can find lucrative work in another city or province, he or she will generally leave the family in the region of their birth so that the children may go to school and the remaining family members can enjoy better medical care.

Sometimes both spouses leave, often separately, in search of work, leaving the child to be raised by its grandparents or other family members.

At my previous Chinese company, we had both workers and senior managers who lived this migratory lifestyle. If they were lucky, they could spend weekends with their families. Many returned once per quarter. Many in the service industries see their families only once a year, usually during the mass migration that is Spring Festival.

And how do they do it, I've often wondered. How do they avoid the sense of separation? How do they avoid the sense of isolation and loss?

Abraham Maslow (1908–1970) was an American psychologist best known for the development of Maslow's hierarchy of needs. In it he postulated that humans could not achieve self-esteem or self-actualization—the fulfillment of one's potential—until they first had food to eat, a safe place to stay, and had established connection with the world around them.

And this is where the Chinese have an edge over Westerners and why the migration pattern of work is sustainable in China. The Chinese are always connected, no matter where they are. They are connected to their families, they are permanent citizens of the cities and villages in which they were born, and they are ultimately connected to every other Chinese person on the planet.

That represents a powerful social and emotional anchor that fewer and fewer Westerners enjoy, which perhaps helps explain the increased use of selective serotonin reuptake inhibitors (eg, Prozac), benzodiazepines (eg, Valium), and anxiety inhibitors such as Xanax that are in such common use in the United States today. (To be clear, I have nothing against this trend. I am simply noting the importance of connection, sometimes which we find among family and friends, sometimes which we find in prescription medication, and sometimes which we find in alcohol and drug addiction.)

CHAPTER 11

FOREVER A FOREIGNER

China is not a melting pot. In places like the United States and Australia, all but a small portion of the resident population is from someplace else. In China just the opposite is true. Out of 1.3 billion people, there are fewer than 600,000 foreign residents, or .05 percent of the resident population, according to government statistics.

Even the native population is relatively homogenous. There are fifty-six officially recognized ethnic groups in China, whose ethnic cultures are both celebrated and protected by the Chinese constitution. Under Chinese law all ethnic groups are equal, granting each the right to self-rule, protection of their culture, and the right to speak and write their own language.

Twenty-three of these ethnic groups, however, have populations of less than 100,000 people. Only eighteen of the minority ethnic groups have a population in excess of one million people, and the largest among them, the Zhuang, have a population of just over fifteen million. Fully 93 percent of all Chinese, in fact, belong to one ethnic group—the Han Chinese.

Everyone outside these fifty-six ethnic groups is a foreigner, a distinction that has gone by many names over the years, but a distinction that is nonetheless clear and ingrained in the culture.

The Chinese are admittedly conflicted by the idea of foreigners. At times foreigners are idolized as paragons of personal qualities that the Chinese would like to see more evidence of in their own society (eg, charity). Sometimes, however, foreigners are demonized, and rightfully so in many cases, as the embodiment of the lowest and worst instincts of the human race (eg, condescension, chauvinism, hedonism).

Gary Moreau

Either way, whether by conscious choice or lack of practice, the Chinese are not assimilative in their attitude toward foreigners. If you are not Chinese but speak the language fluently, you are merely a foreigner who speaks Mandarin. If you were born on Chinese soil, you are merely a foreigner who was born in China. And if you have lived in China for thirty years, you are simply a foreigner who has lived in China a long time. I have a Chinese wife, but I am still openly referred to as a foreigner who married a Chinese wife.

Being a foreigner has its advantages and disadvantages. The advantage is that expectations are low. You are a foreigner. They don't expect you to understand or appreciate their culture. They are, as a rule, quite forgiving of cultural faux pas. And the waitress will not laugh at you when she sees you struggling to pick up a peanut with your chopsticks. She will just bring you a spoon—without the sigh.

If you've lived here for a while, as I have, the isolation does tend to weigh on you. I have Chinese friends. Many I feel very close to. They admire and respect me, and I feel the same toward them. I am nonetheless, not one of them, and I know that line will never be crossed.

Newcomers, moreover, may feel disquieted by behaviors that long-term residents ultimately become accustomed to. They may still find themselves the subject of long and blatant stares, particularly if they venture away from the urban areas and popular tourist destinations where foreigners are less commonplace. Not so much because they are such an oddity as because the Chinese do not consider it rude to stare, a cultural trait that some Westerners find unsettling, but which I have come to appreciate as refreshingly transparent. Westerners stare too. We just do it more deceptively.

There is prejudice, of course, although it is seldom meanspirited or judgmental. Nonetheless, I know that when I inquire about the price of an item I am interested in buying, the shopkeeper is sure to quote a price considerably higher than it would be for a Chinese shopper.

Once you accept the fact that you are a foreigner here, seldom considered a pejorative label, you will find that there is very little blatant discrimination and blatant racism here.

Racism is, in the end, a deductive concept. If your skin is black or brown or yellow, you are presumed by the deductive thinker to behave in a certain way (cause and effect). It is deductive logic that tells me that if you are a young black man with your hoodie up, I should move to the other side of the street.

If you are an inductive thinker, on the other hand, you will merely conclude that here comes a young black man with his hoodie up. You may wonder why this is considered fashionable, but you will only speculate cause and effect, you won't accept them as given. Chances are, therefore, that you won't act upon them.

CHAPTER 12

RACISM & PREJUDICE

During the protests in Ferguson, Missouri, over a white policeman killing an unarmed black teenager and the grand jury's decision not to prosecute, people of all ethnicities took to the streets in an attempt to force a more meaningful discussion on racism and its implications.

As usual, the discussion didn't seem to get very far and protests erupted again in 2015 on the one-year anniversary of the shooting.

But why is racism such a difficult issue for Americans to come to grips with? And why do we continue to argue whether or not it exists?

I believe that the inductively minded Chinese have an explanation that is best explained by their example.

John Blake wrote an article on CNN's website after the Ferguson shooting entitled, "The New Threat: 'Racism without Racists,'" a term used by a Duke University sociologist and the title of a book written by Eduardo Bonilla-Salva.

The premise of the article is that you don't have to be racist to behave in racist ways. In my own words, you only have to be a deductive thinker who believes that cause always controls effect. So long as we don't think blatantly racial thoughts (cause), we are not, by definition, racists. Deductively speaking, of course.

Blake, however, in a stroke of brilliant inductive logic, noted that this line of thought missed the point. Many white people, he noted, say, "I don't see color" and "Justice should be color-blind." If the grand jury made the decision not to indict the officer, then that was the right decision and there's no issue of racism.

Wrong. It is the outcome, not the cause, which ultimately matters, as every Chinese will tell you. It doesn't matter why American culture is racist, it only matters that it is, a fact that is difficult to refute on any objective basis. Study after study has documented it.

In just one study professors from the University of Chicago and MIT, according to Blake's article, sent 5,000 fictitious resumes in response to 1,300 help wanted ads. They were identical except for the name. Some were given names typical of Anglo-Americans while others were given names more frequently associated with African-Americans. The ones given the Anglican names were called for interviews at a 50 percent higher rate.

There are only a few hundred thousand expatriates living in China today, a country with a population of 1.4 billion people. And not one Chinese person I have ever met has ever said, "I don't see color." Not one Chinese, not one, has ever asked me if I'm a foreigner or suggested that, "I didn't notice. You look Chinese to me. I am color-blind."

I am a foreigner, and that is how I am referred to by every Chinese person I have yet to meet. I have round eyes and a big nose, and children in particular are not afraid to stare at me because of it.

However, not once in my time here have I ever been harassed in any way simply because I am a foreigner. Not once has a policeman in a public place asked to see my identification or asked me why I was there. Not once have I been made to feel like a victim of suspicion. Not once!

The point is that there is no attempt to pretend. There is no attempt to see no color. There is no fear to acknowledge that we are different. We can talk openly and freely about our differences because neither of us sees being different as being bad. We are who we are.

I was the only foreigner in my company and ate lunch every day in the company canteen. We frequently spent the time on the topic of the difference between foreigners and the Chinese. Can you fathom a group of African-Americans and white Americans having that discussion in such an informal, relaxed way?

We're all biased. We can't help it. When I see an older Chinese woman approaching a line I am quietly standing in, I immediately brace myself to prevent her from cutting in front of me.

When I am approached on the streets by trinket sellers, I tell them in Mandarin to "bug off" in a manner that might be considered rude in America in order to clear up any potential ambiguity. They are never offended. They are glad to have the clarity so they can move on to the next potential customer and not waste their time on a sale that isn't going to happen.

Unlike the American Caucasian and African-American populations, we are talking the same language. We aren't pretending that our behavior is only defined by our values.

Behaviors (effects) can also reinforce biases (causes), of course, and the Chinese realize this. As China's continued development leads to more and more outbound tourism, the government has initiated a massive educational campaign to teach the Chinese how they will be expected to behave when traveling abroad. Wait in line. Don't spit. Don't urinate on the side of the road. Cover your mouth when you sneeze. (Spitting and sneezing, by the way, are issues of traditional Chinese perceptions of health, not civility.)

It's not judgmental. There is no attempt to be color-blind. It's very matter-of-fact. It's an informative dialogue.

And it occurs at every level. My Chinese wife often asks me if I find a particular Chinese woman attractive. The Chinese and foreigners often have different perceptions of beauty in both men and women, and she is just curious to learn. She doesn't pretend the difference doesn't exist. So I don't pretend the woman in question doesn't exist or is not pretty. I answer her honestly and often in a level of detail that few American husbands would ever share with their American wives out of fear of starting an unwanted fight. My wife has never challenged me on my answer, however, either at the time or in the future. She doesn't pretend I am not a man. She only cares how I act upon it.

CHAPTER 13

REVERSE PREJUDICE: TRYING TOO HARD

As an American I've always been a foreigner. Like all Americans other than the relatively small minority of indigenous Native Americans, my family is from someplace else. In my own case the migration took place a couple of generations ago, but the timing doesn't redefine the reality.

America, often referred to as "the melting pot," was built on a culture of assimilation. The ability of US culture to assimilate foreigners has long been considered one of the country's great strengths: the symbol of a culture built on equal rights, transparency, and goodwill toward those who are different from us.

This inward assimilation, of course, is getting a lot of press at the moment, both from those who wish to limit the pace of immigration and by those who prefer not to be assimilated to the same extent that prior generations of immigrants desired. What gets far less attention, however, is the inverse of the American cultural trait of assimilation. It is the cultural tendency of Americans to *seek* assimilation, however temporary or superficial, when we are the foreigners in a foreign land.

Americans traveling abroad have earned a universal reputation for being a little loud and a little pushy at times. And while I have witnessed this myself, I have also witnessed similar behavior in tourists from every corner of the globe. The fact is that people who employ a strong transmitter-oriented communication style are likely to get both loud and frustrated when they are unable to get their point across.

The truth is that most Americans universally and genuinely want to "fit in" when they find themselves in a foreign culture. Business travelers in particular often obsess about it. American companies sending employees on a foreign assignment frequently provide extensive training to assist in cultural understanding and assimilation on the implied assumption that cultural integration is universally expected, even admired, by the host culture.

I see it frequently in many foreign business people traveling to China for the first time. Once they learn that I have worked here for many years, they are often brimming with questions about what to do or how to behave in a wide variety of social situations they may or may not encounter. They are anxious to do the right thing.

Tourists also exhibit similar enthusiasm for "going local," as it were. One older widower in the small town where my former in-laws live went abroad for the first time in her life on a group tour to India. She came back so enthused with her experience that she redecorated her home with Indian art and took to wearing traditional Indian clothing around her small rural village. Amused, but ultimately weary of her overindulgence, her neighbors started to joke, "It's time for Sally to take another trip."

I too used to accept that cultural assimilation is important and underscores the generally respectful and civil nature of American culture. After all these years in China, however, I have acquired a different perspective—one that I believe may help to explain the general political and cultural isolation that we as Americans sometimes find ourselves in.

It came together for me in an "aha" moment I had while attending training that we were providing for our field sales organization in Shanghai some time ago. The trainer was an independent professional who came highly recommended and certainly lived up to his billing. He was Chinese, but attended a prestigious US university so he certainly had an informed opinion on American culture and social habits, In talking at some length with him, he genuinely likes and respects America and its people.

In a section of the course that addressed how to interact with people of different nationalities and ethnicities in a positive and effective way, however, he put up a series of photographs showing President Barack Obama and President Vladimir Putin greeting various foreign monarchs, emperors, and religious leaders. It was a lesson in contrasts.

In each case President Obama could be seen bowing deeply while look-ing straight down at the floor—in a way totally outside the American cul-tural norm—to the foreign leader he was being introduced to. President Putin, on the other hand, was pictured standing erect, offering a firm handshake, and looking his host directly in the eye. And in each picture of President Obama, the trainer had added a speech bubble to the receiving dignitary, saying, "Dude, what the f--k?" (It's a topic for another time but many Chinese swear in inappropriate settings because they learn English, in part, from American movies.)

As a quick but important aside, contrary to what a lot of Americans believe, the Russians and the Chinese are not any more culturally aligned than, say, the Chinese and the Swedish. President Putin, however, is widely admired in China, and this trainer's perspective on the difference between President Putin's and President Obama's approach to meeting foreign mon-archs, I think, explains why.

The essential message is that when you are interacting with others, particularly if they are somehow foreign to you, you should be friendly but strong—respectful, but not compliant to the point of suggesting in-sincerity. In each of these pictures, President Obama was going so far to assimilate—to follow what he thought was the proper way to pay respect to the individual receiving him—that it came off as being a bit phony, even insincere. At the very least he looked a bit weak, as if compliant to a degree that would naturally breed distrust.

President Putin, by contrast, exhibited respect, but did so with su-preme confidence that enhanced the sincerity of his greeting. He came off as a man who was genuinely interested in meeting his host *and* a man you could trust.

I offer no opinion as to which, if either, characterization is accurate. However, the lesson did provide clarity to me regarding my own education in how to be a foreigner.

When I first arrived in China, I was often an anxious wreck in social settings. An introvert by nature, I nonetheless wanted to do the right thing. It was, of course, my job. But more importantly I desperately wanted to fit in. Introvert or not, I wanted my new Chinese colleagues and neighbors to like me. Don't we all?

The social protocols of Chinese culture, however, are complex. Even after reading a half-dozen books on the topic, I still found it confusing to attend a business dinner where people were constantly offering toasts and making short speeches.

There were so many variables. Sometimes you stand up; sometimes you sit down. Sometimes you come around the table; sometimes you toast from afar. Sometimes you suggest "bottoms up"; sometimes you don't. To say nothing about the protocols involving how to hold your glass and who should hold his glass lower, exactly how low to go, where to clink, and so forth.

But then I learned to be a foreigner. I learned to accept the simple and obvious fact that I am a foreigner and my Chinese hosts know it. I couldn't convince them otherwise no matter how much I assimilated the language and the culture. In the end, I will still have Western eyes and a big nose.

But here's the important part of the lesson: *That's OK for them.* They know I'm not Chinese, and they know I'm never going to be Chinese. So they cut me a whole lot of slack when it comes to cultural protocols.

The thing is that they respect me for being strong and sincere. The rest is largely irrelevant. I can relax. They can relax. Everybody has a better time.

Of course I still participate in the cultural traditions. But I no longer think of it as a forced march. I participate to the extent that I want, and then I let them continue on their own. I no longer feel like I need to understand or even participate in every cultural activity that's going on around me.

But the lesson doesn't stop there. I can honestly say that in learning to be a foreigner, I have come to be a whole lot more comfortable in my own skin. Life is no longer the intense test of social protocol it once was for me. I am perfectly comfortable taking it as it comes, and that makes me both a better listener and a more effective communicator. And that, in turn, makes me better at getting along and working with people—all kinds of people.

So when the day comes that I move back to America and a foreign family moves in next door, I will not care if they speak my language or follow my customs. They are foreigners. They should be who they are. As long as they are trustworthy and sincere—and strength does imply sincerity most of the time—we will get along.

And should I ever get the chance to meet a monarch or a religious leader, I know exactly what I'm going to do. I'm going to "pull a Putin." I'm going to shake their hand, look them straight in the eye, and say, "Hello. I am a foreigner. Please forgive my ignorance of your culture. But it is indeed a pleasure to meet you."

To my fellow American foreigners, I say, "It's OK to be a foreigner. Don't try so hard. Relax. Be who you are and let others be who they are. Everyone will get along better that way."

And keep your voice down. Speaking loudly or becoming openly frustrated will not help them understand you.

LIVING IN CHINA

CHAPTER 14

THE CHINESE EDUCATION SYSTEM

Getting a good job in China is not just an opportunity; it is an obligation. You are expected to take care of your elders in their old age, so you are expected to have the most successful career you can. Otherwise both you and they will lose face in the extended family and community.

In the past, that meant getting into a well-respected university. While the informal economy of day workers and unregistered migrant laborers and tradesmen is enormous, the best jobs have historically been in the government or the large state-owned enterprises that dominate key industries such as energy and transportation. For these jobs, patronage aside, the university you graduate from goes a long way in determining which doors of opportunity will be open to you.

The universities are officially ranked—tier one, tier two, and so on—and you never choose your university based on what academic programs they excel in. You go to the highest ranked university you can get into and major in whatever they offer you. The school, not your major, will determine the professional opportunities open to you upon graduation.

It is a great system for convincing students to buckle down and work hard. It is almost impossible to simply cruise through high school and graduate without having learned all that much.

Several unintended consequences handicap Chinese graduates in today's global world, however. The first is that there are only so many seats at the top tier universities. That makes admission to the best schools a zero sum game. You can only attend if your classmates only qualify for a less prestigious school, which obviously doesn't reinforce team-building skills.

The second unintended consequence is that the educational emphasis is inevitably focused on rote learning—the absorption of the kinds of facts that are likely to be asked on the standardized national exam known as *gaokao* (in fairness, Chinese educators are actively trying to change this).

Both of these factors have contributed to one of the biggest problems China faces in its future development—a severe management gap. Many young Chinese entering the workforce are bright and hardworking but are equipped with the wrong skills for today's global marketplace. They are great at engineering and science, which is why they can so easily copy anything.

However, they are not always equipped with the communication skills necessary to sell their ideas or defend their positions. And collaboration, which is arguably the cornerstone of the commercial world of technology, does not come naturally.

This has caused many within China to question China's ability to ever produce a company like Apple or Google. Are the Chinese creative enough?

I believe the question is misdirected. The Chinese have an abundance of creativity. Just look at their art, their poetry, their theater, and their architecture. It is among the most creative mankind has ever produced. And China has been producing it for thousands of years.

I believe the issue is one of curiosity rather than creativity. The current education system does not emphasize learning for the sake of learning. Learning is taught only as a means to an end. Good enough is enough.

It is an inductive view of education. Results (knowledge) are all that matter. The means to achieve them (collaboration, analytics, creativity) are all lacking. That makes the Chinese both great at copying and solving previously encountered problems (and explains why the government seems to always use the same playbook). It is not, however, a productive way to teach people to solve new problems or address new challenges. The temptation is always to revert to the tried and true.

That, however, is not the approach by which people like Steve Jobs built their innovative empires. They built them on raw curiosity, the desire to know simply for the sake of knowing, as well as absolute notions ("putting a dent in the universe" as Jobs put it) that are often too vaguely defined to be understood by the rote learner.

There is another unintended consequence of the Chinese education system that is getting much attention among the Chinese themselves and falsely reinforcing some of the educational attributes that are sure to hurt China in the collaborative global economy of the future.

There was a study by Amy Hsin and Yu Xie, two sociologists from the City University of New York and the University of Michigan respectively. The study was an attempt to understand the well-documented fact that Asian Americans achieve at a much higher rate than other ethnic subgroups in the United States.

Amy Chua, a Yale law professor, famously attributed the achievement gap to harsh (meaning good) Asian parenting, coining the phrase "tiger mother" and igniting a firestorm of controversy among American mothers offended by the implied stereotype of the lax and coddling Western parent.

I do remember a parent-teacher conference several years ago here in Beijing in which my wife and I shared with my daughter's teacher her disappointment that her report card scores were not as high as a Chinese boy in her class with whom she was friends. The teacher, an Australian as I recall, immediately noted, "You can't compare your daughters with the Asian kids. The Asian kids leave school and immediately go into private tutoring whether they need it or not. As an educator it drives me crazy. The kids need much broader development at this age, and a little playtime with other kids is a good thing. Your daughter is doing just fine. Tell her not to worry."

The theory of the tiger mother has two fundamental flaws. The first is that it fails to incorporate the statistical impact of selection. Not every Chinese family can move to the United States. I would dare say that for the same reason if you tested the average foreign student in China against the overall Chinese population, you would find the foreigners' scores to be consistently higher.

The second is, again, an unintended consequence. Chinese students are under tremendous pressure from their parents and their teachers to perform well on standardized tests. Most Chinese students start their day at seven o'clock and don't finish until nine that evening. That burden leaves little time for play, and their physical and social development can suffer as a result.

You might protest that the performance of China at the 2008 Summer Olympic Games and other international sporting events contradicts this generalization. On the contrary, it reinforces it. China has an abundance of internationally elite athletes, but they are pulled out of mainstream society and its education system at a young age and put through a parallel education system designed to develop the most gifted athletes in isolation (the Soviets employed a similar system).

The need to reform the Chinese education system is likewise being reinforced by the divergent trajectories of the availability of a university education and the impact of a slowing economy that continues to rely heavily on infrastructure and real estate investment.

The Chinese university system now produces seven million graduates per year, a sevenfold increase in approximately fifteen years. The current economy, however, which has yet to pivot to the kind of service economy (eg, financial services or medicine) the government has promised, cannot absorb that number of university graduates, particularly given the previously mentioned deficiency in the skills of deductive thinking, communication, and collaboration that are critical to an advanced modern economy.

The same trend happened in the West, of course, during the Great Recession. The difference is that the Chinese graduates have virtually sacrificed their childhoods on the promise that a good score on the gaokao and a diploma from a respected university were a guaranteed ticket to a good job and a comfortable life.

The resentment, understandably, is palpable, and the government is scrambling to address the problem. While social unrest is an obvious concern, there is also the risk of a major brain drain as these graduates pursue careers outside of China, denying China of the talent it will most definitely need as the economy attempts, as it must, to move up the value chain.

The good news for the future is that the Chinese put great value on education. The rest is just process and can be fixed. Applying the same enthusiasm they bring to every challenge, I have no doubt that the Chinese will continue to produce a performance-driven workforce with the creative and collaborative skills necessary in the modern global economy.

CHAPTER 15

WOMEN IN CHINA

My home in Beijing (they call them villas here) is an investment property owned by a successful Chinese couple. (This is commonplace. Real estate is the investment of choice in China.) Because the house was being renovated during the early days of my assignment here, I went back to view it several times prior to making a commitment. On each occasion I met with the husband, who was both easygoing and fluent in English.

Although my wife and daughters were still living in the United States at the time, we eventually agreed this was a house we could call home during our time in China, and I informed the Realtor accordingly. She in turn arranged a meeting with the landlord to negotiate the final price and sign the paperwork.

When I showed up on this last occasion, however, it was the wife, not the husband, who met with me. I was certainly OK with that, but I was curious to know the reason for the change in players, particularly given the immediately obvious fact that the woman spoke little English. So I took the Realtor aside in search of an explanation. She explained, with more than a hint of exasperation, "Now you're talking money. Before you were just looking. In China the women handle the money."

And in the years since, I have generally found that to be true. A lot of the products my former company produces and sells are sold through distributors, many of which are small, private husband-and-wife teams. And with few exceptions it is the husband's role to establish and maintain the personal relationships that are so critical to business in China while the wife handles the books, the banking, and the buying. Most of these men,

I suspect, are clueless when it comes to how much money they or their companies have.

This is not a new development. When I traveled through Asia meeting with suppliers more than twenty-five years ago, I don't recall ever meeting with a single woman with a seat at the table of decision-making in most of the countries I visited. The meetings tended to involve a lot of people at different levels of the organization, but all were men. (I recall one occasion when a female executive traveling with my team was asked to remain in the hotel while the men went out to dinner. The request came not as a result of the activities planned. Our hosts simply didn't know how to deal with her presence.)

In Hong Kong, by contrast (Mainland China was not accessible to foreign business at the time), the companies tended to be family affairs where the matriarch and the daughters played prominent roles in all meetings and social activities. The daughters, in fact, would often take the lead when it came time to negotiate price.

Mao Zedong famously noted, "Women hold up half the sky," and advocated equal pay for equal work. The rights of women are explicitly protected in the Chinese constitution.

The Constitution of the People's Republic of China

Article 48. *Women in the People's Republic of China enjoy equal rights* *with men in all spheres of life, political, economic, cultural and social, and family life. The state protects the rights and interests of women, applies the principle of equal pay for equal work for men and women alike and trains and selects cadres from among women.*

While few countries can match China's record for gender neutrality, there clearly remain further opportunities for improvement. Women certainly occupy positions of great power in the Chinese government, but no woman has ever served on the seven-member Politburo Standing Committee that rules the Communist Party of China. Only 5 percent of the Central Committee are women, although it must be noted that the overall parliamentary representation of women in China is higher than in the US Congress.

The culture remains largely patriarchal. By custom and tradition the men are often granted the final word (at least that's what they are allowed to think) and the best seat at the dinner table. (Due to the group-dining orientation of all Chinese cuisine, of course, dining tables are invariably round, so there is no "head of the table" per se. There is, however, still a protocol as to who sits where.)

Nonetheless, women have made more advances here than in many Western countries, including my own. Of my own senior management team, precisely half are women, as are half of the graduates from China's universities each year.

Nearly all women have careers. As a practical matter, stay-at-home-mothering is just not an option financially. Live-in grandparents typically provide childcare and household support such as cooking).

And contrary to the tradition of dowries, wherein the bride's family provides assets to support the bride in her marriage, it is the young men of China who are expected to provide "red envelopes" (red envelopes stuffed with cash) to their potential in-laws to prove their ability to provide for their future family. (Remember that older adults generally rely on their adult children for their retirement support, giving the process of accepting a husband for your daughter not unlike "due diligence" in the mergers and acquisitions world. And, of course, future in-law red envelope values are soaring due to both the high cost of housing in China and the gender-bias of birthrates influenced by the one-child policy, which has created a scarcity of potential brides in some areas.)

While China has a long history of literary excellence when it comes to love, it strikes me that marriage here is approached more pragmatically than in the West. Young women of marital age, or so I'm told by my Chinese friends and colleagues, tend to waste little time on relationships that are unlikely to lead to marriage—love or lust aside. And even on initial dates, young women are likely to ask direct questions about income, job security, debt, and investments. "Do you have a car?"

"Do you have any debts?" "How much do you earn?" "How stable is your employer?"

For every yang there is a yin, of course, and China's marital customs are no exception. Young women are under great family pressure to marry before they become too old—what is colloquially referred to as "a left-over woman"—to the point that there is a market for boyfriend rentals—a young man with a good job to take home over the Spring Festival holiday to get your overbearing parents to back down a bit.

And, of course, it's always difficult to draw the line between accepted custom and institutional oppression when it comes to matters of gender. There's little question that there are statistical gender biases among certain professions. Women are overrepresented in the service industries and underrepresented in the top ranks of the largest state-owned enterprises.

On balance, however, as the father of two young daughters, I don't hesitate to say that I am pleased with the role models Chinese women provide for them. While the women may not rule the roost at every level, they do control the money, and that in itself goes a long way toward ensuring equality of treatment and opportunity.

And the dragon ladies of lore? Well, I have found a universal confidence among the women of China that is refreshingly genuine and well-grounded. They are more likely to be aggressive than coy when engaging male colleagues, and I have to admit that when I make a trip to the local markets to shop, I consciously avoid the female sales staff when it comes time to negotiate a price. In my experience, they tend to be much tougher negotiators.

If anything, I believe that the men of China are more than a little afraid of the women. And I say that with all due respect. Bravado aside, when the women speak, the men listen—or cower, as the case may be.

Dragons or not, the women definitely do hold up half the sky here. And even if the men hold up the colorful half that the rainbow passes through, the women have the half with the gold. This is the reverse, I think, of what you find in many Western cultures, in which the women get the pretty and the men still hold the power.

CHAPTER 16

E-COMMERCE IN CHINA

E-commerce is exploding in China, growing at 45 percent per year and accelerating. While it still represents a relatively small percentage of the total retail sales made in China, many analysts are confidently predicting that it will eventually leapfrog traditional brick and mortar retail stores here.

Two things had to happen to make that possible. The first was that the e-tail platforms had to develop a payment system that was trusted and reliable. And they did.

The second was that they had to figure out how to deliver products in a timely and inexpensive manner so that even household items could be sold online. And they accomplished that as well, creating an e-commerce logistics ecosystem that can deliver packages across large urban centers such as Beijing and Shanghai for as little as $15.

What's propelling the explosion, of course, is the usual suspect of lower prices. That's particularly true in China because brick and mortar retail is essentially a real estate game, and real estate in China is famously expensive and completely controlled by the government, not the free markets. (You cannot actually own land in China. The land belongs to the people of China. You can only acquire the right to use the land for a specified period of time, and that is controlled by the fiduciaries of the people—the government.)

That means that at the large foreign box retailers that are visibly present here, you might be shocked by how high the prices are. While the labor is cheap, the rent is not.

Another development that makes China uniquely ripe for e-commerce dominance is congestion coupled with the fact that, due to cost and the regulatory hurdles needed to open a modern trade box store, the brick and mortar penetration of China is extremely low at a time when traffic congestion in the major urban areas is making it less and less convenient to leave the house. If I can order something in my pajamas that is inexpensive and will be delivered tomorrow, if not today, I'm not about to fight the traffic to reach the nearest big box retailer or shopping mall, which may be an hour away, depending on traffic. (The e-tailers get around the congestion by using specialized scooters to move your package the last kilometer.)

I ordered a fifty-inch flat-screen television from a famous Japanese supplier online. It arrived the next day, and the man who delivered it was an obvious expert. He set it up, adjusted everything to its optimal setting, and took all the packaging with him. He also gave me the telephone number of a local service center. If I ever had a problem, just call, he said. And he arrived on a small motorcycle with a metal box attached to the top. The smaller packages were inside. The television was strapped to the top.

To give you a sense of how big e-commerce might become in China, consider what happens in one special day, November 11, each year. It was invented by the marketing wizards at Alibaba, which along with JD.com controls something close to 90 percent of the e-commerce conducted in China.

Now known as Double 11, given its date, this e-commerce extravaganza was originally called Singles Day or Bachelor's Day. The idea was simple. Chinese singles, which are often referred to as sticks, are by definition left out of the amorous gift giving of Valentine's Day. Singles Day offers those so neglected to self-indulge without remorse—at great savings.

On November 11, 2013, exactly three weeks prior to the United States' own Cyber Monday, the Chinese once again recalibrated the global yardstick by which all things mind-boggling are measured. Alibaba, which owns B2C online platform Tmall and C2C online platform Taobao, attracted 402 million unique visitors who collectively spent $5.75 *billion*, an 83 percent increase over the prior year—in one twenty-four-hour period.

Alipay, Alibaba's equivalent of PayPal, processed 188 million payment transactions, more than the number of transactions processed by Visa worldwide in any given day, on average. And more than twenty-three times the average daily transaction volume processed by PayPal.

With days like this, it is no wonder China has become the largest e-tail market in the world. Alibaba, it seems, has come far closer than any other company to attaining that elusive Western dream of selling one widget to each of the 1.3 billion Chinese.

———

On top of the convenience factor, there is the previously noted issue of communication style. Being receiver oriented in their communication, the burden of communication falls with the listener, not the speaker, as it does in the United States and most Western countries.

Rather than the word *burden*, however, I've come to use the term *choice* when differentiating the speaker and listener orientation of communication. The Chinese, in other words, have no trouble simply tuning out the voices around them. While the cacophony of shrill and overpowering promoters one encounters in the grocery store on a Sunday afternoon is enough to drive me to the verge of insanity, the Chinese appear to not even notice their presence.

Taking that one step further, I wonder if the Internet isn't ideally suited for the Chinese model of communication. It's certainly cheap, an endearing quality to even the richest of Chinese. It's convenient, of course, which we've already discussed. And all of the annoying negatives of the online world, like the constant onslaught of unwanted pop-ups, the crush of junk mail, the millions of poor-quality web pages that seem to have been thrown together by a group of five-year-olds over cookies and milk, are not burdens at all to the receiver oriented, who effectively just tune them out.

And if you surf a few popular Chinese websites, Taobao included, you'll see that Chinese websites do bear a startling resemblance to a crowded grocery store awash in promoters dressed in silly costumes shouting their call to commerce. The only difference is that what the stores attempt to achieve through the relentless din of promoters, the websites seek to achieve through the use of overpowering graphics in constant motion. Both are overwhelming to our Western senses, the difference being only the path (audible versus visual) to sensory overload and the headache that often accompanies it.

The Chinese, however, see these websites through their eyes, not ours, and they're obviously effective. How else do you explain the fact that enough people logged onto Alibaba e-tail stores during the early hours of 11/11/13 to register 10 billion yuan in purchases *before* 6:00 a.m.? (They reached that same milestone in 2014 in the first thirty-eight minutes after midnight, the official start of the promotion.)

But what are the implications of this nearly incomprehensible e-tail revolution for the Middle Kingdom and the rest of the world it increasingly influences?

I would certainly be concerned if I were a traditional Western retailer looking to pave my way to riches in China with brick and mortar. And any Western company, no matter how low-tech or otherwise grounded in traditional channels of commerce, had better come up with a way to integrate the Internet into its commercial platform in a meaningful way.

Overall, I think the e-tail trend is generally good news for foreign companies looking to get in on the commercial action in China, particularly if they are just now showing up at the party. The cost of developing an Internet presence is not prohibitive (although the cost of getting any traffic may be), and the reach is universal on day one.

I would suggest, however, that you leave your Western web designers at home. They are bound to design websites that are appealing to your eyes but may not be so appealing to the Chinese you are attempting to lure into your universe. If you want to get your point across, it's always better to communicate in the same way your audience does.

The more intriguing question, and perhaps the most critical for those of us wishing to build strong long-term businesses in China, is where will it all stop? Will China, as it has in so many ways, slingshot past the rest of the world in the role ultimately played by e-commerce? And is e-tail so uniquely suited to Chinese culture and the realities of Chinese life today that it slingshots past itself? Instead of life playing out online, as appears to be the social trend in most Western cultures (think Facebook, Twitter, and so forth), will the online world play out in real life in China? And what will that look like?

Rather than the online world looking more and more like the physical world, will the physical world ultimately imitate the online world? Instead of using the online world to capture sales leads that are then closed by traditional sales teams, for example, will the role of the sales team become one of feeding leads to the online platform for follow-up and closure? Instead of using dating websites to arrange a shared activity, will we use activities to arrange online relationships?

These are intriguing questions for companies operating in China. Because, as we know from experience, change occurs quickly here. So if the online world is going to turn the real world on its head, I would bet dollars to donuts that it will happen first here in China.

As Confucius said, "Wherever you go, there you are." A fitting thought indeed for an online world in which you can be, quite literally, everywhere at once.

CHAPTER 17

THE INTERNET

There were more than 600 million Internet users in China at the end of 2013. And by the end of 2014, China became the largest e-commerce market on the planet.

Beyond its massive scope and reach, however, there are a couple of fundamental differences between Internet in China and the Western World Wide Web. And both, not surprisingly, mirror the fundamental difference between the deductively grounded world view of the West and the inductively holistic world view of the Middle Kingdom.

The first relates to e-commerce and reflects the importance of relationship in Chinese culture. While much of Chinese culture turns on personal obligation, all relationships are personal. And because the Chinese cannot personalize institutions to the extent that Westerners often do, there is a natural suspicion of all commercial institutions.

As a result, Amazon, which is synonymous with e-tailing in the United States, is a distant laggard here to industry leaders JD.com and Alibaba (Tmall & Taobao), the latter two accounting for close to 90 percent of the massive e-tail market in China. The Amazon model is a brand model built on the strength and credibility of the company's core brand—itself. JD.com and Alibaba, by contrast, both provide e-tail models that serve to facilitate peer review to the point of actual shopper branding through a complex system of peer endorsement that ultimately rates both the product *and* the reviewer, resulting in a community of virtual *personal* relationships that ultimately drive buying behavior.

The second difference between Internet China and the Western WWW is a little more obvious and a lot more controversial—at least in the West. While the United States and other Western countries have resisted any temptation to regulate or otherwise limit the use of the Internet, the Chinese Internet is highly regulated.

The Chinese, as a result, cannot access Facebook or Twitter or YouTube or any of the other Western social media outlets that been virtually woven into the fabric of Western culture. (There are Chinese versions of each, but they are not simply translated copies. They are Chinese in both style and social structure.) Nor can they access pornography—in any form. (Some estimate that as much as 30 percent of all Internet traffic in the West is porn.) There are laws on the books that prohibit using the Internet to spread false rumors or malicious lies. And yes, there is censorship of political content determined to be offensive or inappropriate.

And, for the most part, the Chinese abide. Not out of fear or ignorance or even the sense of powerlessness to do anything about it. They abide because, in their world view, everything must be evaluated in context.

While the rational foundation of all liberal democracy is that political legitimacy flows from the individual, the source of all political legitimacy in China flows from the government's collective obligation to protect and sustain the larger Chinese family—the common good. And while it is the fundamental belief that individual rights are the foundation of common good that gave rise to Western democracy, it is the more holistic, outcome-oriented world view of common good that defines the roles of the governing and the governed in the Confucian world view of rites and obligation.

There are, of course, pros and cons to both political systems and the polar world views on which they are built. Within the liberal democracies of the West, the dangers of rogue government behavior is minimized by the fundamental expectation of government transparency and the empowerment of the individual to demand accountability at the ballot box. On the other side of the ledger, however, individuals with money and power can bend the political agenda in ways that potentially compromise the common good. (Take your pick of special interests that control the political agenda of the United States today.)

On the other hand, under the one-party socialist system—there are eight officially recognized political parties in China, although seven of those pledge allegiance to the eighth—the government can act swiftly and decisively in the interest of social advancement. Airports, rail lines, and highways can be completed in a fraction of the time it would take such projects to wind their way through the courts in the United States. And the government can act swiftly to halt the dissemination of false rumor or spiteful content that might otherwise harm innocent netizens or institutions. With such power, however, comes the risk of silencing constructive dissent and productive political dialogue. Of course, the line between promoting the common good and oppressing the common good can be a matter of perspective.

To the Western mind, political censorship is never defensible. As deductive reasoners we believe in absolutes: absolute morality, absolute truth, the absolute belief that all men are created equal, and the absolute source of all government legitimacy. Through such an absolute lens, context is merely oppressive rationalization.

In the world of inductive reasoning that is at the heart of the Chinese world view, context is everything. Outcome trumps process. Achievement trumps language. Rights are both situational and relative.

To the average Chinese person, therefore, the question is not whether the government should censor or not. (They will point out that while the US government doesn't censor, it does snoop, and the end result isn't all that different when it comes to personal rights.) To them it is a question of context. Why? And how does this one piece fit into the larger puzzle?

There is a rational justification for regulation. Like the printing press before it, the Internet is an extrapolator. It is a lever of influence. And levers, through leverage, extrapolate impact. A modestly strong man, with leverage, can move boulders many times his size and mass.

And so it is with the Internet. Individual voices with no established audience can be broadcast across the world. Tiny companies whose products would be lost in the crushing swells of traditional commerce can build global markets with little more than an idea and a keyboard. And dreamers, once confined to their own thoughts, can inspire a legion of followers.

But with every great benefit comes a potential curse. Extrapolation begets exaggeration, and since the Internet is itself a neutral, unassuming lever, veracity is not a prerequisite to its impact. Rumors and myths are disseminated at the same speed as truth and facts. Commercial fraud and products of no redeeming social value (eg, porn) are granted the same access to potential customers that legitimate commercial providers and worthy causes are. Even terrorists who wish to destroy us are given the same power to organize via the Internet as those who wish to celebrate our success.

As Yogi Berra once said, "In theory there is no difference between theory and practice, but in practice there is." The Chinese I know want a better environment, better medical care, and a better life for their children, not to post political dissent on the Internet.

And that, ultimately, is the context within which all governments are measured—the context of hope. When people have hope for themselves and their children, as the Chinese currently do, everything else is mere ideology.

In the end, the Chinese, as they so often do, have taken a less absolute, more holistic approach to managing their virtual community. It is the Internet with Chinese characteristics—characteristics of realism and balance with an eye toward achieving the best outcome for all. In short, individual rights within the context of hope for a better life.

CHAPTER 18

SOCIAL MEDIA

The United States, without a doubt, was able to author the American Century because of its deductive commitment to discreet values of individual freedom and liberty. No political or social system, however, is only individually incremental or collectivist. Incremental to collectivist is a spectrum, and every culture and state falls somewhere along it.

While the United States put its discreet values front and center, it was, nonetheless, likewise a collectivist world view that allowed those discreet values to flourish. The commitment to family, to community, to country provided a fertile medium for those discreet values to positively influence the American culture and spirit without pushing the country into anarchy and repression.

That collectivism, however, the dike between individual liberty and social disintegration, is under both direct and indirect attack. It is weakening to the point that we are forced to live in fear. Totally innocent strangers are being gunned down in places built for relaxation and entertainment, our schools are shrouded in death, and our children are forced to endure the security normally associated with places of incarceration. And "lone wolves" terrorize our public places and force us into the isolation of our homes.

Contrary to popular perception, Western social media, I fear, is not helping us to connect individually or to the world around us. We can form vast "social" networks, but they aren't really social at all. They aren't even real. They are networks of electrons alone.

A tweet can reach millions, but it is not collectivist. You cannot hold a neighborhood picnic on Facebook. YouTube is, by definition, a self-centered medium of expression.

A friend of mine often cited the saying, "Are you listening to learn or listening to respond?" Social media thrives on the latter. Responding is its lifeblood. Which means, in turn, we get little practice at really listening in the wired world. We learn facts, but we learn little about more holistic notions like world view, motivation, or overriding beliefs. Certainly social media has put the final nail in the coffin of the Socratic method, which has given us so many important social advancements.

American politics, I would likewise argue, is in its current state of morass and paralysis due to the loss of collectivist policy-making and the current individualism of all things political. A sound bite, like a tweet, is by definition incremental and one-sided. There is no listening. There is no response. There is no dialogue.

Corporations are now embracing social media in order to communicate with their customers. But while the stated intent is positive, the underlying motive may not be. Will corporate social media promote transparency and truth, much less advance society, or merely enable the dissemination of distorted truths in an effort to sell products and services? Will their overwhelming presence alone distract us from the personal connection that is so important to both a healthy society and one that is advancing in terms of social justice and opportunity?

The commercial world has always been there, of course. In the past, however, our exposure was intermittent and in our control. We decided to go shopping. We decided when to pick up a magazine or newspaper full of advertising. We decided when to open a piece of traditional mail that was clearly there to promote a product or service.

Today the corporations decide. They are always with us, relentlessly pursuing our attention through the smartphone, the tablet, and every other electronic handcuff we carry with us night and day. There is no break. There is no break at the beach. There is no break while out for a walk in the woods. Never. We are under their potential influence twenty-four/seven.

And now the game is rigged against transparency and objectivity. Corporations routinely hire social media "influencers" with large followings to discreetly promote their products. Celebrity endorsements have been with us for a long time, of course, but they were obvious and transparent and did not violate the personal ethos that gave rise to social media in the first place.

The Chinese, of course, are as wired into social media as the Americans are these days. Perhaps more so. They have their own versions of Twitter and YouTube and use them with abandon. But these Chinese platforms are designed and used with distinctly Chinese characteristics.

WeChat, the Chinese version of Twitter, is designed and used for ongoing social dialogue rather than simple pronouncements from a tweeter to an audience of "followers." Surely mundane facts are exchanged on WeChat, but they are part of an ongoing dialogue of getting to know one another and building trust. WeChat groups are the new rural villages of old—the new neighborhoods of the electronic age.

In essence, social media in China, despite uninformed Western accusations of censorship and repression, are designed to reinforce collectivism in an urbanizing world. They represent true virtual communities that exist at multiple and diverse levels rather than the single issue or personality isolation created by most Western social media.

CHAPTER 19

FUNERALS IN CHINA

The Western press got a good snicker in April 2015 when it was widely reported that China's Ministry of Culture had warned of a crackdown on the practice of hiring strippers to perform at funerals. According to these reports, it was becoming more and more popular in the Chinese countryside.

To be honest, I've never heard of the practice. And I have yet to find any Chinese colleague who has either.

According to the accounts I've read in Western media, the explanation for this practice is unclear. One account suggested it was a way to attract more attendees to the funeral. Another suggested it was a reward for migrant workers who had to travel a long way to participate. (One friend of mine punned that right or wrong, it showed good "thinking out of the box.")

Pornography of all forms is illegal in China, and they're serious about it. In all of my time here, I have never seen any vendor selling a pornographic magazine or DVD, even in the black markets where you can easily buy a fake Rolex or LV bag.

In general, I believe the Chinese are quite conservative when it comes to matters sexual. While I know that attitudes are changing here, I would bet that the percentage of young couples who have intercourse before marriage is lower here than just about anywhere on the planet.

Having said that, the attitude toward sex and sexuality is different here than in the West. In most Western countries, sexual love and marriage are inseparable concepts. You can't have one without the other, which is why infidelity remains overwhelmingly frowned upon in the United States despite a mass liberalization of sexual norms.

But that is a Jeffersonian view of marriage. It's all about the individual, both in terms of happiness and individual obligation.

But the Chinese have a Confucian world view. The individual is subordinate to the family, both immediate and extended. The survival and harmony of the family trumps everything.

That is not to say that Chinese women welcome, or even accept, infidelity or patterns of aggressive sexual behavior. It is to say, however, that they generally view sexuality through a different lens—through the lens of family stability and well-being.

That's also not to say that Chinese women are timid or feel in any way that they suffer at the hands of patriarchal cultural norms. If anything, as I've noted before, I think that Chinese men are generally afraid of the women, who in many ways hold the reins of power in China and are fully aware of the fact (a culture built around family has to be matriarchal in many ways by definition).

So even though you can't buy pornography here, you can go to the auto show, where scantily clad young female models stand next to vehicles on display. (In Shanghai the government recently told carmakers they were going too far and to cover up the models.)

And there are plenty of provocative billboards and store signs around town, although most feature Western models, perhaps in deference to traditional Chinese conservatism. (It is not because most Chinese prefer Western notions of beauty. I believe most Chinese men and women prefer Chinese norms of beauty.)

This all contributes to yet another example of Chinese duality. There is sexuality here. But it's not Western sexuality. It just is. Like life on a farm, if you will, but with LV handbags and carefully coiffured hair.

So, do they really have strippers at Chinese funerals? I have no idea. I can only say that if they do, they don't think about it with the snicker most Western readers are likely to have. To the inductively minded Chinese, whatever the reason for it, it just is what it is. If you asked an attendee at such an event why the girls were there, they would undoubtedly reply, "Because someone invited them," and look at you like you are just as inexplicable as all of the other foreigners.

The government of President Xi Jinping is most definitely cracking down on openly lewd sexual behavior. I believe he is an extremely moral man. But his is not Judeo-Christian morality; it is Confucian morality. He wants to protect the family and the culture, and he believes these behaviors serve to undermine those things.

Chinese morality is harmonious, not absolute, which is undoubtedly why this story got little coverage here in China. Not because the government prevented it—after all, they put out the warning—but because there would be no value in it to the Chinese reader. It wouldn't sell newspapers.

Doesn't that, in a way, make them more sophisticated on the topic? Duality and irony. Yin and yang. This is China.

Sexual love and marriage are Jeffersonian soul mates built on the supremacy of individual happiness and obligation. The Chinese world view on marriage is all about the family and the harmonious survival of the ancestral line.

To the modern Westerner, looking sexy and being sexy often go hand in hand. Not so to the inductive Chinese. Looking sexy is a self-contained concept.

There is no pornography in China. It's illegal, and this set of regulations is enforced because it undermines the harmony of the culture and extended clan. That doesn't mean, however, that sexuality itself is banned.

CHAPTER 20

FASHION

Try as I might, I just can't seem to get my mind around Chinese fashion or design. In the famous words of US Supreme Court Justice Potter Stewart, when attempting to define pornography, "I know it when I see it." But I'll be damned if I can describe it, much less define it. Words, for once, completely fail me.

My fashion tastes tend to simple elegance on a woman and timeless simplicity on a man. And while my tastes in artwork cover a wide spectrum of styles and eras, the colors are typically rich and the imagery straightforward.

The furniture in my home is eclectic, but my material of choice is most certainly wood. Cherry is my favorite, but you'll find plenty of mission oak as well. And while I do have several pieces of traditional Chinese furniture, I have more contemporary Danish furniture than anything else.

I do truly enjoy old Chinese architecture, however. The ornately decorated temples, walkways, and royal compounds fascinate me to no end. I admire the fine craftsmanship and am genuinely stirred by the rich colors and textures.

More than anything else, I am dumbfounded as to how anything so intricately complex in detail could, as a whole, appear to be so inherently balanced and visually integrated.

Where do they start? When an ancient architect and master builder sat down to create a new building for the imperial grounds or a new temple, where did they begin? Even great art, it seems to me, needs a center of gravity. There must be a grounding point around which everything turns.

An artist cannot create a masterpiece instantaneously. It is a slow, methodical process that requires a multitude of starts and stops, necessitating a consistent starting point that ultimately brings the entire work together both visually and functionally.

And if there is such a center of effort in Chinese architectural design, to borrow a term from the world of physics, I'll be damned if I can find it. It eludes me completely.

A Wikipedia entry that references a 2006 book entitled *Chinese Houses: The Architectural Heritage of a Nation* (Knapp, Spence, and Ong; Tuttle Publishing) states, "An important feature in Chinese architecture is its emphasis on articulation and bilateral symmetry, which signifies balance."

That much I get. Balance is everything in Chinese culture and the foundation of the Chinese world view. And I understand the basic principles of fêng shui. Once you accept the existence of *qi*, by whatever name, it's really pretty logical, even to the deductively oriented Westerner.

As a quick aside, a German company built a new plant across the street from our own about a year ago. And for a while it appeared that their gate would directly face ours from the north, which had our plant manager convinced that we would have to purchase large stone lions to guard our gate and prevent our neighbor's bad luck from cursing us. In the end, however, somebody apparently set them straight, and they built their gate perpendicular to the street and our own. Crisis averted. No lions needed. Bad luck can't make right turns, apparently.

This emphasis on symmetry and balance, however, does not fully explain the intricacy and complexity of Chinese architectural decoration. Yes, it is balanced and symmetrical. But it is also finely detailed and complexly intricate. And it all comes off as both appealing and in some strange way, inexplicably calming. While it would be logical for such busy intricacy to create a visual sense of dizzying confusion, if not anxiety, it has quite the opposite effect.

Which, in an appropriately tangential way, brings me to the world of Chinese fashion.

For the fashion houses of Europe and New York, China is the new frontier, full of promise and opportunity. Hardly a week goes by that there isn't some CEO or designer from New York or Paris in Beijing giddily proclaiming his or her intent to dip deeply into the pockets of the nouveau riche of China.

And if evaluated solely by the sheer scope and scale of Chinese affluence, to say nothing of the number of LV handbags hauled back from shopping sprees to Paris and Dubai each year (the two most popular outbound tourist destinations for Chinese tourists venturing out of Asia), that's probably more than just wishful thinking. At least by the numbers.

Or is it? For the land of opportunity it is in virtually every industry, relatively few foreign companies have made money here. And while the foreign fashion industry has the advantage of powerful brands and creative energy, an area where the Chinese have yet to excel, the product is easy to copy and even easier to take costs out of.

And while the Chinese have the money to acquire the real McCoy, I believe there are some fundamental realities that may ultimately rain on the parade of fashion brands seeking to dress and accessorize the men and women of China.

For starters, the Chinese are not as deeply aspirational toward foreign cultures as you might be led to conclude from their enthusiasm for German automobiles. As I have noted many times, the Chinese on average want nothing other than to be Chinese. They are perfectly content in their own skin.

While the first ladies of the G20 are often seen wearing clothes designed by the most prominent designers of the New York-Paris-Milan axis, First Lady Peng Liyuan is frequently seen wearing the work of Chinese designers little known outside the Middle Kingdom.

And while I can't remember the last time I saw anyone in Beijing wearing a Mao suit, officially known as the *zhongshan zhuang*, named after Sun Zhongshan (Dr. Sun Yat-sen), President Xi wore an updated version while attending formal diplomatic events on one of his diplomatic trips to Europe and received enthusiastic accolades from the home crowd here in China.

And then there is what I might call the identity factor. Westerners often assume that Asian cultures promote uniformity rather than individualism. While the Chinese are very proud of their heritage and their ethnicity, I don't see that in the Chinese culture. While the Chinese want to be Chinese, they don't want to be a clone of the Chinese man or woman standing next to them. They value individual identity.

But how do you stand out in a country of 1.3 billion people, virtually all of whom share the identical hair color and similar facial features? It's not easy, and apparel and fashion accessories are one of the few avenues open to them.

Which is why I believe the Chinese will always be more inclined to create their own individualistic fashion trends than to follow the fashion trends defined by others, be they the designers who rule the fashion world or the celebrities who give their designs broad popularity.

A quick stroll down the streets of Beijing or Shanghai would seem to bear this out. While it's clear that people, particularly the young, have chosen their wardrobe with some deliberate care, it is unclear exactly what specific style or design statement they are seeking to make. While my own mother taught me at a young age not to mix stripes and plaids, I can detect no such universal fashion guidelines at work here.

But somehow, as in their architectural design, they pull it off. Despite combining design elements that appear to have no common denominator, they generally end up with a "look" that somehow hangs together.

Not surprisingly, I think, the Chinese approach to both architecture and fashion seems to follow the inverse process to the one employed in the West. While a Western fashionista builds a look from carefully selected design elements, the Chinese fashionista appears to start with a holistic impression and work back from there.

As a result, it would appear there are few rules to follow. Almost anything goes. And if the resulting look is something only you can readily decipher, perhaps you've achieved your objective—standing out in a very big crowd indeed.

CHAPTER 21

TOMB-SWEEPING DAY

On April 5, 2015, while the Christian world had just celebrated Easter, China was celebrating the Qingming Festival, also known as Tomb-Sweeping Day. There is, as one would assume, no connection between the two.

Tomb-Sweeping Day is celebrated on the first day of the fifth solar term on the traditional Chinese lunisolar calendar, also known as the Han calendar. This is the fifteenth day after the Spring Equinox. (In Taiwan the holiday is always celebrated on April 5 to mark the anniversary of the death of Chiang Kai-shek in 1975.)

The Qingming Festival can trace its ancestry back to the Cold Food Festival (Hanshi Festival). Although first celebrated in 636 BC, it took on its present form in AD 732 when Emperor Xuanzong declared that ancestral respects could only be paid once per year during the Qingming Festival.

It is, as the name implies, a time to pay respect to your ancestors. Families typically gather at gravesites—which are frequently conical mounds of dirt—particularly in the countryside to both pay respect and to let the ancestors know that the family tree still lives on.

And because the Chinese spiritually claim little distinction between life and death, except where it unfolds, they often leave food and alcohol at the gravesite for the deceased to enjoy.

They also burn joss paper money, otherwise known as ghost money, to bring wealth and good fortune to those who cannot earn it on their own.

Other articles made of joss paper may also be offered. You can buy paper Ferraris, iPhones (yes, the iPhone 6 debuted this year), and mistresses.

While the Qingming Festival goes back a couple of thousand years, it only became a national holiday in the People's Republic of China in 2008. Chairman Mao Zedong was not a fan of superstition and wanted to rechannel many such Chinese traditions into a stronger commitment to the State.

All of this undoubtedly seems strange to most Westerners. Many undoubtedly wonder how the Chinese can continue to be so superstitious in this era of science and technology.

Superstition, however, is a decidedly deductive concept. To believe in superstition, you must believe in linear reasoning and assume that cause and effect are both singular and scientifically explained. Most Chinese hold no such beliefs.

I don't believe the Chinese even think about whether or not the offering of money and mistresses has any impact on their ancestors. It is tradition, and to the inductive thinker, tradition is sacred because life is circular.

And I have to wonder, although I disclaim any expertise on the topic, if the Ferraris and the iPhones aren't so much for the living than the dead. Perhaps they want to show their ancestors that the family thrives. Or perhaps they believe that their ancestors, if pleased, can help the living attain these things.

Whatever their true beliefs, Tomb-Sweeping Day, like virtually every Chinese holiday, is a family holiday. It is a time when families gather over food and drink both to celebrate the past and to grease the wheels of future prosperity.

CHAPTER 22

MEDICAL CARE IN CHINA

Within twelve hours of my family's arrival in China in 2007, we were sitting in a medical clinic in Beijing, my youngest daughter, then four years old, sobbing uncontrollably from the pain in her ears. Turns out she had just endured a fourteen-hour plane ride with a severe double ear infection (talk about parental guilt!).

Within three months of my own arrival, I was in immediate need of a hernia operation and simply did not have the time, being new on the job, to return to the United States for it. So under the knife of Dr. Chen I went.

I've also had teeth extracted, a colonoscopy, a minor stroke, and the usual battery of human illness, and my daughters have had concussions, athletic injuries, and the normal array of fevers, skin irritations, and general maladies of youth.

So yes, I feel qualified to write on the topic of medical care in China.

Broadly speaking, there are three medical systems in China. The first is traditional Chinese medicine, or TCM, which has been around for thousands of years and which is the form of medical care that first comes to mind for many Westerners when thinking about China. It remains widely practiced and utilized, but it is by no means the only form of medical care available in China.

The other two are simply two variations on the theme of Western medicine (although the term "Western" is a bit presumptive on my part) practiced around the world. The difference between these two "Western" medical worlds is strictly a function of how much you can afford to pay, although I would be careful about drawing inferences of quality from that distinction.

TCM, like Western medicine, works at many different levels, from seasonal soups to keep you healthy (*Hang dou* and *Liu dou* in winter and summer, respectively), to acupuncture to address more serious illness and affliction. At every level, however, the focus is the same—*qi*, the natural energy or life force that circulates through the body in channels called meridians.

TCM was built on various philosophical and Taoist interpretations of nature. By definition, therefore, it is all natural. The emphasis is not on repair or adaptation, but restoration. "Cures" seek to remove barriers to flow or to accelerate flow but not to modify or alter the *qi* itself. That, after all, would be playing with the essence of life.

As a mirror to the universe, TCM operates on yin-yang theory, the inhibitory and physical being the yin and the active and excitatory being the yang. They are opposing but inseparable, each acquiring meaning and definition only relative to the other.

TCM is not fringe medicine. It remains very much mainstream in China, often preferred by even the most educated and urbane of Chinese. And while many Westerners consider it to be unsupported by modern science, we must remember that science is merely a methodology for explaining reality. It is not a body of knowledge unto itself. Something is unscientific by definition if it merely cannot be explained using the scientific method. But since the scientific method is built on the exclusive foundation of deductive reasoning, that prerequisite excludes a lot of what is otherwise very observable and very real.

When most Westerners think of TCM, they think of acupuncture, but the practice of inserting sharp needles into the skin that most Westerners are familiar with is only one form of acupuncture. All are designed to promote the normal flow of *qi* and bring the yin and yang back into harmony. How that is done depends on the ailment, but the subtly and complexity of the process has led to the identification of 400 primary acupuncture points, or holes, along the twelve main meridians of the body.

Cupping is another common form of acupuncture practiced here. It commonly involves lighting a cotton swab soaked with alcohol, holding it inside a small glass held upside down and designed for the purpose, removing the swab, and placing the glass on the bare skin, normally the back. The cooling air inside the glass creates a vacuum that in turn sucks blood and harmful bodily fluids to the surface.

There is no bleeding per se, and the glass is not hot enough to burn, but the process does leave a bright red circle on the skin that takes several days to go away. And since the process typically involves a number of glasses up and down the back and shoulders, it can be a bit shocking the first time you encounter someone whose cupping marks are visible.

Yet another form of acupuncture is called *gua sha* and traditionally involves scraping the back in long, brisk strokes using the polished horn of a water buffalo. Again the idea is to promote the flow of *qi* through the meridians, restoring the proper balance of yin and yang in the body and drawing blood and harmful fluids to the surface. It also results in subcutaneous blemishing or ecchymosis, which, to put it simply, makes it look like you've endured a very painful thrashing.

But I have experienced gua sha and cupping firsthand, and they are only mildly uncomfortable. I underwent the procedures both out of curiosity and a desire to get over a nasty cold, the most common ailment for which gua sha is prescribed, although I have also heard the Chinese say that it is good for releasing anger as well.

Does TCM work? I am not a doctor, but scientific or not, I do accept the idea that most things in life come down to a question of balance and that science has done an incomplete job of explaining the reality we experience firsthand.

And the one aspect of TCM that I believe is indisputable is the inseparable nature of health and illness. If we live healthier lives, we will, on balance, suffer less illness. Both deductively and inductively, that seems rational to me.

In this respect I believe the Chinese are well ahead of the West. Organic is mainstream and has been for some time. It is Westerners who are introducing the Chinese to processed and packaged foods. As one Western NGO worker who has been here for twenty-five years noted, when he first arrived, the only consumer goods on the shelves were Coca-Cola and Nutella. Everything was sold bulk—and unprocessed. Now the shelves are lined with the same processed snack foods, candies, and sugar-laden drinks you will find in Frankfurt or Saint Louis.

One area where I have come to totally endorse Chinese thinking, because I feel so strongly about it, is in the use of ice to cool beverages. The Chinese never put ice in a beverage. They prefer not to drink it even cold or chilled. The most common drink in China, particularly in the winter months, is plain warm water.

And it's not out of concern for the quality of water that goes into the ice. They don't use ice because the Chinese have known of the need for hydration for generations and they know that the key to hydration is absorption. (The problem with most health supplements, you may know, is that they never get absorbed. They get ingested and then eliminated, having had almost no helpful effect along the way.) And the key to absorption, the Chinese believe, is thermal consistency.

In other words, the Chinese believe that all beverages should be as close to body temperature as possible. That in turn will facilitate the absorption process. And that, I have to say, makes a world of sense to me, no matter which world view you bring to the process.

As a quick aside, there is a material environmental issue relating to the use of ice to cool drinks as well. Just think of how much energy is consumed in the United States alone on the production of ice for beverages. It has to be huge. And you can get quite used to the idea of drinking beverages at room temperature. I can attest to that, although I admittedly have yet to convince my daughters.

As briefly referenced earlier, many of the cultural norms that so offend Westerners traveling in China are in part based on the Chinese perspective on health. The act of clearing your throat of phlegm and spitting it out, as an example, is not designed to gross out foreigners. It's done because the Chinese believe that the phlegm and mucus caught in the throat is full of harmful bacteria and should be eliminated from the body as soon as possible.

And while they don't cover their mouths when they sneeze, they do not do so in part because it grosses *them* out to think of depositing those germs on the back of the hand or into a handkerchief that will ultimately be comingled with their intimate clothing for washing. (I have also read accounts from Western doctors that caution against restraining a sneeze too forcefully.)

On balance, I have found the Chinese to be more concerned with health than many Western cultures, including my own. This contrasts sharply with the public environment in which they live, but I think it is a natural expression of the Chinese world view, based as it is on a foundation of yin-yang theory.

Balance. It makes sense to me.

———

Given that even the most developed countries struggle with the challenge of providing adequate medical care to their citizens, how do you meet that enormous challenge in a country of 1.3 billion people who earn on average a mere $9,000 per year? Chairman Mao found a way, and it worked undeniably well. Between the Communists' rise to power in 1949 and 1980, life expectancy in China rose a quarter of a century, the most dramatic increase ever recorded, according to *US News & World Report.*

They did so through the now-defunct cooperative medical system (CMS), a rural-based system that reflected the agrarian identity of China at the time. The CMS was a three-tiered system whose front line of care was what came to be known as Mao's "barefoot doctors"—rural residents, mostly farmers, with some basic medical training. Communal health centers, funded by the communes they supported, and county-level hospitals made up the second and third tiers.

The system fell apart, however, when Deng Xiaoping opened China's arms to the world and much of the economy was privatized and nudged into the currents of free market forces. But while the system looks much different today, the government has once again brought 95 percent of the population under the umbrella of health insurance (as broadly noted in the debate over President Obama's health-care reform in the United States, 15.4 percent of the American population had no health insurance at the time).

So how do they do it? One could easily write a treatise on the topic, but I have neither the time nor the expertise to do so, although I can say that the Chinese health insurance system is a hybrid of the single-payer systems found in Canada and the UK and the private insurance system found in the United States. Like so many things here, it is quintessentially Chinese.

I can offer a few observations that I think must factor into the equation somewhere, somehow. I believe each reason for China's ability to cover such a wide spectrum of its population with healthcare, however, is just another facet of the Chinese deference to practicality and quest for balance in the face of the conflicting pressures inherent in the challenge of providing affordable but competent health care on such a massive scale.

My first observation is that there is an acceptance here that not all medical services require the same level of training and regulatory oversight. Nurses, pharmacists, and other medical practitioners appear to be far more empowered to handle routine medical needs than in the West. Not all medical procedures, after all, require the attention of a board-certified physician who has completed seven to eight years of schooling and apprenticeship and whose every move is scrutinized by legions of administrators and regulators (all of whom add cost to the system).

My second observation is that there is less of a sense of entitlement when it comes to both cosmetic imperfections and quality of life. While I admittedly don't have the data to support it (I'm not sure it even exists), my sense is that they're not doing double knee replacements on seventy-year-old men or removing unattractive but otherwise harmless birth defects or scarring. (The wealthy, of course, are different, but they're different on their own dime.)

This undoubtedly comes from the decades of hardship endured by most Chinese but is nonetheless reflective of a cultural acceptance of the fact that much of what happens in life is beyond our immediate control. (Hence all the cultural devotion to bringing about "good luck.") You might call it the "life is hard, get over it" perspective.

My third observation is that the citizens themselves—the would-be patients—bear a considerable portion of the burden for their own health care. While health insurance coverage is broad, it is relatively shallow, and hospitals, clinics, and pharmacies, like most businesses in China, operate on a strict cash-in-advance basis. The Chinese, as a result, actively save for their medical care. When one of my previous workers was hurt on the job, we sent someone to the hospital with him, corporate cash in hand, to pay for his medical care. No credit, even for American multinational corporations with long histories and good credit ratings.

And as you might expect in a culture where family bonds trump virtually all other obligations, this presumed self-reliance extends to the family as a whole. In Chinese hospitals nurses and orderlies do not perform many of the housekeeping and basic care functions expected of them in Western hospitals. Family members, whose constant presence adds to the sense of overcrowding in most hospitals, are expected to empty bedpans, bathe the patient (assuming this does not involve serious medical risk), and provide food and drink, a simple expectation that greatly enhances the capacity of the hospital system and reduces the ongoing costs of operation. (There are always people for hire who will perform such chores if no family is available.)

Finally, whatever the root cause, virtually all the Chinese I've discussed the matter with seem to have at least a rudimentary knowledge of disease, the body, and the basics of remaining healthy or recovering from a minor illness. And they accept personal responsibility for doing so to the extent they can.

Yes, most of the men smoke, and alcohol is often consumed, again by the men, in copious quantities (cultural norms are changing, particularly among young urbanites, but I have met few women who smoke cigarettes or drink alcohol). Still, every Chinese person knows to eat fruit with every meal (at the end of the meal—preferably thirty minutes later, to be exact—to assist with digestion), and the urban parks and numerous outdoor public exercise venues set aside by the government are generally brimming with people early in the morning regardless of age or physical limitations.

But, of course, even the healthiest lifestyles can't preclude the onset of illness, and if you're the one it hasn't spared, the quality of care available becomes of paramount importance.

For those who can afford it, private hospitals and clinics provide world-class care and facilities. In the hospital where I had my surgery in Beijing, every patient has a private room equipped with the latest in medical and personal electronics, the food is first rate—and served by the staff—and the doctors are all Western-educated and fluent in English. Priced accordingly, of course.

And there is, I'm certain, wide variation in the quality of facilities and care offered within the medical system that serves the bulk of the population. In the end, I'm really not qualified to assess the qualifications of Chinese medical care in general, but I can tell you that when a fellow expatriate's daughter fell off a kitchen counter and broke her neck, the private hospital staffed with Western-trained doctors insisted she be admitted to a Chinese hospital because, as her parents were told, "That's where the doctors with the most expertise in this type of injury are." And, I'm happy to report, she fully recovered without a trace of the original injury. (On the first night they had no empty rooms, so her gurney was simply pushed to the side of the hallway, and he slept on the floor underneath it.)

There are, nonetheless, a few notable differences between what you may find here and what foreigners are accustomed to in their home countries. The first, of course, is the distinct possibility of overcrowding. The patient rooms tend to resemble the wards of old, and beds are often placed wherever there is room. As a result, privacy is generally nonexistent, a reality reinforced by the constant presence of family members taking care of their loved ones.

And while the government is pushing reforms to address the problem, doctors and other medical professionals are notoriously underpaid, relying in the past on financial incentives provided by the pharmaceutical companies and gifts from their patients, leading some to conclude that patients were chronically over-medicated, and the poor, without the means to provide adequate gifts to their medical providers, were underserved.

Again, I offer no conclusive research on the topic. From everything I read, and all the Chinese I speak with on the topic, however, my sense is that the government is actively taking steps to address this issue, although I can attest to the fact that gifts are still given by at least some patients. (I have yet to hear of any medical system that is deemed perfect by all the citizens it serves.)

Perhaps the greatest difference flows from the kind of practical perspective you would expect to find in a society less concerned with legal rights and risks than the day-to-day realities of survival. After my own hernia surgery, the surgeon asked extensive questions about my employment situation before providing his prescription for physical activity, ultimately suggesting that, "If you have to go to work, you have to go to work. If you can stay home and heal, that is, of course, best. Relax. Life is short." Good advice, but a little less rigid and prescribed than one might receive from a Western doctor understandably concerned with the constant threat of malpractice litigation.

All told, I find the medical system here to be like many institutions in China—pragmatic. You can't sue the state-owned hospital for a gazillion yuan if there is a mistake made in your care, but somehow I suspect that the average Chinese has access to more medical care, TCM or Western, than the citizens of many countries at comparable levels of economic development. Infant mortality, in fact, fell from 50 per thousand in 1980 to just 15.2 per thousand today, still above the United States at 5.9, but below Mexico at 16.3.

So, if I were asked where I'd rather receive medical care, the answer, of course, is that I'd rather not have to make that choice. I do believe, however, that I am living a healthier lifestyle here in China and I have no fear about becoming ill or injured here. Wherever I happen to be, I am confident I will get good care with less paperwork. I may not be able to sue for malpractice, but I'm personally OK with that. Life is full of risks. We can't mitigate them out of existence even if we try.

In the true spirit of yin-yang theory, we just have to find the natural balance, as the Chinese so often seem to do, between what we hope to gain and what we stand to lose.

CHAPTER 23

THE MID-AUTUMN FESTIVAL
(AKA THE LUNAR HARMONY FESTIVAL)

The Gregorian calendar is the official civil calendar of most major countries in the world, including China. Saudi Arabia and Ethiopia are two exceptions.

The Gregorian calendar was created in 1582 by a slight modification to the Julian calendar in order to bring the date for the celebration of Christian Easter in line with the date chosen by the First Council of Nicaea in 325. The Gregorian calendar is a solar calendar, meaning it aligns with the earth's rotation around the sun and the seasonal solstices and equinoxes that are its byproduct.

While introduced to China almost immediately after its creation by Jesuit missionaries, it was not adopted as the official calendar here until 1912. Until that time China used the Chinese calendar, which contrary to popular myth, is *not* a lunar calendar. It is a lunisolar calendar, defined by both the lunar phases and the solar seasons.

That said, Chinese culture, without a doubt, is lunar-centric. As a result, in China the second most important holiday of the year (after Spring Festival, of course), is the Zhongqiujie Festival, known in English as the Mid-Autumn Festival, or more simply, the Moon Festival (the same festival is celebrated in Vietnam and on the same date but by a different name in Korea).

The Mid-Autumn Festival is celebrated on the fifteenth day of the eighth month of the Chinese calendar, when the moon is at its fullest and its roundest (ie, in perfect balance). It is, without a doubt, my favorite Chinese holiday and has been celebrated in China since the Shang Dynasty

(c. 16th to 10th century BC). This year it fell on Sunday, September 27, 2015.

Part of the attraction is simply the time of year and the typically pleasant weather that accompanies the holiday. The summer humidity has broken, and the skies are typically richly blue and smog free.

In the West the lunar phase that gives rise to the holiday is known as the harvest moon, Mother Nature's signal to bring the crops in. It is a time of reaping the bounties of the spring and summer, making it by definition a time of replenishment.

Not surprisingly, however, the Chinese take a more holistic view of replenishment and draw a much less definitive line between the worldly and the spiritual and the relative needs of the body in both regards. To them the moon, like water, is a symbol of rejuvenation—a broader, more holistic view of replenishment.

The Mid-Autumn Festival is a gift-giving festival, and logically the most common gifts involve food. Moon cakes, specifically, are the gift of choice. These are small, dense cakes sometimes filled with sweet paste but always embossed with characters of good luck and fortune. (They are, of course, always round in shape, denoting balance and equilibrium.)

The real attraction of the Mid-Autumn holiday to me is not the celebration of material replenishment, but the concurrent celebration of the basic emotional replenishment and rejuvenation that can only come through connection with family and friends.

The theory is simple enough. There is only one moon. And everyone on the planet can see it. Only its position in the sky and the time of its ascent and setting differs—wherever you are in the world.

The most important custom of the day, therefore, is for families, who have gathered to consume the bounty of the new harvest over a special dinner, to retire afterward outdoors to look up at the moon and remember friends and relatives who are doing the same thing elsewhere in the world. It is, if you will, a lunar mirror that allows family and friends to replenish their love and connection despite the separation of distance and time.

And how great is that?

That custom likewise symbolizes what I consider to be one of the most endearing aspects of Chinese culture—the notion that the universe is a vast ecosystem that exists not to support us or to nourish us or to provide us pleasure, but just so that we can be a part of it. Whether made of cheese or billion-year-old star fragments, the moon is as much a part of life as is the water we drink and the air we breathe—and we are part of them.

When you think of life in this way, it is easy to see how life becomes both more and less personal in nature. We are who we are, but who we are likewise has a more shared quality to it.

It is not *the* moon; it is *our* moon. It is, in fact, us. And we are it. It cannot be owned. It cannot be harvested. In many ways, it cannot even be described, although many a poet and writer has tried.

It can, however, link us all together. It is a source of our connection—our shared identity—even our shared cycles of birth, rejuvenation, and mortality.

And in this time of ever-increasing segmentation and fragmentation—regional, ethnic, religious—is not the moon the one thing we can share equally? No matter where you live on the planet, what ethnic group you are part of, or what religion you practice, is not the moon—the lone moon—the one thing that is both neutral and shared by all?

The same can be said of the sun, of course, but the sun is not unique to our world. And while the moon moves the tides, it exerts a more benign power, a power more poetic than life enabling—or threatening.

The world is getting both smaller and more fragmented. Nations are dividing into ever-smaller states. Markets are fragmenting. Identities are both exploding in number and finding expression in ways both more and less personal.

This is a day when we can all, whatever our differences, look skyward and remind ourselves of the core things that still unite us all—the planet we share, the personal seasons we endure, the connections between us that ebb and flow like the tides.

It matters not what language we speak or what deity we worship. It matters not whom we consider our friends or our foes. It is the one thing that is common to us all and benign, neutral, and so vastly powerful all at the same time.

I would, therefore, like to offer a simple suggestion to all the diverse people of the world. On this one day each year, when the neutral but powerful moon is at its fullest and most perfectly round, let us celebrate not our diversity, but our connection beneath the great lunar lantern in the sky. We can call it the Festival of Lunar Harmony.

To be clear, this would not be a lunar festival. This would be a festival of human connection. The moon is merely the reagent used to bring out the common thread of all humanity. It is quite all-inclusive. No one is excluded. We need only to look at the night sky in affirmation of our collective identity as global citizens of something greater than our race or ethnicity, our gender, our nationality, or even our passions.

Try it. And pass it on. It would be the ultimate yin-yang experience. In balance, harmony. In harmony, connection. In connection, peace. And in peace, fulfillment, and the sense of belonging that we all yearn for and that the world so desperately needs.

CHAPTER 24

SPRING FESTIVAL

Take all the holidays celebrated in your country and by your culture, roll them all into one, and multiply by a multiple of whatever, and you will begin to have just some appreciation of the significance the Chinese give to Spring Festival, otherwise known as Chinese New Year, or the Lunar New Year.

It is, of course, a secular holiday, although there are behavioral customs still practiced by many that undoubtedly have their roots in Chinese folk religion and the yin-yang foundation of Taoism. All of these, however, have little to do with worship and everything to do with ensuring good luck in the coming year.

Luck is another facet of superstition, and the Chinese, as inductive thinkers, look at it much differently than Westerners. Luck is luck, but the Chinese believe you can greatly influence the chances that good or bad luck will come your way. Fêng shui is a methodology, for example, for maximizing the potential for good luck and minimizing the potential for misfortune through the harmonious management of your physical surroundings.

There are many rituals, therefore, from when and how to sweep out your home, to not having your hair cut for the first thirty days of the new year that exist for this purpose. Interestingly, I find that fewer and fewer Chinese actually follow all these rituals, but I have yet to meet the Chinese who wasn't aware of them.

The rituals, however, are only a small part of the Spring Festival tradition. By far the most important aspect of the holiday, and the one I find so endearing, is the complete and total emphasis on family. Families are together, no excuses, no matter what the distance that needs to be traveled.

When Mao Zedong defeated the Nationalists to form the People's Republic of China in 1949, the population of China was only 542 million people, about one-third of what it is today. Mao appreciated, however, that the biggest challenge facing his poor country was feeding itself, since agriculture in China was, and still is, a labor-intensive, albeit glorious, occupation.

Mao, therefore, conducted an active political campaign to convince women both to join their husbands in the fields of China and to have as many children as possible. Within a decade the Chinese population swelled by an additional 100 million people. Ultimately, the population grew so rapidly that in 1979 China introduced the family planning policy, informally known as the one child policy, to slow the rapid population growth that was threatening to overcome the country's social infrastructure.

Formal family registries (*huji*) were first introduced in China during the Xia Dynasty (c. 2100 BCE–1600 BCE) as a basis for taxation and social control and are still in use in other parts of Southeast Asia, including Japan, although they are used for very different reasons.

In China, the current system of registry, known as hukou, was first introduced in 1958 when it was redefined to be a residency registration system as much as a system for family registration. Your access to social benefits such as schooling for your children, government-provided housing, and medical care was greatly limited outside the area of your hukou, or place of registration—normally your place of birth.

As Deng Xiaoping would state some three decades later, "Some shall get rich first," and the government knew that as the country developed, the urban areas would be the first to realize an enhanced standard of living. The hukou system was therefore used to limit the flow of rural workers into the urban areas so as not to overwhelm the country's urban modernization.

It still exists today but in modified form. And while the rights of migrant workers, whose numbers are still measured in the hundreds of millions, are getting much more attention by the government and society at large, your hukou still determines a lot when it comes to the residential opportunities available to you and your family.

Like everything else in China, you have to understand the hukou system in context. When the system was first set up, all workers were divided into urban workers and rural workers—the latter of which are still often referred to as peasants. It's not a nice word, for sure, but not meant in the context most Westerners take it. Many English-speaking Chinese say s--t, as well, when referring to human excrement, because that's simply the word they know for it. It has no bearing on their education or sense of civility.

While the hukou system sounds downright oppressive to most Westerners, you have to remember that as inductive thinkers, everything is relative to the Chinese. They don't think in terms of absolutes.

When it introduced the hukou system, the government had no intention of eliminating urban migration in the sense that residency is strictly controlled in the sci-fi world of *The Hunger Games* or by the Berlin Wall in former real life. It merely wanted to slow it down. (The same is true of the Great Chinese Firewall on the Internet. The government doesn't want to stop English-speaking Chinese from accessing foreign websites. They simply want to slow the process down, which is precisely why they don't just take China off-line.)

Today, the hukou system is at the core of the Spring Festival holiday. Many rural husbands and wives typically leave their village to find work in the cities, often living thousands of miles from their families and each other. The children stay with their grandparents so they can go to school and get the medical care they are entitled to within the jurisdiction of their hukou.

During Spring Festival, however, Mommy and Daddy return home, creating what is believed to be the largest human migration on the face of the planet. The statistics are mind-numbing. According to government statistics reported in *China Daily*, during the official forty-day Spring Festival travel period that began February 4, 2015, the Chinese will collectively take 2.8 *billion* trips. At any given time, a population larger that the entire United States will be on the move.

During one ten-day period, some 250 million Chinese will travel by train alone, many without the benefit of a seat as the trains are packed to capacity by the necessity of demand. I have personally met people who stood for as long as sixteen hours on a train to return to their hometown for the annual festival.

As a result, the country shuts down for up to a month. Not literally, of course, but pretty close. Officially, it is a three-day national holiday that the government turns into a seven-day holiday by converting weekend days into normal workdays. This year, for example, Sunday, February 15, and Saturday, February 28, became "normal" workdays to allow seven days of uninterrupted time off during the heart of the festival. (New Year's Day is February 19, but it could be argued that February 18, when families gather over the New Year's dinner and to watch the national gala on television—and light fireworks, of course—is the most important day of the festival.)

Not every company shuts down, of course. Retailers and service providers are all open throughout the holiday. And companies like my former employer (glass furnaces cannot be shut down) continue to produce during the holiday, although they do not ship, as the trucking companies, most of which rely on migrant workers, do shut down, as does China customs and all the banks, making it virtually impossible to export anything.

When I first arrived in China, I considered shuttering production for the festival so that our operators could spend the time with their families until a Chinese colleague set me straight. They would be heartbroken, I was told, as we pay them, according to government regulation, three times their normal pay to work over the holiday. They line up to volunteer.

Again, while a deductive thinker might find it distasteful to violate an absolute holiday tradition, an inductive thinker will always consider the results to be paramount. When else can you get nine days of pay for three days of work?

———

The cultural and ethnic homogeneity of China is self-evident. But imagine a holiday that has thousands of years of tradition, is central to your culture, and is celebrated with equal enthusiasm by every last citizen. And it's apolitical!

That is Spring Festival.

There is no wrong on this one. There are no court cases about what can be displayed on public property. There's no parsing of words to keep everything politically correct. Everyone—without exception—celebrates it. And because it is completely apolitical, the companies get to join in the fun as well.

For companies that serve the retail trade, the Spring Festival retail season is as important as the December holiday selling season is to US retail. For all companies operating in China, however, Spring Festival is also a season of gift giving and celebration.

Chinese culture is a gift-giving culture. If you've happened to witness a flight heading to China with returning Chinese tourists, you've undoubtedly noticed the bags and bags of duty-free goods being loaded onto the plane. For the most part, those are not for personal consumption. They are gifts for relatives, friends, and colleagues.

At Spring Festival employers give gifts to their employees, their customers, and other key business partners, including the government bureaus they work with on a regular basis (remember, no lawyers but a big government). My former employer normally gave a set of glasses with that year's zodiac animal embossed on the bottom. If it is a national company and it doesn't make a product suitable for personal use, it will often give its widespread customers a gift indigenous to the province in which it is based, such as a certain kind of fruit or local craft.

Even the government gives gifts. I often received gifts from the government officials responsible for our industrial zone in thanks for being a good corporate citizen, for providing jobs, and, of course, for paying taxes. The practice of government gift giving, however, has come to a screeching halt since the new administration came to power and issued what came to be known as the "eight rules." As part of their effort to make the government more transparent and accessible to the average citizen, and to stamp out corruption and frivolous spending on excessive dining and entertaining, the central government has put the kibosh on government gift giving at taxpayer expense. (While some of these gifts went to employers, many went to other government officials, particularly those in a position to impact career paths.)

That simple directive had far-reaching impact on the Chinese economy and is, in fact, realigning entire industries. The hospitality industry, in particular, has been hit hard. Restaurants that once counted on a steady stream of government banquets and entertainment are scrambling to rebuild their customer base. And this past Spring Festival, the calendar industry was in near collapse due to a memo published in October by the Commission for Discipline Inspection of the Communist Party of China, reaffirming that no taxpayer funds should be spent on the purchase of printed gifts, including calendars.

Companies take the Spring Festival center stage when they host their Spring Festival annual dinner. Virtually every company holds one, and every last employee is invited—and attends. I honestly don't know if attendance is typically mandatory, but I can't imagine an employee not attending. In addition to missing out on a good meal, some fun entertainment, and a goody bag to take home, I would guess such an omission would score high on the Chinese scale of harbingers of bad luck.

My company's practices were pretty typical.

It is a good-sized company and the factory operates 24/7/365. Glass plants are built around their furnaces, and furnaces are designed to run continuously. The company, therefore, had two identical Spring Festival dinners, usually one or two days apart, so that all employees could participate, and no one had to report to work afterward.

The "dinners" start at 3:00 p.m., although no food is served before six o'clock. The time in between is primarily consumed by the employee talent show, during which individual employees or groups of employees play musical instruments, sing songs, or perform skits of their choosing. The top manager, of course, kicks it all off with a short "state of the union" address and best wishes for the new year, and there are games scattered throughout the show designed to make the senior management look ridiculous and thus give everyone a good laugh at the boss's expense. (It's a humbling experience, I can attest.)

But the real show belongs to the employees themselves. And it would be difficult to overstate the enthusiasm and the dedication they bring to the task of putting on a show for their colleagues. Employees with a particular musical talent tend to perform on their own, but the singing and skits, sometimes serious but often comical, are often carried out by groups of employees. Department performances are common, but not mandatory. A group of young single men from different departments got together to perform their version of *Swan Lake* one year—tutus and all (if costumes are involved, the company will pay the cost).

One of my favorite aspects of the show is the unwritten rule that department managers are expected to both participate and to humble themselves. It's a healthy process, and in the many years I attended these events, I never witnessed any behavior that would or should make anyone uncomfortable or embarrassed. It's all in good fun and treated as such by all.

The meal is generally sumptuous and follows a protocol not dissimilar to the family reunion dinner. Beer and wine are generally served, although many choose not to drink, and I have never witnessed any employee drinking more than he or she should. No standing up on a table and telling the boss to go *you know where*. The Chinese are simply too polite for that, and somehow I don't see them wasting free beer on what is likely to be wasted effort. They're too pragmatic.

Toward the end of the meal itself, the members of the senior management team rise as a group and go from table to table—no exceptions—to toast the employees seated there, thank them for their hard work, and wish them and their families the best in the coming new year. It takes some time, but I for one think it's a nice tradition, and the employees seem genuinely appreciative.

After the management group has made the rounds, the floor is open for others to do the same. If you're lucky, individual employees, or more likely, departments, will come en masse to the head table to toast the management team. And departments are likely to toast one another, particularly where there is a working relationship or some direct reliance involved. For example, the sales department will often make the rounds toasting the tables of the production employees, and the shipping employees are likely to toast the folks in customer service. (In case you're wondering, alcohol is not mandatory. I generally toast with orange juice. Everyone is fine with that, and no one has ever attempted to goad me into switching.)

And while this is all happening, the most anticipated event of the whole day and evening begins—a progressive and seemingly endless series of raffles, uniformly known here as "lucky draws."

Because it is a gift-giving culture, many of our employees, myself included, receive gifts from suppliers and other business partners throughout the year. As an American company, however, we have strict and well-intended policies about the acceptance of gifts that give even the appearance of potential compromise of the impartial conduct of our business. We don't make employees give the gifts back, since that would be offensive to the many business partners who are simply making a well-intended and culturally normal gesture. But we do ask that our employees report the gifts and except for gifts of nominal value turn the gifts into the human resource department, which will include them in one of the Spring Festival dinner lucky draws (it's a pragmatic compromise, to be sure, but everyone appears to be OK with it).

The company chips in as well, and while not everyone walks away with a lucky draw prize, there is a nice gift for everyone who attends—one year we gave a nice backpack to everyone—and the winners of the bigger lucky draws are generally quite thrilled with their winnings. One year's grand prizewinner walked away with a big-screen television, for example.

In the early stages of the progressive draws, however, we normally have a wide range of prizes that we allow the lucky employee to choose from. And I kid you not, I have seen all the Apple iPods sit on the prize table until all the large bottles of cooking oil and five-pound bags of rice have been claimed.

As I've said so many times, of all of the gifts China has bestowed upon me, none has been greater than the gift of perspective.

For most Chinese families, Spring Festival begins with the reunion dinner, held on New Year's Eve. Traditionally, however, the celebration of the new lunar year begins on the eighth day of the last lunar month, known as the Laba Festival. This year, by lunisolar coincidence, that was January 27, 2015.

Like everything associated with Spring Festival, the purpose of the Laba Festival is to bring prosperity in the coming year. Its modern-day custodians, oddly enough, are the Buddhist monks who serve warm Laba porridge made with rice, beans, nuts, and fruits on that day. In Beijing, which is inevitably cold this time of year, you can see a long line of office workers on their way to work waiting at the many Buddhist temples in the area for some of the sweet and warm soup.

I find the image of Buddhist monks serving Laba porridge in the heart of Beijing to be both interesting and informative. Interesting for obvious reasons. China officially governs by the tenets of socialism with Chinese characteristics, and embracing and celebrating its spiritual and religious tradition is clearly one of those characteristics.

It is important because it highlights a recurring theme throughout Chinese culture that is critical to understanding the true nature and meaning of Spring Festival. At its core Spring Festival is not so much about celebrating the old or new year as it is about maximizing the chances that the coming year is a good year—which is to say, a prosperous year. And following classic yin-yang philosophy, that means keeping bad luck at bay as much as it means promoting good luck. Both efforts, while diametrically opposed, are necessary to achieve the desired result.

It's all a bit fatalistic, but I've come to accept that there is something to the perspective. Let's face it: a lot of what happens to us in life is beyond our control. Why pretend it isn't? Most success stories could have easily been a tale of woe, and many who struggle in life were only a hair away from the lucky break that would have made things very different indeed.

That's not to say, in the least, that successful people don't earn their success. I think they do. But it's not guaranteed. I think successful people, as much as anything else, have learned how to maximize the odds that a lucky break will find them. And one of the most effective ways to maximize those odds, of course, is to maximize the sheer number of *opportunities* for good luck to come your way (ie, hard work). Isn't hard work, after all, a core quality on which almost all success is built, and doesn't it, by definition, simply increase the number of hands you are dealt in life? An old colleague used to say that in baseball, as in life, it only takes one hit in ten to get into the Hall of Fame.

Is it really such a leap of faith, therefore, to think that drinking a bit of tasty porridge served by a friendly Buddhist monk on a cold January morning might lead to good things in the coming year? I can't *quite* get there, admittedly. I'm a foreigner. But I do have some sense as to why and how people buy into such beliefs. (In the West we call them superstitions, but that's such a pejorative term that I've stopped using it.)

Which is the perfect segue into the reunion dinner, called Nian Ye Fan, that officially kicks off the Spring Festival holiday for most Chinese families. It's the most important dinner of the year, by a wide margin, in a culture that attaches great importance to food and the dining experience. Hasn't history taught us that the ultimate prosperity is having enough to eat?

Nian is the name given to the mythical beast that according to legend arrived on the first day of the New Year and ate all the crops and livestock, as well as some of the villagers, especially children. Food was set out to appease the beast, and once the villagers noticed that the beast passed over a child wearing red, the color red became ubiquitous with the holiday—and with everything celebratory in China, for that matter.

But a quick digression. Normally the Chinese government includes New Year's Eve as one of the three official Spring Festival holidays. This year, however, they didn't. This year the holiday officially starts on New Year's Day. And I suspect they did this because they placed a good bet that most employers would give employees the day off on New Year's Eve anyway. And most companies did.

In my company's case, we decided to pay them at the holiday rate anyway, both because we thought it was the right thing to do and because we were afraid no one would show up for work if we didn't. Who could blame them? Miss out on the most important family meal of the year without getting anything for it?

So either the government is inhumanly clever, knowing that most companies would do what we did, or even the Chinese government, as thorough as it normally is, is capable of oversight. Personally, I think the former option is the more probable. Inductive thinking, after all, fosters pragmatism and cleverness.

But back to the reunion dinner.

As noted, it is perhaps the most important family event of the year. And because no one wants to be blamed for any potential family misfortunes in the coming year, I suspect there are few excuses short of making money and contributing to the family's prosperity that will get you out of it.

It is strictly a family affair, not a time for building relationships. Foreigners are almost never included. That said, however, the woman who works in our home, known here as an *ayi*, invited my wife and daughters to her family home in a nearby village one New Year's Eve while I was in Germany on business over Spring Festival. It was a sign of genuine affection for my wife and daughters, for sure, but also indicative of the importance placed on the event. In this very kind woman's value system, no one should be left alone for Nian Ye Fan.

Some families choose to dine out. Very seldom do the Chinese entertain in their home and virtually never for business or outside the family. On most occasions they meet their guests at a restaurant, although private rooms are almost always available for such occasions. Needless to say, getting a reservation is extremely difficult on New Year's Eve unless your family has been patronizing the restaurant for a couple of decades, and the meal itself—like virtually every product and service in China—is priced to market supply and demand. A New Year's Eve meal at a decent restaurant will set you back.

Most families, however, prefer to dine at home. As with a US Thanksgiving dinner, preparations are made days in advance, and the food is bountiful. And there are some protocols to follow.

One of the great symbols of wealth and prosperity in Chinese culture is the fish, which it why it adorns a good majority of the souvenirs sold here. As a result, fish is a must-have for any reunion dinner. Traditionally, the fish was left uneaten, in tribute to Nian, I suspect, but I am told that many families today do consume the fish.

Beyond the serving of fish, the Nian Ye Fan menu generally follows regional preferences and specialties. In the north, that means dumplings, or jiaozi, often served later in the evening. In the south, a glutinous cake called niangao is prepared and shared with friends and relatives over the coming days.

Of course, there is drinking involved. And here, as in many Asian countries, drinking is a group activity. If you want to take a drink, you should make a toast. It doesn't have to be long or eloquent, but it's impolite to just sit there and suck down your alcohol in isolation. You can toast a specific person or persons, or you can toast the table as a whole. To avoid the time and effort required to clink everyone's glass, you can simply tap the glass a couple of times on the lazy Susan in front of you that is common to every Chinese restaurant.

The drink of choice on such festive occasions is *baijou*, often referred to as Chinese wine. Believe me, however, that is a mischaracterization if ever there was one. Many Westerners liken the taste to rocket fuel and it has the same impact on the senses. But it is, after all, the number one spirit in the world in liters consumed each year. (I predict that once some enterprising bartender finds something you can mix it with that won't catch on fire, baijou will become an international phenomenon.)

And rockets it is, once the New Year's Eve celebration gets fully underway and the fireworks come out. In a country in which citizens are not allowed to own guns or weapons of any kind, fireworks are commonplace and readily available. Some of the bigger cities have put restrictions in place. Beijing, for example, no longer allows fireworks in the central part of the city after New Year's Eve in 2009, when construction workers accidentally set ablaze the nearly finished luxury hotel next to the new and already iconic CCTV building known as the Big Pants.

I simply can't do the fireworks scene justice with my simple vocabulary. It is unbelievable. They are everywhere. They are loud. And they go on all night—yes, until the sun rises!

It can get a little dicey. In addition to the risk of fire, there is always the risk of injury. And you don't even have to be involved. Our ayi was riding her bicycle home one afternoon when she passed a field in which some men were setting off some kind of rockets. They were sticking them in an empty beer bottle, but of course the bottle fell over once the rocket was lit and proceeded to scream right into her thigh, knocking her off her bicycle. She wasn't seriously hurt, but it was a nasty burn that kept her hobbling for several days.

A bit of bad luck, for sure.

To avoid that kind of thing from happening in the new year, it is tradition to clean your home thoroughly in the days leading up to the new year to make room for the good luck that is sure to arrive on New Year's Eve. (It's also a good idea to get a haircut, in part because the yin-yang extension of that says it is bad luck to cut your hair during the first thirty days of the new year.)

Once New Year's Eve arrives, however, it is customary to lock the broom and dustpan away just in case an obsessive family member decides to do some final cleaning and accidentally cleans out the good luck that has just arrived.

Without a doubt, the one thing that has come to define Spring Festival the most for me is the air of unqualified and unbridled optimism. In a word, hope. The Chinese universally believe, no matter how much hardship they have endured, that the coming year will bring better fortune.

I admit that like a lot of Americans, the December holidays were not always a joyous occasion for me. The days were short, the weather cold, sometimes miserable. While I love my family, like most families, we are a little dysfunctional, and the holidays just seemed to remind us all that we weren't the Cleavers. (*Leave it to Beaver* was an American TV show featuring the Cleaver family—an irreproachable middle-class suburban family. It launched in 1957 on the same day that the Soviet Union launched *Sputnik*, by coincidence.)

Spring Festival is different. I have yet to hear of a single person who suffers from the holiday blues. Everyone looks forward to Spring Festival. Everyone embraces it. Everyone has a smile on his or her face.

I think the reason is that while Spring Festival is all about family, it's not about *the* family. It's not a forced march. It's not about what kind of family you have or whether you are a functional family or a dysfunctional family.

In short, it's not so much a celebration of family, which is where most families fall short (what are we celebrating?). It's about rejuvenation, the promise of a new day, the chance to start over.

It's a massive reboot. Sweep out the old; make room for the new.

And here's the thing with hope—it's not a zero-sum game in the vernacular of mathematical gaming theory. Everybody can win. Your fortune does not have to come at the expense of someone else's misfortune.

Isn't that the problem with most relationships, including family? In most relationships isn't there always one person with just a little more power over the relationship than the other? And isn't it that imbalance that creates the potential for strife and distress. Sure, there are exceptions. But even the exceptions prove the rule. Successful relationships are successful because both sides put aside that imbalance in the interest of the relationship. In failed relationships one or both parties does not or cannot.

On the other hand, no one can own hope. Everyone can possess it in equal abundance. Circumstances often make that difficult, but it's not a limitation of hope itself.

It is this overwhelming sense of collective joy that has come to mean so much to me during Spring Festival. I wonder if we Americans haven't lost our ability to experience this most powerful of emotions. With all the emphasis on individualism and personal achievement and reward, I wonder if we haven't lost the ability to know the true joy of someone else's achievement or good luck. And I wonder if we haven't lost a bit of what truly binds a culture and a people. Would there be so much strife in Western societies today if we could truly share joy?

But for every yin, of course there is a yang. And hope's yang is the emotion of anger and hatred. Hope cannot exist in imbalance with anger.

Thankfully there is an anecdote for anger and hatred, and the Chinese understand it well. It is forgiveness, and it is a critical part of their holistic world view.

If Spring Festival is a celebration of hope, it is also a time for forgiveness. There are no good children who get presents and bad children who get sacks of coal. They all get red envelopes with money stuffed inside.

Service workers, like the barber or the masseuse or the woman who works in your home, get red envelopes, but it is not so much custom as opportunity. Some expect it for sure. And it's always appreciated. But it's somehow bigger than entitlement. It's a symbol of things to come. More than payment for service past performed, it is a key to the lock that opens the door to the future.

On the third and fourth days of the lunar new year, it is customary for the husband to visit the home of his in-laws, if not to grant or beg forgiveness, to at least give thanks for the gift of his marriage.

Hope, forgiveness. Hope, forgiveness. The continuous circle of a rich and bountiful life. Hope, forgiveness.

CHAPTER 25

SEX, DATING & CHILDBIRTH

S ex, of course, is not childbirth, but it starts there, so a little context might be helpful. I think of it as falling into three categories: economic, social, and reproductive.

Economic sex is prostitution and exists in every country in the world. In poorer and less developed countries, it's easy to understand why it does. It all comes back to Maslow's hierarchy of needs. People have to feed themselves, and if all other avenues have been exhausted, there is and always will be a male market for sex the world over.

Prostitution, however, is clearly illegal in China, as are all forms of pornography—you cannot buy even a copy of *Playboy* here, and all pornographic websites are blocked. In addition to cracking down on corruption, the current government has clearly made the crackdown on prostitution a priority—in part, I suspect, because the two issues can be interrelated. In Dongguan, a large manufacturing center in Guangdong Province in the heart of the Pearl River Delta with an immense migrant worker and expatriate population, the Xi government conducted a massive attack on the sex trade, shutting down more than 3,000 venues that were rumored to have employed nearly 300,000 people in one way or another.

In terms of social sex, surveys conducted by both the government and others suggest that attitudes toward casual and premarital sex, like everything else in China, are changing. It is often referred to as a sexual revolution not unlike the one experienced by the West in the sixties and seventies, but from my observation, I don't think the change rises to the level of "revolution."

On balance, I believe, the Chinese remain quite conservative when it comes to sex. While public displays of affection were considered totally taboo among people of my own age, it's not all that evident among the young people of Beijing and Shanghai even today. By Western standards it's all pretty tame.

Young women certainly dress more provocatively than they did a couple of decades ago when men and women were encouraged to dress in a similar conservative fashion, but I think much of that is driven by young women's perception of fashion rather than a desire to look sexy.

In ancient China, of course, marriages were arranged. But while that is no longer the case today, the process of choosing a spouse strikes me as more objective than emotional here. Seldom, I'm told, will a man or woman take a spouse with a vastly different educational, economic, or social background. In a culture of filial piety and obligation built around family and relationships, marrying someone completely outside your "league," to put it bluntly, is considered a recipe for disaster.

China, of course, has traditionally been patriarchal, and while modern Chinese women enjoy all the same political rights as men and are evident in both private and public leadership positions, it is still viewed that when a man and woman marry, the woman is joining the family of the husband. Which partly explains why male suitors are still generally expected to provide well-stuffed "red envelopes" to the parents of their potential bride. (One of the rites of engagement still commonly practiced in the lead-up to the wedding is for the parents of the groom to prepare a special bedroom for the new couple to stay.)

And while virtually all young women now have careers, the career potential of a potential husband appears to get ample consideration in a young woman's final choice. Questions about income, property, and investments are considered appropriate, or so I'm told, once a dating couple starts to get serious.

It's a stage reached fairly quickly, from what I've seen. It is not uncommon for young women in my own office to publicly acknowledge that they have no boyfriend, only to announce their marriage a few months later.

There is little question that young women are under immense pressure to marry. In addition to carrying on the family heritage, of course, there is the practical question of who will take care of the grandparents when they're old.

And not long after marriage, it often seems to be the case, comes the child. Boys, of course, remain the preference, although that remains more true in rural areas than in the large urban centers. Still, the national gender bias of newborn babies remains at 117 to 100 when 103 to 100 is considered natural in the West.

China is ahead of the United States when it comes to maternity benefits, although you are expected to get a certificate from the government before you get pregnant. Maternity benefits are determined locally, but at a minimum new mothers are given three months off with full pay; that can extend to six months, depending on a variety of factors, including where you live and the age of the mother. Even upon their return to work, nursing mothers must be allowed liberal time to nurse their child should they desire to—at home.

There are many rituals and traditions relating to both the newborn baby and mother. Most are falling out of favor among young mothers, but one that is still followed to a surprising degree is the belief that a woman who has just delivered a baby should not bathe or leave the house for one month after the delivery. The reason, as you might suspect, comes back to traditional Chinese medicine and that, of course, inevitably involves issues of yin and yang. A mother who has just given birth needs to retain her inner warmth (yang), which will dissipate through her pores should she bathe. This concern undoubtedly dates back to the days when few Chinese had access to warm water, but it is still considered appropriate by many Chinese, even today.

And then there are the eggs, which recovering mothers are expected to eat in abundance. One colleague told me that her own mother, having just delivered my colleague, ate at least ten eggs per day for the first month. Eggs, for that reason, are often given as gifts by visiting friends and relatives following a birth.

Gary Moreau

I'm sure unwed mothers, other than divorcees or widows, exist, but I have yet to meet one. And while getting married today is a fairly simple affair involving going to the appropriate government office and registering, divorce appears to be equally simple and is increasing in frequency, even though it was considered a source of shame just a generation ago.

When the ever-practical government of Beijing put a limit on the number of homes any household could own in an effort to control rapidly rising housing prices, there was a material spike in the divorce rate—a development virtually everyone believes was created by the desire of wealthy couples to get around the property restriction (surely another excellent example of the law of unintended consequences).

CHAPTER 26

THE POLICE

I grew up in a small mill town in Upstate New York (the real Upstate, not Westchester). It had three police officers—the chief and two deputies. All three had been born and raised there and knew everyone by name.

For a young boy, that could be a handicap. I recall one winter evening when a couple of friends and I were throwing snowballs at passing motorists, until we saw Chief Reilly coming down the street in his patrol car.

We scattered for the bushes nearby and thought we were pretty clever in selecting our hiding spots. However, Chief Reilly came to a gentle stop right in front of us and without getting out of his car, got on his loudspeaker. He addressed each of us by name and told us to stop throwing snowballs at cars and go home. "It's too late for you boys to be out. And I'll warn you now that if I catch you again, I'll have to have a talk with your dads."

And he drove off. We went home and did as he said.

At that age I never questioned what the role of the police was. They were just there. Chief Reilly was just, well, Chief Reilly. He or his deputies usually stopped by the school at the end of the day to direct traffic and make sure the many kids who walked to school—I rode my first bus to school in the seventh grade—got on their way home safely.

The chief could be a serious man but was always ready with a friendly smile. He was a moderately sized man, but not muscular in any way. One of his deputies had the same build as Barney Fife (Don Knotts) in the classic television series, *The Andy Griffith Show*, in which Griffith played Andy Taylor, the sheriff of Mayberry.

It would be unfair to conclude that we lived in a homogenous white middle-class community. It is true that there were relatively few African Americans in the community, but they were there and not in segregation. A large number of Native Americans resided there, not on the reservation the next county over, but among the rest of the citizens. We had immigrants from all over the world, including India, various countries in Southeast Asia, and many parts of Europe. We had a large Italian population and a large Irish population, but many of those were second generation whose parents had come through Ellis Island and been put on trains taking them to where the government at the time thought people of that nationality should settle down.

I don't recognize the US police I see in the news today or when I return to the United States to visit. Barney Fife, I dare say, would never get hired to be a policeman in the United States today.

As I've traveled the world, I've begun to notice that in a certain way, the police are a mirror to the society they serve. The bobbies of England project British gentrification and tradition. And the gendarmes of France project French virility and the ever-present whiff of superiority. (I am French by heritage, so I feel some entitlement to make such an observation.)

And what about China? Well, they don't really project much at all, because it is clear in China that the main role of the police, at the risk of over-generalization, is to protect the state, not the citizens. There are many levels of police that belong to many different arms of the government, but they all fall into one of two camps—power or bureaucracy. In both cases, however, as an individual citizen, you are not their *raison d'etre*, as it were.

While the police in America are there to protect the rights and safety of the individual, the police in China are here to protect the rights and safety of the group (ie, the country at large). The difference shows not the difference between Chinese and Western culture, but the reason(s) for the difference—collectivism and individualism.

One whole branch of police is responsible for traffic control. They don't carry weapons. And they don't really control traffic. I've never seen a motorist get a citation for speeding or running a red light or anything else.

If there is some special event that is clogging up traffic at some obscenely congested intersection, they will often be there in relatively large numbers, but usually standing off to the side observing more than directing.

When there is a traffic accident, by law you are expected to try to negotiate a settlement on the spot with the other driver (assuming there were no injuries, of course), but the traffic police will intervene if necessary, and as I've observed, play a role somewhere between arbitrator and judge. The court system, in its infancy, will not welcome your complaint, so everyone has an incentive to settle.

The most powerful police are the military police and unlike in the United States, they carry full domestic civil authority. They do carry weapons, always work in pairs, are inevitably quite tall and fit, and march more than walk. You will see them at the airport if there are visiting dignitaries in town, but they are not there to answer your questions. And chances are you won't feel inclined to ask them. They are a serious-looking lot.

Having said that, China's military by all estimates is quite large. But it sticks to itself. As the world witnessed during last year's demonstrations in Hong Kong, civil order is generally left to the local police. The People's Liberation Army (PLA) keeps a low profile. They have no need to campaign for public support, as they might feel they must in Western countries, although they do get involved in humanitarian crises such as earthquakes and floods.

Of course, such large human tragedies are a potential threat to the security of the country, and so it's easy to understand why they would be called in, although I believe sheer compassion for the victims is also a key motivation.

The "normal" police, as it were, are not unlike my Chief Reilly. The police wield immense power in terms of their ability to access records, do background checks, and monitor suspects. But they appear to wield it with great reservation. They certainly set priorities. If the threat and/or consequences are thought to be relatively mild, they will be inclined to encourage you to work it out or wait for further evidence of intent before getting involved, in much the same way Andy Taylor might have.

I have had a couple of opportunities to enlist the help of the local police, and one involved an international con that could have been costly to my company. The local police did get involved. They were professional, thorough, and extremely civil and courteous throughout the process. And it was stopped.

On the other hand, an executive from our corporate offices left a brand new iPhone 6 on a treadmill in the gym of the hotel where she was staying. When she went back to retrieve it, of course it was gone, despite the fact that there were no other patrons in the gym during the time she was there. She was certain one of the gym attendants had taken it and wondered if we shouldn't call the police and ask them to go there and get it back.

While such a response would undoubtedly have led to action in the United States, I assured this executive that the police here would take no interest in the case. There was no threat to civil order or the safety of the state, and after all, she had left the phone unattended. Most inductive-minded souls of any nationality would have taken advantage of their good fortune.

One thing you will find here is that it is next to impossible to take investigative matters into your own hands. There are no private investigators—not legal ones, at least. Access to things such as phone records and Internet usage records are considered the exclusive right of the police and the government's overall security organization.

While the Chinese police may not spend too much effort trying to locate the thief who stole your bicycle, they are, by the same token, very unlikely to rough you up (recent Internet video would suggest there are exceptions, but you'd have to admit the situation behind it is a little more involved than merely wandering onto a highway). They simply don't have the motivation and are likely to weigh the risk of greater civil disturbance against any desire to teach you a lesson or project their power.

So while many Westerners may perceive that China is a "police state," just the opposite is true. The police here remind me very much of my own Chief Reilly and his deputies. They want nothing more than to keep the peace, and they're willing to use personal discretion and judgment to do so.

As in most countries, they mirror the society they serve. There are strict limits as to how far you can go in threatening civil disorder, but within those limits people are pretty much left to work it out between themselves. Yin and yang—a harmonious equilibrium between a massive population wanting to improve their lives and the men and women assigned the duty of optimizing the common good.

CHAPTER 27

RULE OF LAW

The 370-member Eighteenth Central Committee of the Communist Party of China held the Fourth Plenary Session in Beijing in October 2014, and as reported by most Western media outlets, the primary topic was "the rule of law." However, as Steve Zhang, professor of contemporary Chinese studies at the University of Nottingham, pointed out, the Chinese agenda for the meeting could be translated as "rule *by* law," not "rule *of* law." The plenum, in other words, had little to do with independent jurisprudence as we think of that ideal in the West and more to do with federalizing some of the discretion historically enjoyed by local government officials.

In reality, all cultures and the political systems that govern them need to find a balance between inductive and deductive reasoning. Overly deductive political systems, such as most Western democracies, ultimately become paralyzed by the emphasis on ideals and values over results.

Overly inductive political systems, on the other hand, can become hotbeds of corruption and, ultimately, anarchy. Moral codes are by nature deductive in nature. And without them, resources are allocated inefficiently, people lose confidence in the government, and the whole system collapses.

President Xi Jinping, I believe, understands this better than anyone else. Deduction must be returned to the Chinese culture and political system, or the party will lose its legitimacy and ultimately the economy and society will be plunged into chaos.

His prescription, I believe, is Marxism with Chinese characteristics, many of which are borrowed from the philosophy of Confucius, to give basic Marxist ideology more of a Chinese identity and the added credibility of an historical association with China at the peak of its global power.

This, I believe, is why President Xi spends so much time referring to the "Chinese dream" and defining that dream in idealistic terms full of uniquely Chinese values.

I further believe it is also why China is in no hurry to embrace the Western ideals of democracy, individual rights, or the rule *of* law anytime soon. The results simply aren't there. As long as the West remains mired in political and economic stagnation, the inductively pragmatic Chinese are yet to be convinced that their way is not the best.

CHAPTER 28

SLEEP

One of the more intriguing dichotomies of the modern Chinese life-style is their resolution of the inherent conflict between the desire to get things done and the rest required to have the energy to do so.

It starts on the plane ride over. The plane takes off, the meal is served, the lights are dimmed, and with few exceptions the Chinese are sound asleep while the Westerners work, watch movies, or just fidget about try-ing to get comfortable and somehow survive the excruciatingly long flight. Upon landing, however, the Chinese jump out of their seats, often before the plane has come to a complete stop, lunge for their personal belongings in the overhead bin, and push their way to the front of the plane to make sure they can deplane as quickly as possible (to be fair, this scenario has softened immensely since I first began traveling here, but the description will still ring true for those coming here for the first time).

And on the commute to work each morning, you can't help but notice that many of the Chinese crammed onto the bus next to you at the stop-light are likewise sound asleep despite the crush of twice as many bodies as the bus was designed to hold. (A Chinese colleague and I both laughed when we got on an empty elevator at a US hotel and saw a large placard warning that the spacious elevator had a legal load limit of eight people. In China there would be no fewer than twenty people on that same eleva-tor.) Once they've arrived at their sparkling new office building, however, they climb aboard the elevator and without fail, reach out and push the button to close the elevator doors with an enthusiasm suggesting that the time otherwise spent waiting for the elevator door to close would be an unforgivable waste.

As a quick aside, the "Chinese elevator culture," as I have come to call it, is fascinating at many levels and is symbolic of multiple dualities. Beyond the rest/action dichotomy that is the subject here, it also speaks to the duality of change and activity. While the Chinese pride themselves on the pace of change they are able to accommodate, in doing so they often confuse activity with action. Having ridden countless elevators around the world, I have yet to witness any compelling evidence that the "close doors" button on any elevator actually does anything. I suspect it is there only to create the illusion of responsiveness when in fact the doors will close whenever they have been preprogrammed to close. That appears to never have occurred to most Chinese, who without exception push the button anyway, often repeatedly, as if the button somehow reacts to exasperation.

Confronted with this dichotomy, many visitors, upon first witnessing a Chinese person sleeping on a park bench or other public venue, may conclude that the Chinese take a rather laidback approach to work. It's not unlike the feeling New Yorkers get when they fly to the Caribbean for holiday and upon taxiing up to the gate look out their airplane window to see the tarmac workers lounging about or asleep on the baggage conveyor pulled up to the next plane over.

What the Chinese have mastered, however, is not the art of laziness, but the art of extending their personal battery life to its maximum, in the same way that Caribbean baggage handlers have learned to survive in the oppressive heat of a Caribbean airport. In essence, they are not avoiding work, but recharging so that they can work even harder and longer.

While always jealous of their effortless ability to shut down, I have become an ardent admirer of the idea of resting when you can. In addition to being good for your health it is the ultimate in lean living, for those of you with knowledge of manufacturing systems and processes.

Again, however, another dichotomy. By eliminating the waste of daydreaming, at the same time, they have eliminated much of the creative benefit of physical idle time. It's great if your work is completely task-oriented, but can be limiting if your work requires both thought and inspiration. While I can wash dishes strictly on the basis of time and motion, writing does not always lend itself to such linear scheduling. If I'm struggling to construct an intelligible sentence, I will often force myself to take a break and come back to it, in much the same way a basketball coach uses a time-out to change the negative momentum of a game.

Many famous Westerners, of course, understood the power of a good nap as well. Thomas Edison, John F. Kennedy, Napoleon Bonaparte, John D. Rockefeller, and Ronald Reagan were all accomplished nappers, according to research posted on huffingtonpost.com. The Chinese, nonetheless, appear to have once again taken a good idea to an entirely new level. That's what happens, I guess, when you have 1.3 billion people on a mad dash to lead more comfortable lives.

But alas, as I write this, I am in the United States on a business trip; it's 4:00 a.m. and I am, of course, unable to sleep.

Maybe it's genetic.

CHAPTER 29

PERSONALIZING SUCCESS

A friend recently told me a sad story about a young woman who had been attending university but had become depressed and dropped out to return home. After isolating herself in her parents' home for several months, she announced that she was feeling much better and wanted to return to university.

All of the necessary arrangements were made, and her mother took her back to the dormitory, where she shared a room with several other young women. Only students were allowed in the living area, so her mother waited outside for her daughter to take her things to her room so they could go to dinner.

Upon reaching her dorm room on the ninth floor, however, the young woman set down her bags and jumped out the window, landing not far from where her mother waited on the sidewalk.

It's an awful story and I still lose sleep over it. And it has made me think—a lot!

There is depression and suicide in China, just as there is elsewhere in the world. But while I have seen no statistics on the issue, it has always struck me that the Chinese are, on balance, a happy people compared to most Western cultures. Seldom is there rage in the air, even on the highway, where I've often thought road rage shootings would be the most common cause of death, were people to drive in the United States as they do here.

One distinction has occurred to me. The United States likes to think of itself as the land of opportunity—a meritocracy. And to an extent, it is.

Work hard, get a little lucky, and you have a good chance of getting ahead in life.

As a result, however, we tend to both personalize and be a little judgmental about career success. The mere fact that we call people who have acquired wealth "successful" is telling. It suggests that their success is both personal and earned.

Unfortunately, of course, the reverse can also be true. Poor people are often characterized—consciously or not—as somehow deserving of their poverty, either through a lack of effort or natural talent.

The Chinese have a very different perspective on the issue. For starters, they don't personalize wealth. "He's rich" is simply a statement of fact, not a personal judgment. People who have acquired wealth are considered simply "good at business," not accomplished. It's not a pejorative assessment. Nor is it a statement of personal respect or admiration, however. Envy, maybe.

Part of the reason for the difference is the simple fact that wealth is relatively new to China. Among my own generation, everyone was poor. There were no financial distinctions.

Even today, despite the appearance of Ferraris on the streets of the major urban areas and the proliferation of sleek glass office towers and upscale apartment buildings, there remain hundreds of millions of Chinese who continue to live in difficult, impoverished conditions.

Economic development, of course, brings many benefits. But it likewise brings many challenges.

The young Chinese of today are under enormous pressure to perform well in school, get into a good university, and move into a promising career. The fact that the care of the elderly is considered a family obligation only adds to the pressure.

And yet there will ultimately be the realization that opportunity is not the same as economic equality. Most Western democracies, particularly the United States, continue to have highly stratified divisions of wealth and income distribution, and the problem is getting worse, not better.

We're already getting glimpses of the trend. As I have written before, like many Chinese, I believe the protests in Hong Kong were more about economic opportunity than democracy. Young people simply aren't seeing the opportunity they have always been told would be there. Housing costs are skyrocketing, and there is more and more competition for the best jobs.

Ditto for Taiwan. While the Western media have universally labeled the 2014 elections there as a black eye for Beijing and the result of a surging desire to maintain Taiwan's political independence, that is not the narrative I hear from the Taiwanese business people I interface with every day.

The political integration of Taiwan and the mainland is a *fait accompli*. It's already happened. Taiwan is a de facto Hong Kong.

What these elections were about, according to this alternative narrative, is frustration among the young people of Taiwan about the polarization of wealth and the lack of universal economic opportunity.

The mainland is beginning to face similar social challenges. There are now seven million university graduates in China every year. And without the double-digit growth China has known for the last two decades, the economy is straining to employ them at the level they expected when they devoted their childhoods to the grueling lifelong process of getting into the best universities.

The undeniable reality of the world is that there are no pure meritocracies. There are only degrees of meritocracy. Some degree of social acceptance of this reality, for whatever reason, is essential to civil order.

As I've noted many times, I believe this is why President Xi Jinping refers so often to the Chinese Dream. And why he is so diligent about rooting out government corruption and the appearance of government waste and insensitivity. Marxism is a conceptual counterweight to the excesses of unregulated commerce.

The West has deductive logic to thank for its relative civil order in the face of polarizing wealth and income (although cracks, under different names, are appearing more frequently). This deductive perspective has enabled the cause and effect thinking that is essential to the acceptance of a black and white moral code that, ironically, creates some tolerance for injustice and inequity.

At the same time, to the extent that deductive Western culture encourages people to personalize wealth and career success, we are planting the seeds of our own civil unraveling should we not address the growing problem of income and wealth disparity. "Now it's personal" is a great enabler of anger and retribution.

For the Chinese, it is the cultural tendency not to personalize wealth and success that holds society together. I believe this is why the government feels it so important to strengthen the party and why so much effort is being placed in reeducating government officials, members of the media, and ordinary citizens in the core ideals of Marxism. At the end of the day, one of the core tenets of Marxism is the depersonalization of wealth and financial success.

When the Chinese start saying, "He is successful," rather than, "He is good at business," the tide will have turned, and the risk of civil dissatisfaction will be greatly enhanced.

For now, however, other than in the cultural outliers of Hong Kong and Taiwan, I see little evidence that this is happening. The people I drive by every day, most of whom lead difficult physical lives, are still smiling, happy to be who they are and very happy to be Chinese.

CHAPTER 30

GUANG CHANG DA MA

Pass by any public park in China in the early morning or evening, and you are likely to see a group of women, and some men, swaying in unison to the beat of any one of the numerous genres of Chinese music. These are the *guang chang da ma* of China, and the majority of them are on the older side of forty (literally translated, it means public square/Daddy's elder brother's wife).

The exaggerated gestures and extensions generally fall somewhere on the visual spectrum between tai chi and ballet, but the music is almost always deafening and inevitably distorted by inexpensive speakers pushed well beyond their limits.

There are many theories as to why this public dancing is so popular. Fitness, of course, is the most obvious, but the sense of social connection, particularly for the retired women, has to be one of the attractions.

While the *da ma* have been doing their thing in the countryside for decades, if not centuries, they have recently created some social urban tension, and the government has stepped in to regulate their activity. Liu Guoyong, chief of the General Administration of Sport's mass fitness division, recently declared, "Square dancing represents the collective aspect of Chinese culture, but now it seems the overenthusiasm of the participants has dealt it a harmful blow with disputes over noise and venues."

As a result, Mr. Liu announced, square dancers would be required to perform one of twelve officially approved routines and more than 600 instructors would fan out across the country to demonstrate the officially sanctioned choreography in the coming months.

Most see the dispute as a battle between the rural collectivism of those who lived through the era of Mao Zedong (and now live in the city) and the more individualistic urban perspective of China's youth.

While that's undoubtedly true, I suggest that the explanation for the dispute has as much to do with the evolution of communication styles in China. When the Chinese answer the phone, they do not say, "hello." They say—or sometimes shout—the word *wei* (pronounced "way" but with more vigor), which essentially means, "I'm here" or "You have my attention."

And so it is in conversation. You must never ask a Chinese person a question until you get his or her attention first. Otherwise you are sure to get the answer, "What?" They won't hear you. Remember, they are receiver oriented and don't receive automatically.

It is perfectly normal for elderly men out for a stroll to drag along a small, tinny radio that is blaring away Beijing opera as they walk. Restaurants routinely put loudspeakers suitable for a rock concert on their steps to let passersby know they exist. Every driver honks his or her horn with abandon. Every other driver ignores them.

This is China. It's loud.

What is most typically Chinese about the *da ma* saga, however, is that no one can comprehend how regulating the choreography is going to reduce the noise pollution or reduce the congestion in China's urban parks. It's a classically bureaucratic solution at best.

And it most certainly will not contain the activities of the *da ma*. The "official" routines and the unofficial routines will coexist in harmony. It will be yet another example of the duality of Chinese culture and socialism with Chinese characteristics—the yin and yang of Chinese governance. The "official" almost always has an unofficial counterpart—like the rules of the road and the way people actually drive.

That's where you end up when your world view is circular rather than linear—always seeking harmony through the balance of yin and yang, official and unofficial.

CHAPTER 31

PARKS & PERSPECTIVE

Having grown up in a rural American village of 3,000 people, I always knew the world as a park. The park was where I went to play Little League baseball. (I was a catcher because they got to wear the cool equipment. Never any good, of course.)

I first learned the value of public parks when I moved to Beijing, a city of twenty-two million people. China, in total, has 119 national parks, and Beijing itself has dozens more. And Beijingers, for their part, make very good use of them.

Fêng shui, of course, puts a lot of emphasis on trees and plants and water, and while that may not directly explain the generous resources devoted to parks in China, the general thinking is in there somewhere. The Chinese love plants and flowers in a very fundamental way.

The city planners in Beijing also love to plant trees, both to help with air quality and to add visual beauty to the city, and because the city sits on the eastern edge of the Gobi Desert that has, in the past, been the source of sandstorms that turn the air orange. (It is fairly infrequent today.)

The devotion to family also contributes to the utilization of public parks. In a city with the density of Beijing, there is no such thing as the ubiquitous American barbeque on the patio or deck. There aren't any patios or decks.

The parks in Beijing are not the place where the loners go. They're filled with families, and one of the things I enjoy most about them is the number of three-generation families you see. My parents are both deceased, and my own children live in the United States, so it gives me a certain sense of connection being among so many extended families.

To really use a park, you have to know how to relax, and Americans, in general, aren't very good at that. If we're not working, we're on the rowing machine or working in the workshop or mowing the lawn. The Chinese, as much as they are focused on their health, don't have rowing machines or workshops or lawns.

Americans are universally thought of as uptight and in general, we are. I believe it's because we're too damn deductive. We need to explain everything, or our universe becomes unsettled. Cause and effect. Cause and effect. (When I have corporate visitors from the United States, they inevitably ask me why the bottoms of the trees are painted white. I can guarantee that few Chinese have even noticed the fact, but the reason is insects, in case you're wondering.)

The Chinese are not uptight at all, except when it comes to money. They're inductive in their world view. They could care less why the bottoms of the trees are painted white unless there's a business opportunity in it. They are white because someone painted them white. That's all the Chinese need to know.

I think there is a lot to be said for the Chinese world view. As hard as the Chinese work, and as frenetically as they work when they do, they also know how to throttle down. It's like they have a switch they can flick at a moment's notice. I envy them that.

As an American expatriate working in China, I have a lot of conference calls at night. And when I'm done, I simply cannot just brush my teeth and go to bed. I have to decompress. I have to decipher cause and effect, or my mind just won't shut down. "Why did so-and-so say what she said?" "What does that mean for me?" "How will my region be affected?"

The Chinese have no such issue. They can sit down on a bus and be asleep in mere seconds. They can nap on a park bench surrounded by thousands of other people.

Young people, I've noticed, tend to go out in groups. I have seldom seen young couples that appear to be dating. I'm told that's true all over the world among the younger generation, but it's truly evident here. And when you do see a group of young people here, you don't sense the level of hormonal tension you do elsewhere when a group of young men and women are together. They seem more like brothers and sisters than anything else, and I really believe that is how young Chinese think of their relationships.

Chinese of all ages often touch when they talk. Old men, as well as young women, will frequently stroll arm in arm when they are walking and talking with a friend. It means absolutely nothing about their sexual preferences.

The Chinese love to play cards. Sometimes it's serious. When you see a bunch of taxis parked off to the side of the road, you can be assured there is a high-stakes card game going on. But families play for fun.

And while the Chinese are as enamored with their smartphones as the rest of the world, they talk to each other as well. I often see pairs of people or groups of young people just sitting on the grass talking. I have few American friends who have the patience or the time to just sit on the grass with me and chat.

Wedding photos are often taken in parks, as are advertisements. It's common to see a small army of photographers trailing a beautiful young model around Beijing's parks, with a lens that must be able to see the craters on the moon.

All told, I am enamored with Beijing's parks and visit them every chance I get. I love the trees and the grass and the flowers. But more than anything else, I love the people. They are serene. They are just enjoying. They aren't trying to figure everything out.

My Chinese wife said it best. We were coming up out of the subway once and were on what had to easily be the longest escalator I have ever seen, and I have traveled the world. My immediate thought: "There must be an enormous electric motor powering this thing."

My wife's mouth dropped open in complete disbelief. "You think way too much," she said. "It's no wonder you sleep no good."

CHAPTER 32

THE ART OF SILLY

While the Chinese are generally known to be rather formal and traditional and often inscrutable in their facial expressions, one of their greatest skills is the art of being silly. Unlike many conservative Westerners, they aren't the least bit afraid to put themselves in positions so compromising of normal behavior that you can't help but have a good laugh.

I have pondered this particular duality for a long time, and I've finally concluded that it has to have something to do with the way they view one another. There are definitely hierarchies of power and most certainly hierarchies of wealth, and a lot of deference that goes with both.

In the end, however, I don't believe these hierarchies are viewed personally. Unlike their Western counterparts, most Chinese don't view wealth and power as a byproduct of innate personal traits or skills. Anybody can get rich if he works hard and has a good stroke of luck. No one is predestined for power and success.

In the end I think it comes down to the extent to which you believe life is a true meritocracy. To Americans meritocracy is a near religion. The people who get ahead clearly deserve to—they have superior skills that they are superior at putting to good use.

The Chinese, on the other hand, accept that some people are smarter than others or stronger than others or perhaps have a better head for business. They don't, however, believe that life is a meritocracy. The parents you were born to, the village in which you grew up, the education you had access to are all essentially random and play a big role in your opportunities for future success.

Personally, I'm a bit in the middle. As a writer I believe that most of the successful writers out there are good writers. I also believe, however, that there are hundreds, if not thousands, of equally good writers you've never heard of.

One unexpected consequence of this difference in world view is that you see little in the way of arrogance within the Chinese culture. Foreigners are considered a wee bit odd, but all Chinese more or less consider themselves equals no matter what their financial circumstances or level of career success. You see virtually no behavior that would suggest anyone is looking down on, or feels superior to, anyone else. It's quite refreshing once you appreciate it's there.

At the annual dinner all companies hold prior to Spring Festival, there is always a managers game designed specifically to make the management of the company look silly. Nobody is excused and it's all in good fun. The activities aren't in any way meanspirited or designed to put the manager in a negative light, but if you're not comfortable looking silly, it does take some getting used to.

If you work at it, however, and play along with enthusiasm, you can bring the audience to their feet in admiration. They like a boss with the strength to put himself out there in an otherwise embarrassing situation.

So too it is with team-building events, which every company in China holds with all its employees. We do these in the United States too, of course, but the team-building events I've participated in in the United States were very much competitions. People from the CEO on down were dead serious on winning each event.

And the events themselves were not so much designed to be fun as to highlight some aspect of teamwork in the workplace. Building bridges or boats and figuring out how to turn over a tarp with everyone standing on top of it are common examples.

Team building in China, for the most part, is more about having fun than developing strategic skills or learning to think out of the box. Four-legged races, tug-of-war, and carrying balloons between your legs are more common than figuring out how to roll a ball down several sections of disconnected piping.

Ultimately I've decided it's healthy to be silly. It takes a certain level of maturity and self-confidence to put your pride on the line. And it certainly takes humility, the most important ingredient of leadership in my experience.

I also think it's an excellent way to build teamwork. So what if you can build a bridge that meets in the middle? If the people within the team still think of themselves in some sort of personal hierarchy, their teamwork will be ultimately ineffective.

Teamwork relies on diversity. To really be a team, you have to consider everyone's opinions equally. That rarely happens in the typical Western team-building exercise, where the most forceful personality on the team assumes control, and everyone else just follows along.

To be honest, no one who knew me before coming to China would have ever described me as silly. I was always serious. But my expression was often a false impression. I often struggled with self-confidence and developing a sense of personal pride.

By teaching me to be silly, the Chinese have greatly strengthened my self-confidence and sense of personal pride. Whenever I attend a team-building event or participate in a managers game, I inevitably come away feeling good about myself. I dropped my guard and it was OK. The world didn't come to an end. I wasn't humiliated.

In fact, I had fun. And in the end I've always believed that fun and teamwork are good for business.

Try it. You'll be amazed at the power of silly!

CHAPTER 33

SUMMER IN BEIJING

Before moving to Beijing I lived my entire life north of the Forty-Second Parallel. I know, cold. I know what it's like to walk the streets of Chicago in January with an arctic gale blowing in from the lake. The word *cold* doesn't do it justice.

And yet I have never felt as cold as I do here in Beijing in the wintertime (Thirty-Ninth Parallel). I am chilled to the bone. My extremities ache. I lose my sense of touch.

Which is why I am so dumbfounded when I look at the thermometer and see that the temperature outside is only in the teens or low twenties Fahrenheit (minus 9 to minus 7 C). It can't be. I have lived in places where it is minus thirty degrees F (minus thirty-four C) for days on end and never felt so cold. It's rather pleasant, actually. Silence fills the air, and the snow makes a comforting, quiet swoosh when you walk.

Some say it's the dryness of the air. Others say it's the humidity of the air. No one, however, has ever offered what I consider to be a plausible explanation.

And if that weren't perplexing enough, the reverse is true in the summer. I have never experienced such stifling heat as the heat that grips Beijing in July and August. It's downright oppressive.

But again, the thermometers are either all broken or don't tell the whole story. It's a heat that simply does not lend itself to calibration.

And how do the Chinese handle the sizzling Beijing summer?

As you might expect, they endure it. And they complain notably little. Suffering, as I've noted before, is an accepted reality of life in China, in the end having little to do with wealth or the type of work you do. It just is what it is.

The schools are closed but not for long. The Chinese school year is much longer than the typical American school year, in part because there is an extended break during Spring Festival when virtually all of China returns to its roots for an extended family visit.

And while employment patterns are changing, most Chinese do not get vacation (my Dutch colleagues call them mini-sabbaticals) as we know it in the developed world. The large number of people who work for themselves in the informal economy simply can't afford the time off. And even those who have paychecks signed by someone else get most of their paid time off around the national holidays, two of which (Spring Festival and National Day on October 1) get turned into Golden Weeks of paid holiday by switching weekends with normal working days to put together a string of five to seven consecutive days off with pay. (And seven to eight consecutive work days on one end or the other.)

The Chinese don't worship the sun in the same way many Westerners do. Or more to the point, they don't like to get tanned by the sun. Light skin is a standard of beauty among Chinese women, and most go out of their way to avoid both the darkening and aging that comes with direct sun exposure. Many use umbrellas on sunny days, and bicyclists going to and from work or the store often wear dark face shields that give the appearance they might stop and do some welding along the way. There are no tanning salons here. They would be as financially foolish as opening a store that sold licensed DVDs.

Air conditioning exists, of course, although many Chinese shun it for perceived health reasons. And most hotels turn it off at night to save money (by far the biggest complaint I get from visiting Western colleagues).

Hand fans are common, but I would like to see a scientific study to determine if the cooling provided by the small amount of wind generated dissipates more heat than it creates through the exertion of fanning. Something tells me it's a net loss, but I seem to be the only one with the question, so it goes, to my knowledge, unanswered.

There is one unique aspect of the Beijing summer known among foreigners as the "Beijing Belly." During the heat of the day, men often pull their shirts up over their stomachs in the same way men elsewhere might take their shirts off. I've never quite figured out if this is a compromise to cultural norms of decorum or just a belief that heat escapes more efficiently through your belly than elsewhere. (Hatmakers, I'm sure, would argue that most body heat escapes through your scalp in the wintertime.)

The Chinese do appear to enjoy fishing, although like most activities in China, it is generally not a hobby that brings much solitude.

There are many large and beautiful public parks in Beijing, and the Chinese take full advantage of them for summer outings. But since they don't like the sun and privacy is essentially nonexistent, the practical impact is that the parks turn into congested tent farms on a pleasant weekend afternoon. People enjoy a nice lunch, perhaps a nap, and just generally spending time with family and friends.

Sports are becoming more popular as people acquire the time and means to pursue them. Basketball is verging on a passion. Yao Ming, of course, has had a hand in that, but the American NBA has done a masterful job of marketing itself here. If you're wondering what the superstars like LeBron James do with their time in the off-season months, chances are they will make at least one visit to China to promote the sport. LeBron was here just after announcing his return to Cleveland and received a hero's welcome.

Riding a bicycle, once a transportational necessity for most Chinese (there are more than 10 million bicycles in Beijing alodne), is becoming increasingly popular as a recreational pastime. Although air quality can be a legitimate deterrent to knocking off 100 kilometers on a Saturday morning, most urban roads have segregated bicycle lanes much like you might now find in the Hamptons or Venice Beach. They're used primarily by the millions of Chinese who still rely on a bicycle to get around (and more than a few unscrupulous drivers trying to jump the line at the traffic signal), but they're there nonetheless and make cycling far more convenient than on the vehicle-dominated streets of most American cities.

Gary Moreau

The Chinese who can afford it or have the good luck to have been born close to the ocean love to go to the beach as much as people elsewhere do (without the typical sunbathing, of course), but in my experience, relatively few Chinese know how to swim.

I find that a bit sad, to be honest, given that 75 percent of the globe is covered in water, and taking a dip on a hot summer day is indeed one of life's simple but great pleasures. It has, at the same time, given me immense pride and satisfaction to realize that the vast majority of citizens of my home country have been taught to swim as children. Kudos to all those who helped to make that a reality.

And what about the practical effects of having so many people in such confined spaces in such hot and humid weather? Odoriferous, right?

This is a topic of great debate within the expatriate community. Many Chinese will claim, to the indignant incredulity of many foreigners, that they do not sweat as much as foreigners do. And whether effect or excuse, most Chinese don't bathe with the same frequency that Americans do. Nor do they use deodorant or antiperspirant out of both a sense of frugality and the belief that it is unhealthy to restrain normal bodily functions such as sweating (that's also why spitting is considered good health rather than bad manners – better to get it out if that's what the body suggests).

I can tell you with certainty that the Chinese do sweat. Glass factories are hot places in the summertime, so I say this with a certain degree of expertise. However, I also believe that for whatever reason, they do sweat notably less than Americans in general. A sheen to the skin, perhaps, but seldom do you see the sweat-soaked shirt you would normally find in similar conditions elsewhere.

And when they sweat, they do, of course, emit body odor. I must admit, however, that even in the absence of deodorant, the odor is not as offensively pungent as it is elsewhere. It's more of an organic smell than repulsively rancid-smelling.

I've given this a fair amount of thought and concluded that it all comes down to a few key differences.

The first is diet. Despite all the marketing hype surrounding organic foods and the whole farm-to-table movement in the United States, the reality is that Americans eat a lot of processed foods. Foods may taste better and remain consumable longer, but we are filling our bodies with chemicals that interact in ways I'm convinced we don't fully understand.

The second is hydration. This is an increasingly popular topic the world over, but the Chinese have been obsessed with it for generations, to the point that they drink only warm water to promote absorption. And in combination with their diet, this has the practical effect of limiting the time anything stays in their bodies to hours rather than days.

And while I have not one shred of scientific evidence to support my theory (my full and complete legal disclaimer), I believe that deodorants and antiperspirants stimulate body odor when used over a long period of time. I don't know why. I don't know how. I'm not even scientifically sure it is true. Through experience and experiment, however, I have become convinced that the process of chemically controlling and/or masking our sweat glands makes them more rebellious.

Experiment for yourself, although I strongly suggest you change your diet and your hydration habits first.

All told, summer is not my favorite season in China. It's just a bit too hot and sticky for my tastes. Or, as I sometimes say when the air quality is poor, too hot, sticky, and icky.

But it is a season, and I prefer to live in places that have them. If nothing else, it gives you something to talk about. Or try to, anyway, if you don't speak the language.

CHAPTER 34

FOOD

Writing about Chinese food is a slippery slope, given that Chinese cuisine, like so many things Chinese, is quite regional. Restaurants self-classify by the regional cuisine they offer (eg, they offer Sichuan food, or Hunan food, or whatever).

Being an American company, of course, my previous employer sent quite a few Chinese back to the United States for meetings, training, and such. (That's when the US government would issue them a visa. It is much more difficult than you might think for Chinese nationals to get even temporary visas to the United States, even when it is at the request of a public US company and they are accompanied at all times.)

So at lunch one day in the company canteen, I shared the question with our Chinese Human Relations (HR) manager, knowing she had been to the United States several times and rather enjoyed the American version of Italian food she had been introduced to. She opined, however, that her enjoyment of American cuisine was not shared by her fellow Chinese, going on to share a few anecdotes of Chinese colleagues who had lost considerable weight while visiting the United States because they simply couldn't stomach the food.

She thought it was an intriguing question nonetheless and offered to put out an anonymous online questionnaire (in Chinese, of course) to our rather significant population of employees, from all levels of the company and all departments, who had traveled to the United States. (For many it was their first time to ever leave China. The first time on an airplane for some.)

Participation was almost unanimous, although it was anonymous, so I can't offer a lot of insight into who thinks what demographically.

Before I share the results, let me point out that the Chinese fortune cookie that you receive at virtually every Chinese restaurant in America is not Chinese at all. I have never seen one in China and our employees, without exception, are quite perplexed when presented one at the end of the meal at a US Chinese restaurant. To my knowledge, you can't even buy them here.

There seems to be a consensus that fortune cookies were invented in California, but there seems to be some controversy as to who invented them, with many believing that the inventor was not even of Chinese descent (The original fortune cookie, some believe, contained biblical scripture, not "Good fortune will soon befall you.")

Chop suey, by the way, is another American invention. It exists on no menu in China. And I have yet to see a Chinese buffet restaurant. Buffets are common at breakfast, where the breakfast is usually included with the cost of the room, but dining in China is highly social, intimate, and interactive, which is why most restaurants have private dining rooms. It's not, however, the type of activity that would lend itself to diners getting up and going off to refill their plates at the buffet.

But on to the results:

Sixty percent of those surveyed said the American food tasted "good," although 16 percent thought it tasted "bad," and 24 percent thought it had no taste at all. The same results for smell, which, upon reflection, probably shouldn't be too surprising.

Also on the not surprising side, most of the Chinese surveyed felt that Americans eat too much meat (64 percent thought "too much" or "way too much") and not enough vegetables (36 percent thought "too little" while only 20 percent felt the vegetables were served in quantities that were "too much" and none felt that there was "way too much."

Almost all agreed that the portions in general are too big. Only 12 percent felt they were "too small," but another 12 percent described them as "huge."

I was a little surprised that only 28 percent felt that Americans eat too little fruit (the Chinese eat it with every meal—but always thirty minutes later for digestion). but not surprised that 72 percent think Americans eat too much cheese (28 percent checked "way too much.")

The favorite food category was dessert, with 48 percent agreeing that the variety and portions were "about right."

Fully 88 percent admitted they had dined at Chinese restaurants while traveling in the United States, although I would guess this wasn't always by choice. I suspect their American colleagues sometimes take them to Chinese restaurants on the assumption that they will feel more at home there.

As it turns out, 68 percent of those who had eaten at a Chinese restaurant in the United States said the Chinese food there was "not at all like the Chinese food I eat at home," and 9 percent concluded that the "Chinese" food served in the United States is "not really Chinese food."

Not surprisingly, they are uniformly dumbfounded by the American obsession with ice. As noted before, the Chinese believe cold drinks are bad for your health and prefer to drink water warm or at room temperature.

And we advise our travelers that if a Chinese person is paying the bill to ask if the service has been included. Because China is a no-tipping country, we have found that many US restaurants will add the tip to the bill if they are serving a table of Chinese. As a former college waiter, no complaint from me on that front, but we've also discovered they won't always tell them if they have included the tip, and the Chinese tip out of ignorance anyway.

In the end the Chinese surveyed were all pretty good sports about the cuisine. Eighty-four percent claimed they would look forward to the food if they traveled there again, and no one claimed that he or she would bring food from home (not at all a good idea as far as US customs is concerned).

And what about me?

Many of my American colleagues assume it is a special treat for me to attend meetings in the United States and have the chance to eat my native cuisine. To be honest, it's not. It's not that I don't like the food. But I don't eat a lot of meat, I have generally given up processed meats and cheeses, mostly for the processing, and I generally find the portions to be a bit absurd.

As I've noted so many times, it's a diverse world. There's always a risk in generalizing. Many might be surprised to learn that rice is not a Chinese staple. That's only true in the south and east. In the north wheat is the primary food staple. I eat far less rice here in Beijing than I did when I used to visit my company's office in Milan, where rice is included with almost every meal and is grown in abundance in northern Italy.

CHAPTER 35

THE ENVIRONMENT

Everyone knows that China faces some serious environmental challenges. What many don't know, however, is that China, for those willing to see, has much to teach the world in the areas of energy conservation and recycling.

Industrial environmental degradation is a global problem. Today it's China because the world has moved most of its production here. Tomorrow, clearly, it will be some other developing country where wages remain cheap and the regulatory environment remains what is often called investment-friendly, but which can mean pollution tolerant. Like so many current event topics, I believe it is unproductive to attach emotion to that term. Good people sometimes behave in bad ways either because we allow them to or we, in fact, give them incentive.

To the extent that specific companies and industries degrade the environment, in my opinion, the blame for that rests in part with all the countries that import that company's products. And since governments are merely the institutional face of the people they govern, it ultimately comes back to the people who buy those products.

I think it a little unfair and disingenuous, therefore, to lay the blame for industrial environmental degradation only at the feet of the Chinese. Walmart and Carrefour shoppers everywhere are just as much a part of the problem.

But let's step back from the industrial question. As an individual I have always been frustrated by the environmental degradation I see around the world. The Chinese have helped me understand that I, as an individual, can make a difference.

As an example, China has been charging for shopping bags for years. And at first it is a nuisance. It's inevitable that you'll forget your cloth bags the first few times. Eventually, however, you learn to keep a few in the car or in your bicycle basket.

And why have Americans stopped riding bicycles anyway? Sure, there are the weekend warriors on their titanium racing machines and the mountain biker who can jump over logs in a single bound. Taken together, however, it's a statistically insignificant population.

What about the millions of people who jump into their cars to run to a store less than a mile away? What if they all rode bicycles instead?

And my personal favorite, ice. Think of how much energy is used each day in the simple but energy-intensive task of turning water into a solid.

Is it really necessary?

Restaurant owners and fast-food franchisees like it, of course, because they believe—based on the incentives we give them in an economy that does little to encourage energy efficiency—that the ice costs less than the refreshment. And that's true. But should it be?

Consumers will argue that it's all about taste and satisfaction. Americans like their drinks cold.

But that is an acquired prejudice. It's simply what we're accustomed to. A mother's milk isn't chilled, and babies seem to like it just fine.

In other words, we can get unaccustomed to such heavy usage of ice. I have. I had to. Ice is rare in China, and I grew tired of having to make a special request in a language I was struggling to learn. But I survived. And I've learned to prefer my soft drink or water without ice.

And what about washing machines and dishwashers? In terms of convenience, they are right up there with the electric garage door opener in terms of the greatest inventions of all time.

And the manufacturers and purveyors of these devices would surely defend their products as contributing to the efficient use of energy. Appliance manufacturers today devote their massive research and development and marketing budgets to developing and touting the energy efficiency of their appliances. But when it comes to electrical appliances, what does energy efficiency really mean? After all:

- However energy efficient they are in other ways, electric appliances by definition use electricity. And even if you get that electricity from wind or solar farms, you still have to build the devices to capture and convert those energy sources; you have to truck that equipment to where the sun and wind are; and you have to build infrastructure, which requires energy, to get it to your home. Humans, on the other hand, require far less energy to power a little elbow grease.
- Appliances are not infinitely scalable in their energy and resource consumption. Yes, the more expensive models have settings to adjust the size of the load, the temperature of the water, and the duration of the wash cycle. But this only reduces the amount of potential waste; it doesn't eliminate it.
- Nor is the effort exerted by these appliances scalable. Dishwashers and the detergents they use must be capable of cleaning the dirtiest of dishes. And washing machines, even on the gentlest cycle, are still subjecting your clothes to a level of wear and tear unlikely to be inflicted with handwashing.

So why don't we wash our dishes and clothes by hand anymore? If everyone stopped using these appliances, how much energy would we save and how much would we slow the environmental degradation of the planet?

That, you might quickly note, would result in a massive waste of time, time that we might otherwise devote to ending global poverty or eradicating childhood disease.

Fair enough. However, we could reduce the time wasted by dirtying fewer dishes and clothes.

I grew up in a household where towels went into the dirty laundry after a single use. I realized as an adult that was extreme, so I began to wash towels only once per week.

Gary Moreau

And then I moved to China and noticed that when I traveled on business with my Chinese colleagues, they inevitably showed up at the airport with little or no luggage. Eventually, of course, I learned that they washed their clothes before retiring to bed each night and hung them in the shower to dry.

I've never gone quite that far but have decided that I can wear a pair of blue jeans more than one day, assuming I didn't roll in the mud or spill soy sauce on them.

By now, if you've even bothered to read this far (and I thank you if you have), you may have concluded that I'm simply advocating poverty for all and that we should throw out all the advances in the quality of life that our parents and grandparents worked so hard to achieve over the last hundred years.

But that's not the case at all. I'm all for advancement. I love my iPhone and my iPad, and I'm obviously more than a little enthralled with computers and the Internet. What I am arguing, however, is that we sometimes get confused about what really constitutes quality of life. And we forget that as advanced as our culture has become, trade-offs remain a reality of life we can't ignore.

It all gets back to the circle versus the straight line. Is every issue really black or white, or is there room for gray?

BUSINESS

CHAPTER 36

HORIZON

Before coming to China in 2007, I read an interesting article by an executive in the US automotive industry who had experience in China. He said the difference between the US automotive industry and its Chinese counterpart is that in the United States, we will invest $300 million in a new factory and accept a five-year payback. In China, by contrast, they will invest $50 million and expect a six-month payback. If it works, they will invest some more.

He is correct. But it has taken me a long time to truly understand the implications of that reality.

It is not at all uncommon to see someone invest a great deal of money in a new restaurant or retail store and close it down completely thirty days later. Nor is it uncommon to see multimillion dollar construction projects stop in midstream, sit for a year, and restart again.

Companies, even large ones, pivot in and out of completely distinct industries with total abandon. One of my largest previous distributors decided the margins in distribution were not attractive enough, so he was seriously contemplating opening a chain of movie theaters even though he knew nothing about the business (and streaming and cheap home theaters are killing the industry anyway).

A hugely successful, multibillion-dollar energy company headquartered in the town where I worked was rumored to be moving out of energy and into traditional Chinese medicine because they feared that as the government deregulates the energy industry, margins will fall.

My biggest Chinese competitor at the time, facing increasing competition in the glass industry, negotiated a $190 million investment in the online gaming industry with the explanation that the CEO had played the game for over a year and found it very entertaining (the investment eventually fell through).

My own former company has been making glass for almost 200 years, and we were far from alone among American companies in our long-term commitment to a single industry. There are exceptions. But most successful companies in the United States are doing exactly what they've been doing from day one.

Put in its simplest terms, the difference between American companies and Chinese companies is that the former exist to build long-term value and the latter exist to make money.

As simple as it sounds, it's a profound difference. Each brings a completely different mindset to the task. Which is one of the main reasons, I believe, that Western companies find it so difficult to find the right Chinese business partner when they are so inclined or required to do so by regulation.

Part of the difference flows from the different ways in which the two cultures think about institutions. Americans who build their own businesses often refer to them as a member of the family or the equivalent of a child—a labor of love. To the Chinese, who find it impossible to personalize an institution, a business is merely a way to take care of their family or live a better life.

If I sound judgmental, I'm not. At the end of the day, most people work to put food on the table. Few are fortunate enough to feel true fulfillment through their work. A recent survey found that for most Americans, their most favorite day of the week is Saturday. But their second most favorite day is Friday, not Sunday. It speaks volumes, I think, about the real joy most Americans are getting from the modern economy.

Some do, of course. And they are the ones who write inspiring how-to books or put a face on an industry (eg, Walt Disney, Steve Jobs).

The Chinese legacy is a different animal. Some achieve it politically (Mao Zedong), while others achieve it through wisdom and philosophy (Confucius). Even successful entrepreneurs such as Jack Ma, the founder of Alibaba and the wealthiest man in China, is seldom talked about in terms of his wealth. The Chinese talk of his charismatic leadership, his perseverance, and his determination to overcome obstacles.

So what does all this mean for Western companies doing business in China? I believe there are a few key takeaways.

1. If you can, go it alone. Many Western companies wishing to minimize their risks believe it is wise to find a Chinese partner to help them navigate the complex regulatory and commercial waters of the Chinese economy. In theory, it is a sensible argument. In practice, however, your chances of finding a compatible Chinese partner are very low indeed. They may say all the right things. However, they are wired quite differently than you. Those differences will become apparent, perhaps insurmountable, over time.

2. Focus on the customer. I have always believed that Western business is too consumed with their competition. (I've always felt that we should give our competitors all of our internal cost data, for example, instead of protecting it like the crown jewels. It is more likely to cause them to make foolish decisions than insightful ones. After all, in the end, even we don't really know what it means.) Nonetheless, when you are battling the same foes decade after decade, your competitors can become a proxy for your customers in a way. You collectively define the market. Not true in China, however. Your most troublesome competitor has probably not even entered the market yet.

3. Accept that cash is the only motivator. If you rely on partners such as distributors or retailers or contractors, accept that they will not be motivated by things like long-term mutual commitment or partnership. They manage for cash, pure and simple. Either find a way to go around them or build your model on that assumption.

This is not a good or bad distinction. While Western companies excel at creating long-term value, Chinese companies are extremely nimble and blazing quick at reacting to market trends and shifts. Both are advantageous at different times and in different circumstances.

In the short term, however, I think the most notable manifestation of this distinction is that Western companies will continue to fall short of their expectations in China. It is the most competitive market in the world. (My American counterpart could count his domestic competitors on one hand. I had more than 400.) The idea of selling one widget to every Chinese is a pipe dream.

That is not to say that Western companies cannot be successful here. They can. But they must adapt to the environment and that may mean leaving many of the business processes they hold dear at the border.

Conversely, I believe Chinese companies, for the time being, will find it very difficult to be successful in the West. There are already exceptions. Companies like Lenovo and Alibaba are very sophisticated and very westernized, but they are not yet the norm.

In the meantime, the Chinese business landscape will continue to be one of the most dynamic in the world. Just reading it will be a challenge. What is *really* happening? And why?

Government reform, while necessary and in the country's best interests long-term, will only add further froth to the already churning waters of commerce. In the end, however, the Chinese markets will mature and stabilize; entrepreneurs will find a balance between long-term value creation and short-term cash flow.

And China will continue to wow.

CHAPTER 37

TWO MARKETS

Ever since Deng Xiaoping launched the opening of China in 1979, there have been two markets for every product and service offered in China. The first is where all the foreign companies live—no exceptions. It is a market driven by brand, quality, and, to a lesser extent, price (in some luxury markets the price must actually be *high enough* to compete).

The second market is populated exclusively by Chinese-owned and Chinese-operated companies. The foreign companies simply can't participate in these markets and make money. Price is everything. And the prices, in general, are one-half or less of what they are in the market that the foreigners participate in.

Until recently, everyone was happy. The pie was big enough and growing fast enough to satisfy everyone, consumers included. For a price, Chinese consumers could buy the best brand names in the world, and since many of the products carrying those monikers were now manufactured in China, albeit in a foreign-run plant, the price premium was not as great as it would be if the products were strictly imported.

Those once-distinct markets, however, are now blurring, and blurring fast, creating a boon for many Chinese manufacturers and a potential bust for many foreign-invested companies operating here.

- Economic growth is slowing. GDP grew at 7 percent in the first half of 2015, the lowest in twenty-five years, and many analysts believe it was a spotty growth. Some areas grew at rates as low as 4 percent, far below the level China needs to sustain reasonable employment levels.

- The National Bureau of Statistics recently reported that inflation for the month of July 2015 rose by 1.6 percent year-on-year, up from 1.4 percent in June, and a very low 1.3 percent during the first half of the year. That statistic, however, includes a 16.7 percent rise in the price of pork, a bellwether of China's food costs, a 10.5 percent increase in the price of all vegetables, and is well below government targets, which began the year at 3.5 percent.
- Most industries, in essence, continue to face deflationary prices as a result of excess capacity in many key industrial sectors. The Producer Price Index (PPI), a key measure of factory-gate pricing, fell to its lowest reading since October 2009, the fortieth consecutive month of decline. And the declines are worsening. The PPI fell by 5.4 percent in July after falling 4.8 percent in June and 4.6 percent in May.
- China's exports, according to further government data, fell by 8.3 percent in July, surprising many economists on the downside.
- The world has opened its doors to China on many levels, and Chinese companies are making the most of it. They're now employing the best manufacturing technology in the world, much of it developed in the West.
- Chinese manufacturers, often with the help of foreign technology and/or workers trained in foreign-owned plants, are greatly improving their quality, not to mention reducing their labor content through the use of armies of robots.

And that's just on the supply side of the equation. On the demand side:

- Price consciousness is getting a boost from the slowing growth of the economy. Having suffered with so little for so long personal consumtion in China is driven by need and confidence as much as desire. If there is the mere rumor that the economy is going to slow, they will immediately reduce their purchases of non-essential products and put more emphasis on finding the lowest price – which inevitably favors the local manufacturers – for the essentails they can't do without.

- The Chinese are responding favorably to the quality inroads made by their manufacturers, perhaps because many extended families have one or more members who work for such a company.

The collective confidence of the Chinese people is surging. They are no longer the emerging country to watch. They are it. And proud of it. They no longer need foreign brands to legitimize themselves to the extent they did a few years ago.

Consider, for example, the plight of Apple, whose iPhones were once considered a must-have for rising middle-class Chinese consumers.

In the second quarter of 2013, Apple's market share was halved, much of it lost to Chinese brands such as Xiaomi and Yulong, both little known outside of China. Writing in *China Daily*, Mike Bastin, a visiting professor at the University of International Business and Economics in Beijing, reported that Apple had fallen to seventh place in the world's largest mobile market and suggested that Apple should now drop its sub-brands, such as 5S and 5C, in favor of purely Chinese monikers.

The Apple 6 helped immensely to reverse this trend, but it nonetheless demonstrates just how fickle the Chinese consumer can be and how much Chinese manufacturers have caught up in their functionality and quality without losing their distinct cost advantage.

Apple is not alone. In a July 19, 2013, article on the topic of foreign companies in China, Reuters' Angela Moon noted, "Among eighteen S&P companies with large exposure to China, twelve of them were underperforming the broader S&P 500 .INX index year-to-date..." And in a 2012 survey of members conducted by the American Chamber of Commerce in Shanghai, the percentage of companies reporting profitability or an increase in revenue fell to their lowest levels in three years, and less than half of the companies surveyed reported an improvement in operating margins.

Much of this, of course, is being blamed on macroeconomic issues, such as slowing growth, tight credit markets, and asset bubbles. I believe that much of this emerging bad news for foreign companies, however, is due to the rise of more intense and capable local competition and changing consumer attitudes.

There are many implications of these trends, not the least of which is that foreign companies are sure to increasingly question their commitment to future investment here. Already one of the most competitive markets in the world, the competition is sure to get even more intense, and what is now admittedly a trickle of foreign companies repositioning their China strategies or outright withdrawing from China is sure to gain momentum.

And cost will be at the heart of much of the intensifying battle, an area where foreign companies are currently disadvantaged.

Why?

To their credit most foreign companies who come to China sincerely want to be responsible corporate citizens. They want to pay competitive wages, provide good fringe benefits, meet all regulatory requirements, and pay their fair taxes.

It's true that not all domestic companies share that perspective. It is, as I have noted in several posts on my blog, largely a Western perspective that doesn't always come into focus through the Chinese cultural lens.

The fact that local officials are given wide berth to interpret and enforce national and provincial regulations as they see fit opens the door to local favoritism, whatever its root cause.

Those advantages are being lost to the local companies, however, and I believe they will ultimately lose any material relevance as the national government seeks to ensure a level playing field for all. A level competitive playing field for both domestic and foreign companies won't happen overnight, perhaps, but in my opinion, it will happen, if for no other reason than China has irrevocably committed to become a world leader, and that won't happen if it doesn't adopt impartial rules of competition, a reality the government is well aware of.

Much of the cost disadvantage that weighs upon foreign companies operating here, however, is self-inflicted, and it gets little attention in the general media or business press.

There are many foreign companies with wholly or jointly owned subsidiaries in China. Few, if any, however, are really Chinese subsidiaries. Nearly all are Western subsidiaries operating on Chinese soil.

And there's a huge difference between the two that goes well beyond the desire to be responsible corporate citizens whose presence is welcomed in China.

Of course, some of these incremental costs are mandated by the government of the parent company, such as the incremental administrative costs incurred by US companies in complying with the Foreign Corrupt Practices Act (companies in Europe, it should be noted, face similar requirements) or Sarbanes-Oxley, or any of the regulatory requirements that apply to a US company's global operations.

Other cost premiums, however, are truly self-inflicted. It is my guess, for example, that most US companies operating in China use the Chinese branches of the US accounting, tax advisory, and legal firms they use in the US. Most are extremely capable and language will not be an issue. Their fees, however, may be substantially higher than the local firm that may or may not be equally competent.

In the end it usually comes down to the scale of the risk and reward. If the Chinese subsidiary is a fraction of the size of the US parent it may not always be appropriate to use the same top shelf service providers. And while there may be times when it's more convient for someone on the corporate staff sitting in the US to get on the phone with a service provider in China who went to school in the US and speaks perfect English, is it really worth the substantial premium that will be paid?

And the practice is not limited to the service industries. Chinese subsidiaries of foreign machine-tool, construction, and maintenance companies are often given preference in bidding on key maintenance and expansion projects for wholly owned foreign enterprises (WOFEs) operating in China. Foreign engineering groups, understandably, have a defensible preference to work with companies they are familiar with, who have proven their ability to perform, who communicate in their native language, and whose approach to managing projects is similar to their own. There is, nonetheless, a price premium incurred, often material, for such confidence and familiarity.

Many multinational companies, moreover, centralize critical services such as Information Technology (IT), engineering, and financial reporting, the former of which may yield benefits and the latter of which is mandatory. The issue is not whether or not this adds net value to the company. These services, and all of the trans-Pacific travel needed to support them, ultimately becomes, through cross-charges or performance expectations, the burden of the Chinese subsidiary.

That is not to disparage any of these practices. They are both understandable and, at one level, easily defensible. The game is changing, however, and once-defensible tactics may no longer work.

If foreign companies want to succeed in China over the long run, they wlll be forced to "China-tize" their cost structures. They will have to go beyond localizing their management teams and minimizing the number of expatriates they have stationed here. That trend is old news. They will have to start localizing everything from policy-setting to technical, IT, legal, auditing, and financial services. If they don't, they will find it increasingly difficult to compete with their Chinese competitors on brand and technology alone.

There will, of course, be risks in localizing all sourcing of raw materials, parts, and service—risks that are sure to be noted by the headquarter organizations most directly affected. And there will be regulatory limits to how far foreign public companies in particular can go.

However, there will be little option if foreign companies want to survive here. If Apple, perhaps the most powerful brand on the planet, can be so quickly challenged by heretofore-unknown local manufacturers, how can any foreign company consider itself immune to a similar fate?

———

To understand the magnitude of the difference, consider the development and deployment of the Apple watch.

On Monday, September 9, 2014, Apple CEO Tim Cook unveiled Apple's eagerly anticipated smartwatch, available for purchase on April 24,

2015. To make Apple's first wearable device, the company will rely on a global supply chain that, according to *China Daily*, includes 349 Chinese manufacturers.

Weeks before Apple's announcement, however, resellers on Taobao, the C2C e-commerce platform of Alibaba—yes, the same Alibaba that raised $25 billion in a record-breaking IPO on the NYSE in September 2014—were actually selling and delivering smart watches for less than $50. They aren't called Apple watches, mind you, and they run on Google's Android operating system rather than Apple's iOS.

The screens are identical in size, however, and the D watch, as it is called, has much, but not all, of Apple's functionality. It offers step tracks, calendar, and Bluetooth-enabled remote camera control. The manufacturer of the so-called D watch, YQT Electronic Technology Co., Ltd., admits that the screen resolution is inferior to the Apple product.

Zheng Yi, CEO of YQT, has proudly announced that the company has made *enough* changes (changes to what?) that it intends to file for patent protection of its product.

If this kind of thinking seems out of sync with Western notions of intellectual property rights, Mr. Zheng is certainly not alone. A quote relating to the D watch in *China Daily* reads, "From smartphones to luxury items, there will always be knockoffs. It is a form of compliment. This proves that products are popular."

This, once again, raises the age-old question: Can China innovate or just copy? Innovation, everyone admits, is critical to success in the modern economy and will be essential if China wants to stop being the factory to the world with all the ecological degradation that comes with the title.

Chinese entrepreneurs are certainly giving it a try. The Zhongguancun District of Beijing, sometimes referred to as the Silicon Valley of China, gave birth to an average of forty-nine new start-ups per day in 2014. And the district is now home to 1,600 tech incubators, ensuring a prolonged pace of rapid expansion.

As I have repeatedly noted, the debate over innovation is often mistakenly positioned as an issue of creativity. And if you look at China's long history of art, architecture, and literature, it would be hard to argue that creativity does not exist in abundance here. To me, the missing ingredient is not creativity but curiosity.

The American education system, to its credit, teaches nothing quite as ardently as it teaches curiosity. Admittedly, it doesn't always take hold and requires a twenty-four/seven partnership between parents and educators to truly be effective. But on average, Americans are taught to be curious. How else could the *National Geographic* channel or reality shows about swamp logging survive?

If innovation was simply a function of creativity, it seems doubtful that the tech innovators who have so changed the world would have led the charge. Even Steve Jobs, to my knowledge, was not endowed with creative genius. He was, however, endowed with unparalleled passion and curiosity.

This is where I believe America has missed an economic opportunity over the last two decades. We've spent too much time pushing money around and lamenting our loss of manufacturing jobs (which should surely be lamented; we've wiped out the blue-collar middle-class).

What we should have done instead is devote our ample energies and talents to pursuing the curiosity that got us to where we are. Curiosity leads to innovation, if channeled properly, and it is innovation that defines the most profitable companies in the world.

There used to be a saying in American business that "pioneers get shot," suggesting it was always best to let someone else establish a new market before you went in with a better widget to harvest the spoils.

This is now outdated thinking. Despite losing the opportunity to get the "first hook" in the consumer's brain, as marketers Ries and Trout so aptly noted, there just isn't time to follow the leader. The pioneers will be on to something else, and the market they created may not even exist anymore.

The good news, in my opinion, is that the millennials I know may not be bigger risk takers than my own generation, but I sense they are more curious, and this curiosity should lead to the development of disruptive industries at a pace that the rest of the world may find difficult to follow.

We can thank the educators of our time for making that possible.

CHAPTER 38

GETTING TO CHEAP

There is cheap. And then there is China cheap.

And by cheap I am not referring to the pejorative poor quality for which that particular adjective is normally used. While poor quality can be part of the equation, even at comparable levels of quality, China cheap is still cheaper—by a lot.

Why?

There are many reasons, some of which involve business practices that fall outside the boundaries of acceptable business practices as either self-defined by the company itself or imposed upon it by the government of its home country. This, however, is but one difference and may not even be material, depending on the industry.

The real difference between the costs of Chinese companies and the costs of foreign companies doing business here is much more fundamental and much more difficult to overcome.

The Chinese have a knack for cheap that the rest of the world, in my experience, just doesn't have. Part of it flows from decades of doing without; part of it flows from the related knack for making do; and part of it, I think, flows from the Chinese world view and the personal nature of all relationships. While the Chinese now acquire some ridiculous percent of all of the luxury goods consumed in the world each year, I have a hunch that of all the cultures in the world, they would be the least bothered if they lost it all tomorrow.

They like stuff, but they aren't defined by stuff. They use it to define themselves socially but not to define who they are. It defines what they've earned, but not what they've achieved. Wealth and luck, in fact, are often used in the same sentence.

To the Chinese luxury is an adjective, not a noun. They love to flout it, but they don't internalize it. If you took a treasured Porsche away from a Western man, he might be despondent. If you took one away from a Chinese man, I suspect he would simply shrug his shoulders and move on to acquire his next fortune.

For that reason, while the Chinese are as consumed with legacy as everyone else, they aren't consumed with building or acquiring things that last, except to the extent that such longevity represents real value. Because things such as cars and buildings are not internalized, longevity is more of a price metric than an inherent measure of quality.

Remember that we, as Westerners, like things that are strong and built to last, in part because of our deductive fascination with process. Built to last means built with sound materials and a sound process, and that, by itself, gives us satisfaction because it aligns with our desire to live in an ordered universe, where rationality and deductive logic prevail.

A friend and colleague brought this point home just recently. We were standing just outside a luxury restaurant on a brand new boulevard. But the boulevard was severely flooded due to heavy rain. Virtually every street in the city was flooded, and by flooded I mean the water was the depth of the radius of an adult bicycle wheel.

I casually noted that because the Chinese government was in such a rush to progress, they seldom took the time to do things like put in proper storm drains.

Her perspective was quite different, however. "No," she said, "the reason is that you can't seen storm drains. No one knows they are there. The government would much rather put the money into fancy landscaping and buildings and monuments that openly display the wealth of the city, even if it means a little flooding once in a while."

In their inductive and holistic world view, moreover, longevity is more a function of sustained balance and harmony than a reflection of sound process. The quality of things like building construction, therefore, is an economic variable rather than a reflection of personal values.

When the Chinese build anything, therefore, they generally don't build it to last for decades, much less centuries. In the housing compound where I live, the houses are considered to be of superior quality, but they gut them every six or seven years and start over (and I mean gut—the electrical, plumbing, and HVAC systems are all stripped out in their entirety). I've seen them build a commercial building and tear it down six months later to build something completely different.

The same goes for the equipment that goes into the factories. Good enough is good enough. As long as it produces a product or service that meets market demand, no one is going to care too much if it's going to last into the next century.

And then, of course, there is the infrastructure behind whatever goods or services your company provides. American companies will install energy-efficient boilers to minimize the cost of providing hot water to the washrooms. The Chinese won't provide hot water to the washrooms. You won't even find toilet paper in most public bathrooms. People are expected to carry their own, and it's not that much of a hardship once you get used to it (make a note to self if you're going to be visiting here; I'm serious).

Heating, ventilating, and air-conditioning (HVAC) systems are becoming more popular in office buildings and public spaces, but the systems are not built to reheat lasagna in the middle of winter or make snow cones in the heat of summer. In northern China office workers still wear coats at their desks in the wintertime, and you'll never see a sweater in a Chinese office in the summertime. By far the most common complaint I get from visiting American colleagues is that the air conditioning in their five-star hotel room doesn't chill the room to their satisfaction. (The Chinese, in general, don't like air conditioning for health reasons, and it's my sense that Western science is starting to support their thinking on the topic.)

Then, of course, there are the input costs that every company must incur in order to make their product or provide their service. And, invariably, these are all much lower for Chinese companies, particularly private ones, than they are for their foreign counterparts.

Let's start with labor. It is true that Chinese companies do not uniformly follow the statutes that their own government has on the books. But to say they cheat is to misrepresent the reality.

As I've noted before, the government is pragmatic, and its number one priority at the end of the day is to keep everyone employed. It has to be. Imagine that you're trying to manage a country with more than four times as many people to employ as the United States, and your economy is three-fifths the size.

So, yes, there are Chinese companies that openly flout the labor laws and appear to get away with it. And if one of those companies is your competitor, you are likely to feel more than a little cheated and to assume that the company is doing so by making under-the-table payments to the people who are supposed to be enforcing the rules.

And that may be true. But it may not be. In many cases, I'm convinced, the government allows them to do it simply because the government recognizes that the company can't be competitive if it doesn't. And if it can't be competitive then the local government has that many more people that it has to find jobs for.

That's not to justify the practice or to in any way suggest that the Chinese people should feel lucky they have an employer who doesn't follow China's own labor laws. It is to say, however, that the issue is not as black or white as many Westerners would have you believe. To us it's a two-dimensional process failure. To the Chinese it is a more holistic issue with multiple dimensions, all secondary to ultimate success—and employment.

And then there are the input costs beyond labor that goes into every product or service. Remember that the Chinese economy operates under the rules of *caveat emptor*—"buyer beware." What's fair to the Chinese shopkeeper or OEM supplier is getting the most money he or she can get out of you for the product or service they are offering. If that's five times the real market price, good for them.

There is, as a result, a "foreigner price" and a Chinese price for everything, built on the reasonable assumption that if a foreigner has found his or her way to China for business or pleasure, that person probably have the money to pay more than a local Chinese customer.

When foreign visitors come to China, therefore, and invariably ask about doing some personal shopping, my advice is always the same: "Enjoy the experience. Buy only what you want and need. And know you aren't going to put any shopkeeper out of business with your negotiating skills, however well-honed." If you think you got a good price, mission accomplished. Rest assured, however, that you didn't get the best price.

To foreigners this seems a bit like cheating. To the totally pragmatic Chinese, however, it's just smart business.

And while you may overcome this input cost disadvantage through the use of your latest production technology (Contrary to what many foreign companies do, I recommend you always bring your latest technology to China. Otherwise you won't get in the game.), that advantage will probably be fleeting. The Chinese you compete with will figure out how you're doing it and do it faster and cheaper. That's just the reality.

The question, of course, is whether or not Chinese business can continue to set the global standard for costs once wage rates rise to the level necessary to support a consumption-based economy, one of the stated goals of the current government.

As usual, I'm not betting against them, in part because they are building robots faster than any nation on the planet and in part because they are moving up the value chain, where labor costs are far less of an issue, at an alarming rate.

In the meantime, if you come to China on business or pleasure—and I strongly encourage you to do so—and you want to do a little shopping, either for your nephew or your business, take a Chinese colleague with you. And let them do all the talking. It's their game. They understand what things are worth. They understand China cheap.

It is often reported by the Western media that China is trying to transform its economy from a manufacturing economy into a service economy. In fact, this is more than a little misleading.

I've never seen a statistic on the topic, but I have to believe that the number of restaurants per capita in China has to be among the highest in the world. They're everywhere. And they're all staffed with probably four times as many workers as they will ultimately be as wages continue to rise.

There are certainly more bus drivers and taxi drivers here, both official and "black," than in any three other countries combined. And while modern trade retail is underdeveloped, there are street vendors and markets everywhere you look, while at every traffic light at every major intersection in every major city in China, you will be barraged by people handing out advertisements for this new apartment complex or that new restaurant.

Every household that can afford one, and there are many, has at least one housekeeper. Gas stations still provide attendants to pump your gas. There is a bank on every corner. And since the air is not pristine and the Chinese are fanatical about their cars, auto detailers abound.

And then, of course, there are the armies of people who are sweeping the streets or maintaining the ample landscaping along every major thoroughfare.

Anecdotally speaking, the most common profession in China, by my observation, is fixing flat tires. There is little regulation of the trucking industry, and since cost is an obsession, trucks are almost always overloaded by any standard in the world. A lot of it falls off, meaning that cracked windshields and flat tires are commonplace.

In short, if you look at the issue simply in terms of where people are employed, China is a service economy already. The challenge it faces is how to employ the millions of waiters, waitresses, and dishwashers who will be unemployed once the declining pool of workers begins to push wages beyond the tipping point (China's labor pool shrank by 9.5 million workers over the last three years).

What China is really doing is developing a two-prong strategy. The first is urbanization. While countries like the United States no longer even count farming as an occupation in its census due to the small number of people who work as full-time farmers, half of China's population still lives in rural areas, many tilling the soil.

And since bringing people out of poverty is a game of leveraging population density, China is undertaking a massive urbanization program with the objective of having 60 percent of its residents residing in an urban area by the year 2020.

Now, that doesn't mean they want to move everyone to Beijing, Shanghai, and Guangzhou. In fact, they are trying to strictly limit growth in those existing urban areas because of the pressure that already exists on the environment and the urban infrastructure.

Instead, urbanization in China means bringing the urban to the people. China's urbanization strategy is a process of making the smaller cities bigger rather than bringing the residents of the countryside to the existing mega-cities.

The second strategy rides on the back and reinforces the first. Rather than de-emphasizing manufacturing, China wants to transform it. As the Chinese say, they wants to transform their manufacturing sector from being the biggest to being the strongest.

Simply put, China wants to move up the value chain. Today they dominate the bottom rungs of the manufacturing value chain in many industries, but these are typically the rungs where the margins are razor thin and the competition with new emerging manufacturing markets is the fiercest.

Although designed in California, as the box says, Apple manufactures most of its iPhones in China. By one estimate, however, only 3.4 percent of the profits from the sale of each iPhone worldwide stays in China. The rest goes to other countries that provide higher-value components and services, including the United States and Japan.

China is the largest aluminum producer in the world. Yet most of the aluminum used to build aircraft, an industry in which buyers must be as conscious of quality and innovation as price, is made elsewhere.

In short, China is stuck with most of the environmental degradation, health and safety risks and little of the profit of the now global supply chain. And it wants to change that.

In March 2015, Premier Li Keqiang announced Made in China 2025, a government-led initiative that is China's answer to Germany's Manufacturing 4.0, the merger of IT and automation into cyber-physical systems that will usher in the fourth industrial revolution.

The details of China 2025 are undefined at the moment. But the government has defined the ten industries it will concentrate on and by implication, ultimately wants to dominate. They are:

Biomedicine and high-performance medical apparatus
Information technology
Energy-saving vehicles
Electrical equipment
Aerospace and aviation equipment
Maritime engineering equipment and high-tech vessel manufacturing
New materials
High-end numerical control machinery and automation
Rail equipment
Agricultural equipment

It will be a huge task. There is no question that China has the government capital and the will. But does it have the skills, and do the right people have access to that capital?

If you look at a country like Germany, we all know the names BMW, Mercedes-Benz, and Siemens. But as much as these industrial titans mean to the German economy, the German economy stands on the backs of medium-sized companies, many of which support these industrial consolidators.

In China, by contrast, you find the same duality on the manufacturing front that you find in everything else. There are the gigantic state-owned enterprises (SOEs) and the tiny private businesses that employ a large percentage of the people. In Dongguan alone, an area at the heart of China's industrial manufacturing export boom of recent decades, it is estimated there are as many as 300,000 private manufacturing companies. Many are very small, and it often takes a complex web of them to produce a usable product.

There are exceptions. Alibaba and Lenovo are two examples. These are world-class companies producing high value-added goods and services. At the moment, however, these are the outliers.

To pull it off, and I never bet against the Chinese, the government will have to undertake four wrenching structural reforms all at the same time.

- Banking reform—With the elimination of the gray market on which most small companies historically relied for capital, many small and medium-sized companies have lost access to capital. The state-owned banks that dominate the banking sector are institutionally risk-averse and limit their lending to the large SOEs that have been their historical bread and butter.
- Education reform—Today's rote education system must pivot away from the acquisition of knowledge and focus instead on promoting curiosity and collaboration.
- Legal reform—Leadership in any of the ten targeted sectors will require a lot of intellectual property. If others can come along and help themselves to it, there will be no return on the investment made to develop it, and the constant innovation necessary for leadership in these fields will come to a halt.
- Reform of the hukou system—If labor cannot move freely around the country and bring their families with them, the pool of talent from which these companies can draw will greatly diminish the ability to find the talent necessary for the strength they seek (this will also be necessary for China to meet its urbanization objectives).

And there will have to be fundamental shifts in business and consumer culture. Chinese investors, including business, are short-term in their focus. They manage to cash. Manufacturing strength, however, often requires long-term investment.

It can be done. Of that I'm sure. And at least having a national manufacturing strategy is a good place to start.

CHAPTER 39

INTELLECTUAL PROPERTY RIGHTS

Whenever the topic of intellectual property protection comes up in discussion, my Chinese colleagues inevitably quip, "In China we don't need copyright laws, we already know how to 'copy right.'"

And it's true. Writing in *China Daily*, columnist Raymond Zhou, in discussing "The Chinese obsession with reproducing elements of the existing world..." notes that "The Chinese have a weakness for imitation..." and goes on to note that iconic landmarks such as the Sydney Opera House and the Beijing National Stadium, otherwise known as the Bird's Nest, inevitably get replicated across the country in scaled-down versions.

Mr. Zhou entertainingly notes that man-made structures often become associated with the natural world or objects with which they bear some visual similarity. In addition to the Bird's Nest, Beijing alone is home to the Giant Egg (the National Center for the Performing Arts) and the Big Pants (CCTV headquarters), although he goes on to add that occupants of the latter are less than enthusiastic about the association for obvious reasons.

Zhou postulates that such literal association has its roots in the Chinese language. The original pictograms, or Chinese characters, were often symbolic replicas of the objects they defined and still today exhibit signs of their literal origin. In the character for *mountain*, for example, you can still see the three peaks of the original pictogram, and the character for *mouth* is easy to guess with its wide open space in the middle.

Visual association, however, is a lot different than intellectual property theft. The former is fun. The latter involves serious money and undermines one of the core principles at the heart of all developed economies.

Gary Moreau

Individuals and corporations must have some assurance that the time and money they put into creativity and technology development will yield some return on their investment.

It is a problem, but I do believe the situation is improving. The government itself has put the protection of intellectual property rights high on their agenda, a commitment necessitated by the country's entry into the WTO.

But why is it such a problem? Why do the Chinese not accept the same standards of IP protection embraced by the rest of the developed world? Or do they?

First of all, whenever you talk about theft, you have to accept that in the bowels of abject poverty theft can be as much about survival as morality. If your family is starving, even the most pious man is likely to be tempted to take the loaf of bread cooling on the windowsill of the local baker. And despite the glamour of world-class cities like Beijing and Shanghai, there's still plenty of serious poverty in China.

That's only a partial explanation, however. Corporations are as likely to steal the IP of their competitors as the poor tailor is to knock off a Hermes scarf.

Another part of the explanation comes back to the distinctive world view on which Chinese culture is based. While Western standards of morality tend to be linear and absolute, Chinese standards are much more contextual and shaped by notions of personal obligation. In other words, how you might treat a stranger is held to a different standard than how you treat a member of the family.

And since corporations are institutions, not people, it is perhaps no surprise that the Chinese grant them few moral rights or privileges. They simply do not personalize institutions to the extent that Westerners often do. Remember, to them all relationships are personal.

In contrast, the US legal system recognizes the concept of corporate personhood. Said simply, other that the right to vote, a US corporation enjoys the same rights and privilege under the US Constitution as a US citizen does. This gives the corporation more rights since it isn't limited in its lifespan and its reach is far greater.

226

And intellectual property rights, as practiced in the United States, are not always a fundamental need for conducting business. There are very profitable companies, in fact, who make not a single product or provide a single service. They simply buy patents and other intellectual property and charge others the right to use them. Enterprising or exploitative?

It could be reasonably argued that the consumer suffers from the protection of intellectual property rights. We all know that once a prescription has exceeded its patent protection period, the price drops like a rock. And there is little question that IP protection inflates prices in virtually all replacement markets, where a more efficient producer is prevented from competing due to a patent restriction that may have little impact of the performance of the product.

On the other hand, IP attorneys will vehemently argue that an end to IP protection would mean an end to innovation since a lot of innovation (eg, pharmaceuticals) requires enormous investments and only a small percentage of those investments pay off. Fair enough. Like most things in life and business, it comes down to achieving a sense of balance. It is generally true, however, that when one side of an argument has both huge scale and pockets lined deep with cash and the other is small, disorganized, fragmented, and only has the potential of future profits, it's seldom a fair fight.

For the Chinese there is the conceptual spillover from the Chinese political system that comes into play as well. Fairness, to the socialist, is an issue of equity rather than the rights of personal claim. No one in China, for example, can own land. Whatever claim you might otherwise make to it, the land belongs to the people, managed, of course, under the custodial eye of the government.

But can we equate intellectual property with land? Is intellectual property a natural resource that rightfully belongs to society as a whole? The Western capitalist, as just noted, would offer an emphatic no. Creative entrepreneurs, capitalist theory goes, will not *entrepreneut* if there is no return on their *entrepreneution*.

But where do the two lines cross? When does creation become an issue of timing or even luck, rather than creative genius? And more importantly, when do the needs of society at large outweigh the financial rights of the individual or corporation, whatever the wisdom of the legal argument?

These are tricky questions without simple, concise answers. Without treading into the murky waters of intellectual property law, however, even the most IP-friendly Western legal codes clearly acknowledge their existence. Seldom do Western IP laws grant absolute and perpetual rights of ownership. There are almost always limits to the duration of the protection and a myriad of requirements that the IP holder demonstrate commercial use and/or demonstrate effort to uphold ownership rights.

In other words, the Western bench has sought to define the most classically Western solution to the universal conflict inherent between IP holders and would-be beneficiaries—the win-win solution. IP holders get enough protection to recoup their investment and make some money, but not so much as to deprive society of the benefit of IP that might otherwise have come into existence in a myriad of different ways.

But what if your world view isn't as linear as the Western world view? What if your relational and holistic world view seeks not to achieve win-win solutions, but win-lose solutions. Does the lion look for a win-win solution when it is hungry and there is a herd of antelope grazing nearby?

I also believe the receiver-oriented nature of Chinese communication and the cultural foundation of personal, rather than institutional, obligation comes into play The Chinese, in other words, don't fundamentally look at intellectual property any differently than Westerners do. They just look at it from the opposite direction and draw the dividing line between public and personal property, and personal right and collective good, at a different point along the moral and legal continuum.

Whatever the source of the gap between China and the West in efforts to grapple with the IP dilemma, there is little question that foreign businesses operating here will have to take robust precautions to protect the intellectual property they hold dear. In this case, caution is more than an admonition. It is a necessity.

If you're like most Western companies operating here, that will inevitably mean disabling USB ports on computers, isolating sensitive documents to encrypted servers only accessible to those with an absolute need to know, outsourcing the construction of critical equipment in isolated parts to multiple vendors, and in extreme cases, leaving your best technology at home. (I don't recommend this latter strategy. I can almost guarantee you will not be successful here without it.)

But each of these strategies is once again a testimony to the Western preoccupation with process. Each strategy focuses on the data and technology itself, treating the IP as a distinct and independent entity—a definable institution, if you will.

Here, however, I suggest you take a page from the Chinese world view, by which everything turns on relationship, not process. In the end, you see, your greatest vulnerability is not the processes you employ to protect your intellectual property. Your greatest vulnerability is the people you employ to deploy your processes, the people who have both your knowledge and experience in how to apply it.

This is where your competitors will go when they want to know your secrets. Contrary to a lot of contemporary Hollywood movies and media assessments of the issue, the IP thieves won't infiltrate your secure network or attempt to sneak into your offices in the dark of night in black Ninja uniforms.

They will stand outside the gate of your plan in broad daylight, and politely "obtain" leads from your departing employees until they have correctly identified the one man or woman who has the information they seek. And then they will work, probably harder than you, to make a new friend.

So if you really want to protect your intellectual property in China, secure your people as fervently as you secure your networks. Put the same effort into retaining your people that you put into protecting your trade secrets, and you will end up with better protection than could ever be achieved through process alone.

And you will enjoy the added benefit of employees who are both motivated and loyal, employees equipped to deploy the most powerful weapon in the arsenal of intellectual property protection—a commitment to innovation that leads to a constant stream of new and more valuable intellectual property.

CHAPTER 40

ENVIRONMENTAL REGULATION

Everyone knows that China faces some serious environmental challenges. In a recent scientific study reported by the *Christian Science Monitor*, air pollution in China, on average, kills 4,400 people per day.

President Xi Jinping and Premier Li Keqiang, however, have vowed to take severe steps to reduce the problem, and to date they have lived up to their word, promising to fulfill 20 percent of China's energy needs with renewable, zero-emission energy sources by the year 2030, allowing the world's most populous country and second largest economy to cap its carbon emissions over the same period.

In January of 2015 a draconian new series of environmental regulations took effect, and the government collected $18.3 million dollars in penalties through June, according to government sources. Even more symbolically, the government has shut down 1,186 companies entirely, according to the *Christian Science Monitor,* with another 698 cases resulting in production reductions or curtailment. There were 437 cases of administrative detention and 429 criminal environmental charges levied.

The government is serious, and I admonish any foreign corporation doing business here to take it as their most serious challenge and their most serious risk. Furnace emissions and water discharges are being put on twenty-four/seven real-time monitoring systems, streaming data directly to the local Environmental Bureau on a continuous basis. And the traditional method many companies have used to circumvent such draconian measures has disappeared. You will be held accountable and the standards are world-class or tighter.

———

I am all for strict environmental controls for industry, and the technology is out there to accomplishment dramatic reductions in harmful emissions.

I strongly believe, however, that we as citizens of the world have an equally compelling responsibility to address the problem. China has severely degraded its environment and is killing its people as a result.

To be fair, it is the countries that import their cheap prices—in part achieved by low environmental standards—that have enabled them. We didn't drink the alcohol, but we bought it for them.

Small manufacturers in China have been dumping pollutants into their rivers, in part because Walmart and Carrefour shoppers the world over give them incentive. Not directly, of course. For the most part, they are good people who simply haven't connected the dots.

But low prices are a bit like narcotics. If there is no demand, there will soon be no supply, and the violence will stop. Perhaps that is too much to ask or expect, but it is true nonetheless. Given the magnitude of the problem, however, even a small increase in awareness would have a huge impact.

Most Western retailers have recognized this responsibility but have taken a totally deductive route to its solution—more process. Virtually every major Western retailer now performs social, environmental, and safety audits on its foreign suppliers. And China, of course, is in the crosshairs of their sights.

Deductive solutions are rarely effective when applied to inductive societies, however. And this is no exception. The reality is—and this is strictly my opinion—that these audits are costing American consumers billions of dollars in higher prices and doing almost nothing to address the fundamental issues. In reality, almost nothing has changed.

And here's why. With the exception of Ikea, the giant Swedish retailer for which I have gained great respect as both a consumer and supplier, virtually all other foreign retailers use third-party audit companies—companies who survive on the basis of these audits—to perform their audits for them.

The problem arises in three ways. The first is that the industrial world is a complex place with an infinite number of operating and structural variables. But the auditor has a single checklist into which all these variables must be pigeonholed. In many cases it's just not practical and has nothing to do with the environment, employee safety, or social issues such as wages or child labor.

I can't speak for other countries, but in the case of China, the auditors tend to be young and not very experienced (they are cheap to employ and willing to travel six days per week). They have never seen most of the technology they see in Western factories located here, and they seldom have any training in cause and effect. In other words, they are taught what the checklist requires—the outcome, but not why it is on the checklist to begin with.

As a result, they refuse to discuss anything. They follow the checklist to the letter. They are generally unwilling to even discuss why that particular item may not apply in any given case or why complying with the checklist may even enhance the danger to employees.

There is seldom any attempt to prioritize issues. (Again, Ikea is the exception, which breaks its requirements down into must-haves—you can't ship until you correct this problem—and the rest, which you generally have some time to correct. Ikea engineers will work with you to come up with the best solution.)

The second way is that due to the decentralization of government regulation, each province and municipality is given wide latitude as to how national regulations are administered. The auditors don't care. In fairness, it would probably be too complicated for them to care. The net result, however, is that the auditing company sometimes wants you to do something in direct conflict with the regulatory requirements of the government in whose jurisdiction you conduct your business.

And then there are the employees themselves, who simply don't want to work under the auditor's guidelines.

Chinese government regulators are totally inductive in their thinking. They write regulation after regulation on virtually every topic. But they only enforce the ones that are important to them at that point in time. The rest are just there in case they need them; in case, for some other reason, they find it necessary to punish a company for doing something that they don't like.

Overtime is a good case in point. The national government has strict regulations on the amount of overtime an employee can work. Part of the reason for this is the power of discretion, and part of the reason is the country's entry into the WTO and its desire to show the world that it is a country that cares deeply about its people and is not a "slave" nation. As a result, these overtime regulations are more stringent than just about any other country in the world (remember that these are not issues of how much you pay, but how many hours of overtime the employee works).

But virtually every regulatory jurisdiction in China cares only about two things when it comes to overtime: is the overtime truly voluntary, and is the employer paying at the right rate of pay?

Not so the social auditor. To them—the deductive Westerner, or the inductive Chinese rotely enforcing a checklist created by a deductive Westerner—it is a black and white issue. This, in turn, forces many companies to cut back on the number of hours that their employees are allowed to work, often resulting in resentment among the workers and financial hardship for their families.

Somehow this doesn't fall into the same category as a manufacturer who either doesn't pay his employees or who locks them in a firetrap from which they have little chance to escape should a fire occur. To the auditor, however, they are treated the same. Deductively sound. Inductively irrational.

And the third way that the conceptual objective of these social, safety, and environmental audits are thwarted? You figure it out. There is an army of "consultants" out there who will virtually guarantee that if you hire them, you will pass the audit. An inductive commitment, for sure, but it seems to work.

———

Chai Jing, a former CCTV anchor (CCTV is the government-owned national broadcasting system), became an Internet sensation on February 28, 2014, after releasing her self-described documentary called *Under the Dome*. All in Chinese, it received 155 million hits in the first twenty-four hours and has been the focus of Internet chatter and newspaper editorials ever since.

It's commonly referred to as a Chinese sequel to Al Gore's *The Inconvenient Truth,* but it's more like a 103-minute TED Talk than a typical documentary. And like Al Gore, Ms. Chai has been pummeled by both sides; some suggest that her presentation was not balanced, downplaying China's need for economic growth, and others complain that she did not go far enough.

Ms. Chai addresses three primary questions: 1. What is pollution? 2. What causes it? 3. What can we do about it? And she gives a human dimension to the problem by noting that it was the birth of her daughter that heightened her interest in the issue.

The causes and solutions, in the end, surprised few. Energy and construction are the primary causes of China's now infamously poor air quality. China's only abundant energy resource is coal, which is normally not a clean energy source to begin with, and China's coal is notoriously poor quality. An energy scientist friend of mine familiar with China describes it as "high energy dirt."

The low level of China's gasoline and diesel standards also take a hit in Chai Jing's expose, but again, that is not a surprise to scientists familiar with the situation. But in fairness to her critics, there will be a cost to raising the quality of the gasoline and diesel refined in China and a massive expenditure of capital to realign China's refining capacity. That's not to say it shouldn't be done, but the cost factor is an inconvenient truth, if you will.

Of absolutely no surprise to anyone is her assertion that the biggest culprit behind China's rapidly deteriorating air quality is weak government enforcement. China has plenty of environmental regulations on the books already. They just aren't enforced—or at least enforced uniformly.

The biggest surprise of Ms. Chai's documentary was her clear explanation of what pollution is and why it is bad for your health. Frankly, I have been stunned by the number of relatively well-educated Chinese who have watched the piece and declared, "I had no idea air pollution was so bad for my health. For me it was always just there. It obscures the sun, but beyond that I didn't think much about its impact on my health."

Most Westerners, I suspect, will be shocked to read that and will immediately jump to the conclusion that this ignorance must be a function of government censorship. I believe, however, that this would be an oversimplification.

Certainly the government has not made the health impact of pollution a priority in the national education curriculum. But I think some lack of awareness is both a reflection of how focused the Chinese have been on improving their quality of life and on how they tend to view health issues through the lens of traditional Chinese medicine, not Western science. It's not that pollution is considered healthy to the TCM way of thinking, it's just not addressed in any direct fashion because it was not the issue it is today during the evolution of TCM.

China does have to tackle its environmental degradation, or the country's major cities will ultimately become uninhabitable. But many international cities (eg, Los Angeles, Denver, London) faced similar challenges in the past and have successfully resolved them.

I think it would be unfair not to recognize the ways in which the Chinese are living, consciously or not, in an environmentally friendly way. Everything is recycled. Everything. When a developer is getting ready to replace a building, he will typically just knock it down and leave it for the recyclers to do the rest. By the time they are finished, there is almost nothing that has to be hauled away to a landfill.

Public transportation in every major city is well developed and well utilized. I myself utilize the subway system whenever I travel around Beijing because it is convenient, cheap, safe, and clean.

Virtually all major streets have bicycle lanes that are physically divided from the vehicle traffic, and cities like Beijing have installed bicycle rental stations throughout the city to make it convenient for visitors to bike their way around (you can leave the bike at a different station than where you picked it up). And every subway station and grocery store offers an inexpensive and convenient area to store your bike in a controlled and secure environment.

Environmental friendliness often goes hand in hand with cheap. As I have noted before, whereas a Western developer would install high-efficiency water heaters to supply warm water to the washrooms, the Chinese developer wouldn't provide hot water at all.

I honestly can't say whether Ms. Chai's documentary is adequately balanced or not. As a writer I know it is impossible to satisfy everyone.

I do believe, however, that she has done the country a great service simply by educating people to the hazards of pollution. Now aroused, I believe the citizenry will take it from here.

CHAPTER 41

GETTING IT RIGHT

China has become a popular destination for US and European Executive MBA programs, and a few of them have found their way to my company looking for advice. Since we are located in a national industrial zone and we have a good relationship with the local government, I am often asked to speak with foreign executives considering making an investment here.

Invariably, my advice to both audiences is pretty simple:

- If you're coming here with the idea of selling one widget to every Chinese person, don't bother. You won't. The Chinese market is no more homogenous than any other market. There are a few very rich people. There are hundreds of millions who don't have enough money to be interested in what you're selling—no matter what it is. And the competition is more intense than in any other market you currently compete in. An astounding number of foreign companies who are already here are not making money. And those that are, more likely than not, are making it on exports, not domestic sales. The domestic market, in short, is *not* there for the taking.

- The good news: there are no lawyers. The bad news: there is no case law. The result: commercial disputes are difficult to predict and often impossibly difficult to resolve.

- Pick your location carefully. Foreigners tend to think of China as a giant monolith. And politically it is. But politics isn't where most of us spend our lives, and it's not where most business is done. Local jurisdictions wield enormous power to interpret and administer regulations as they see fit, a reality reinforced by the fact that most regulations are intentionally vague in order to give the government the upper hand in enforcement and to preclude the opportunity to exploit the proverbial loophole.

- Make sure to send your most experienced A players to run your business here. China is not a place to develop your future leadership. They will get eaten alive. Send your best – the person you just can't possibly replace in their current position.

- Put 99 percent of your effort into getting the right local team. Most foreign companies fail in China because they fail to get their management right. Only glance at the resume. The fact that a candidate speaks fluent English and has worked for a who's who of multinational companies doesn't mean that person shares your values. And if he or she doesn't, the damage that can be inflicted can be crippling. It can make everything else irrelevant.

- Understand the culture. Your country leader does not need to speak the language. He or she does need to understand the culture, however. Without that you will make the wrong choice at every fork in the road. Understand how the Chinese communicate; understand the way they negotiate; understand the value they place on relationships versus words.

The people challenge, however, goes well beyond the senior management staff. Personnel development—at all levels—must be the number one priority of any company operating here. Here's why:

- The Chinese are on a mission, a mission to lead a better life and to provide safety and comfort for their families. They manage their careers accordingly. Every job is evaluated in the context of a career path. If they aren't constantly enhancing their personal market value, they will leave immediately.

- The pace of change here is incomprehensible until you are immersed in it. Your organization must be constantly updating its skills and its perspective. My entire organization is in training, both internally and externally, from the unskilled laborer to the highest level of management.

- As a foreign company, your workforce will inevitably be young. Even the most experienced executives with the skill set and the desire to work for a multinational company will have twenty years of experience or less. More often than not, you'll have a thirty-year-old in a position that would normally be occupied by a fifty-year-old in in the West. And since the market isn't about to give you time to catch up, you must find a way to give your organization two years of experience every six months.

And the $64,000 question from most of the groups I meet with: what about the corruption?

It exists in every developing country. China is no exception.

In the 2012 Corruption Perceptions Index compiled by Transparency International, however, China ranks eightieth in the level of perceived corruption, well behind Denmark, Finland, and New Zealand, the three highest scoring (least corrupt) countries. The United States, however, scores only nineteenth, and Italy is just eight places ahead of China. China is, in fact, twenty-five places ahead of Mexico, a key US trading partner, and fifty-three places ahead of Honduras and Russia. All told, China places in the upper half of countries assessed.

Yet it is a big problem and the government would be the first to admit it. I know of big multinational companies who have pulled out of China because they ultimately concluded that they could not be successful here while at the same time remaining true to their corporate values and code of ethics.

I believe, however, that the government understands the need to wipe out corruption at all levels of society. Not just because it is a prerequisite to China becoming a true global leader and political and economic superpower, but because corruption, at its core, creates huge inefficiencies in the economy. When wages are no longer dirt cheap and the rule of commercial law is firmly established, China will have to compete on the overall efficiency of its value creation.

241

Gary Moreau

Retailers must ultimately stock their shelves with the products people want to buy. And companies must ultimately buy raw materials and supplies from the vendor who provides the best quality at the lowest price. Any personal financial transaction that compromises those objectives will ultimately bring the whole system down. In the world of efficient markets, honesty and integrity are essential to long-term value creation.

You can compete here. You can thrive. You just need to live your values, live them consistently and transparently, and never, ever forget the importance of getting the right management in place. Everything else flows from that.

CHAPTER 42

THE EMPLOYEE PERSPECTIVE

Talent development is a hot topic in the corporate world these days. Assess the competencies. Define the gaps. Execute a plan to close them. And out the other end comes an all-star team that can vanquish the competition and achieve even the loftiest goals.

A great theory, to be sure. But if it were that simple, of course, every team would be a championship team, and no company would ever have to report bad earnings or eliminate jobs. And since there are still plenty of companies in this latter camp, we can conclude that this is a worthy but ultimately elusive goal for many companies.

For most companies it is more practical and productive in the short term to play to the strengths of the team they have rather than trying to acquire or develop the strengths they don't currently possess.

Every team, of course, is different by definition. Teams are made up of people and people come in all shapes and sizes and with all kinds of different strengths and weaknesses. And that's just as true in China as it is everywhere else on the planet. (And in the end, that is the strength of diversity. Why do we always want to homogenize everything?)

But at the risk of over-generalization, I believe there are a few strengths that you will—or should—find in almost every Chinese organization. Understand them, and find a way to play to them in pursuit of your company's goals, and you will greatly enhance your chances of success.

To understand those strengths, however, you must first understand the common denominators from which those strengths originate. There are only a few that are truly critical.

The first is what I refer to as the survival mentality. While socialism with Chinese characteristics has lifted more than 300 million people out of poverty in just one generation, most Chinese still live with a survival mindset. A good many remember what it was like to live in a world of scarcity and hardship. And even if they've never lived in such conditions, they know that it's not so far away as the crow flies. The single-minded drive for financial security—and the insipient fear of losing it, therefore, continues to define a great deal of China's economic behavior.

For the consumer, cheap reigns supreme. Forget what you hear about the success that luxury brands have enjoyed in China. Price still drives the lion's share of personal consumption. The luxury market is big only because of the fact that you have 1.4 billion consumers here. The average consumer still focuses almost exclusively on price, and even those that are interested in luxury are likely to look for it at duty-free stores or in the gray markets.

For employees, similarly, it's all about take-home pay and/or personal development that they believe will ultimately lead to greater take-home pay. We lose employees every day to employers who offer lower pay and fewer benefits, but a lot of overtime.

The second key common denominator is that whatever education your workforce has received, chances are that it was an education built entirely on rote learning, a process designed to instill knowledge, but not curiosity and the analytical thinking that curiosity ultimately leads to. As a result the Chinese are generally proficient at generating mountains of data but often fall short when it comes to deciphering what it all means.

The third is that within Chinese culture—a culture that turns on relationships—all relationships are personal. Institutional loyalty is a foreign concept to them. In their world view loyalty is a human quality that cannot be extended to institutional entities.

There are, of course, pros and cons to every human attribute, and these three are no exceptions.

As famed psychologist Abraham Maslow, author of the human hierarchy of needs, taught us, until people are confident that they have secured sufficient food and shelter, they are unlikely to think too much about broader and longer-term needs such as belonging and self-fulfillment.

As a result, if you stock your restrooms with plentiful amounts of toilet paper, you are likely to find it quickly depleted. And if you think you are clever enough or personally dynamic enough to arrest employee theft or the acceptance of inappropriate gifts from business partners, you will be proved wrong. (This is not a cultural issue. My own American grandmother, who had lived through the Great Depression, routinely emptied the container of sugar packets found on the tables of restaurants into her purse. When challenged by her embarrassed grandchildren, she noted that it was built into the cost of the meal.)

On the other hand, you will find it easy to find employees who are willing to work overtime, even on holidays, to help you satisfy short-term needs. And financial incentives are particularly strong motivators.

Most importantly, a survival mindset is not selective or situational. They will treat your money just as carefully as they treat their own. Which, again, comes with pros and cons. They may not choose the best long-term solution to problems in order to save money up front, but they will, if you task and reward them accordingly, complete tasks in the cheapest and quickest possible way. (Note to self: Be careful about perceived hypocrisies. Your Chinese staff will fret about spending ten RMB ($1.50), so there can be issues when your visiting foreign colleagues stay at the nicest hotel in town and dine on Peking duck night after night. Don't expect your foreign visitors to live like the local Chinese. Just be sensitive to the optics.)

So how do you play to these strengths? I have a few simple suggestions.

First, assign your team very specific tasks, no matter how difficult, and let them go. Chances are they will get it done. They may get it done with the metaphorical equivalent of bailing twine and chewing gum, but they will get it done with amazing speed and at minimal cost. (Their Western counterparts are likely to be appalled at this, accustomed as they are to doing everything with titanium and something akin to space-age polymers.)

Secondly, define the key analytics that are most critical to your business and teach them, as a rote-teacher would teach, to the people you want to use them. They will use them and once again, they will use them with mind-boggling speed and efficiency. Almost all Chinese are well versed in the mechanics of mathematics. Incredibly well versed, in fact, by contemporary Western standards.

And thirdly, in choosing your managers—expats or Chinese nationals—don't be fooled into assigning your strongest taskmasters. Assign your best leaders, your best team-builders. Assign people that your Chinese employees will believe they can learn from and who have the desire and skill sets to nurture that relationship.

It took me a while to learn these lessons, to be candid, but once I did, I was able to achieve far better results with a fraction of the frustration. In the end I spent my time on coaching, developing the right analytics for people to use, and developing and assigning clear tasks with clearly defined personal benefits to the people assigned to carry it out. And then I get out of the way.

When I tasked a team with the objective of obtaining ISO certification, they achieved 9,000, 14,000, and 18,000 certification in just over six months. They didn't quite understand the need, mind you, which would have killed the project in most Western organizations, but I worked very hard to earn their trust and when I told them I wanted it done, they went out and did it. It was personal.

The ultimate lesson here—and it admittedly took me a while to learn it—is that if you come to China and simply shoehorn in your Western management and personnel systems and methods, you are likely to be both frustrated and disappointed.

If, however, you adapt your management systems to the strengths you will find here, you will be astounded by what you can achieve.

POLITICS

CHAPTER 43

CHAIRMAN MAO ZEDONG

I don't want to turn this into a historical treatise because then most of my most desired readers will put it down. I want to promote understanding, not history.

But you can't understand China today without knowing a little about Mao Zedong, the founder of the People's Republic of China and it's first leader.

Chairman Mao (1893–1976) was born in Shaoshan, Hunan Province, the son of a peasant farmer who became wealthy as a result of extensive landholdings.

Mao was a Communist, of course. But more than that, he was Chinese and was heavily influenced by Peter Kropotkin, a Russian anarchist who promoted a society of mutual aid and cooperation free from any central government, frequently using evolution and examples from animal behavior to make his case.

Convinced that feudalism and capitalism ultimately fabricated poverty through false scarcity and the creation of privilege, Kropotkin's theories of mutual support were ultimately the philosophical basis for the rise of trade unions and help explain Chairman Mao's lifelong personal kinship with workers and laborers.

At the time Mao was fighting the Nationalists, the average Chinese farmer was poor and illiterate. Very few had any education at all.

How, then, could these poor farmers consciously choose a particular political and economic ideology? One can easily surmise they were incapable of formally debating Marxist-Leninist ideology versus Adam Smith and Thomas Jefferson.

So why did they become Communists? That's the point. I don't believe they did. They became Maoists.

Mao represented many things to the Chinese. He was, first and foremost, Chinese and proud of it. He wanted nothing to do with Western culture or Western institutions that during his lifetime, he had seen concentrate vast amounts of the country's wealth in the hands of a few Nationalists who went to great lengths to adopt Western culture.

More importantly, what Mao advocated was a peer-to-peer economic system perfectly aligned with the Chinese cultural traditions of personal relationships and obligations. Why, he asked, should Chinese soil belong to a handful of feudal lords when it requires the toil of an entire nation to bring it to life?

With vision well beyond most of his counterparts in Asia and elsewhere in the world, his national dream was inclusive. As Mao once noted, "Women hold up half of the sky." Why, therefore, should they not enjoy equal rights with men, giving women a role in Mao's peer-to-peer world view? (Mao's father pushed him into a forced marriage—the first of his four marriages—when he was seventeen, and some believe this influenced his strong feminist support.)

Was Mao a modern-day Confucian? Confucius lived during the dynastic era, which was highly structured and hierarchical, so on that basis you would have to say no. And while Chairman Mao is known to have studied Confucius, he is said to have voiced a preference for popular novels such as *Romance of the Three Kingdoms.*

Still, Mao's political philosophy turned on obligation, just as Confucius's did. He merely changed the focus of the obligation to the state—which, as a Communist state, was a collection of peers, not a hierarchy of royalty.

Mao was well-known for his propagandist speeches and posters. And if you look at the iconic posters of that time, you will quickly notice one thing—they all center on people. They all represent the Maoist Chinese man and woman—chin up, strong, and proud. In a word, committed. And what is commitment but obligation acted upon.

If you look at the government posters of most Western democracies at the time, you will note a different emphasis. In the United States you would see Uncle Sam, who isn't a person at all. He is institutional imagery. Or the Lady of Justice holding the iconic scales of jurisprudence. Again, institutional imagery, not personal imagery.

Each form of imagery both reflected and reinforced the respective cultures. But there is no question that Mao Zedong both personally and ideologically reflected the perfect post-dynastic China—a modern version of Confucian China, with equal commitment to rites and obligations but directed in a new way that offered an acceptable alternative to the Western culture and ideology that was then sweeping the world in the wake of the Industrial Revolution.

Perhaps the best evidence of this is the resurgence of reverence for Mao Zedong in China today and the degree to which the government of Xi Jinping invokes the ideology of the Chinese Dream as an essential ingredient to continued development and advancement.

In many ways the Chinese Dream is quintessential Mao. It is a shared dream; it is an inclusive dream; it is the dream of a people rather than a nation-state.

President Xi does not personalize the Chinese Dream to the extent that the revolution was personified by Mao. But that is appropriate for China at the current time and place.

China is a now a world superpower. And that takes both strength and deference. And I believe it is—and has always been—difficult for liberal Western democracies, with their emphasis on ideals and the institutions that personify them, to accept the dominance of countries aligned with a single personality.

Russia, I believe, bears this out today as it seeks to regain its historical relevance on the main stage. President Vladimir Putin, not the institution of Leninism or Marxism, personifies Russia today. This alone is difficult for many idealistic and institution minded Westerners to accept and tends to isolate Russia on the world stage.

Many Chinese, on the other hand, while adopting a more institutional face to the world in their quest to gain a voice, accept Putin's personalization and admire the independence and machismo it represents. It's not an issue of ideology or intangible institutions like the rule of law. It's personal, and as was the case with Chairman Mao, that is a concept that fits their culture and world view.

One last note about Mao Zedong and his impact on modern China.

Chairman Mao was married four times and had ten children, although other women have claimed that he fathered even more. The child of most significance, however, was his oldest son, Mao Anying, who was born in Hunan Province in 1922. When his mother, Yang Kaihui, was executed by the Kuomintang in 1930, he and his younger brother, Mao Anqing, escaped to Shanghai and were eventually sent on to study in the Soviet Union.

Mao Anying fought with the Russian Red Army in World War II against the Nazis and later served in the Chinese People's Volunteer Army (CPVA) in Korea as an assistant to Peng Dehuai, head of the CPVA forces in Korea, a role assumed to be relatively safe but which nonetheless allowed him to become a military legend fighting beside his Communist brethren in Korea.

Mao Anying and another officer, however, were killed by a South African bomber in 1950 as they were cooking over an open fire in violation of the army's own regulations against open fires that could be easily spotted by enemy bombers.

It is an important story because most people in China today believes that Mao Anying was destined to take over for his father as chairman of the Communist Party of China, creating the beginning of what might have become a family dynasty.

Who knows how that might have changed the path that China ultimately took following Chairman Mao's death in 1976.

But it didn't happen that way. And while most older Chinese talk regrettably about the Cultural Revolution, I seldom hear them speak judgmentally about Mao and his role in it. His methods were misguided, perhaps, but most Chinese appear to believe that his motives were well intended.

In fact, among the older generations who remember him, Mao Zedong appears be more highly revered with each passing day. He smoked and womanized and supposedly drank to excess, but by all accounts he believed in what he was doing and led a simple life that aligned with the workers of the time, more than any world leader since.

A documentary on the current lives of two of Mao Zedong's daughters recently received wide acclaim across China and further reinforced the country's reverence for Mao. Both women, now quite elderly, live simple lives in small rural huts, far away from the glass monuments of Shanghai and the imported luxury cars of Beijing.

The word I most often hear associated with Mao is the Chinese word for "fair." As so many older colleagues have explained to me, back in the days of Mao, "We had nothing. We were very poor. There was never enough to eat, and our living conditions were terrible. But we all suffered together. Nobody was exempt."

And always, without exception, when I hear that story, I hear respect and envy in the voice. For that, at the heart of it all, is what it means for many to be Chinese.

CHAPTER 44

THE MONOLITH MYTH

M any Westerners believe that China is a giant monolith at every level—political, economic, social, and ethnic. In fact, nothing could be further from the truth.

There are nine officially recognized political parties in China. All eight minority parties, however, swear allegiance to the Communist Party of China. It calls all the shots. The seven members at the head of the politburo are the most powerful seven people in China, without a doubt.

And the state-owned enterprises (SOEs) that dominate key industries such as banking, power, and transportation collectively form perhaps the largest centrally planned economy in the world.

When you understand how China really works, however, you will see that it is a loose and diverse federation of localities that function with incredible autonomy and that provide China with a look and feel of diversity that you will find in few other countries on the planet.

The Han ethnicity makes up roughly 93 percent of the Chinese population, but there are a total of fifty-six officially recognized ethnic groups in China, and the rights of each to practice their own culture is officially recognized in the Chinese constitution.

While Mandarin, or simplified Chinese, is the official language of China, linguists generally recognize seven to thirteen distinct dialects, depending on how you classify them, and roughly 250 different languages, when you count the languages spoken in the isolated regions and autonomous administrative territories. Many of these dialects and languages are so

Gary Moreau

distinct, they are unintelligible to someone who speaks a different dialect or language.

There are twenty-two provinces in China, equivalent to the American state, four municipalities (Beijing, Shanghai, Tainjin, and Chongqing) with provincial level authority, five autonomous regions (Guangxi Zhuang, Inner Mongolia, Ningxia Hui, Tibet, and Xinjiang), two special administrative regions (Hong Kong and Macau), and Taiwan (officially considered a breakaway province). And within these political entities are 341 prefectural entities, including counties, county-level cities, towns, rural townships, and other distinct political entities (Taiwan not included).

The national government is comprised of four main branches: the National People's Congress (legislative branch), the State Council (executive branch), the Supreme People's Court and the Supreme People's Procuratorate (judicial), and the People's Liberation Army (military). The Communist Party of China, however, ruled by the Politburo Standing Committee, a group of four to nine people, makes all decisions of any significance. Paramount leader, Xi Jinping, is the general secretary of the Communist Party and the Central Committee and is chairman of the Central Military Commission.

The National People's Congress is the largest parliamentary body in the world, with almost 3,000 members elected for a five-year term. It only convenes once per year, for ten to fourteen days, so its role is largely advisory in practice.

The members of the State Council include Premier Li Keqiang, four vice premiers (the number is variable), five state councilors, and twenty-nine ministers and heads of State Council Commissions that are the working bureaus of the government.

These bureaus typically have identical counterparts at the provincial, city, and economic zone level, however, and these local authorities have wide latitude to interpret and apply government regulations as they see fit. The differences between localities can be staggering and make doing business in multiple localities potentially complex. Relatively simple things such as building codes, fire codes, and labor laws can vary widely by locality even though all such regulations, in theory, emanate from one national regulation or law.

There are also wide regional variations in cuisine and dining. Restaurants are often identified by the provincial nature of their menu, such as Hunan cuisine or Sichuan cuisine. Generally speaking, the more south the province, the spicier the food. Northern cuisine is generally considered quite simple and bland and is seldom found outside the region.

It's almost impossible, therefore, to speak of China as a single entity. When people ask me about China, I generally have to ask them which one they're interested in. There are many.

And foreign businesses considering setting up shop here are strongly urged to get to know the local officials before making a decision on location. The investment and regulatory climate varies widely by locality.

This variety is changing, and the regulatory process is becoming much more uniform and nationalized. The strength of the decentralized system is that it maximizes the power of the government. Since laws and regulations are vaguely worded, that gives the local government broad latitude to determine if and when the law has been broken. Essentially, it is whatever they say it is on any particular day.

In many ways this is an ideal legal and regulatory structure for an inductively oriented society. As one Chinese colleague objectively noted, "If the laws are too precise, people will find ways around them. Better to be vague so that the government can say whether or not you are violating the law on any particular occasion."

While this approach might open the door to official oppression and grossly unfair treatment in a society built on deductive logic and absolutes, it works because of the inductive nature of Chinese thinking and the resulting emphasis on balance and harmony.

Government officials, in my experience, are quite pragmatic in their outlook and almost always willing to work out a mutually agreeable compromise. Their decisions are seldom heavy-handed, and they are always open to further discussion and negotiation.

The key is to understand the government's inductive perspective. They are seldom looking for absolute solutions. They are always searching to find the harmony of balance between your needs, their needs, and the needs of the community at large. Seldom do you run across the overbearing official who is simply standing on principle or the literal, but illogical, interpretation of a rule or regulation.

There are downsides, however. One is the opportunity for rogue officials at the local level to shake down companies within his or her jurisdiction. With foreign firms, in particular, this seldom involves a direct solicitation of funds. More often than not, it involves purchasing a product (eg, fire exit signs) or service from a company with a close relationship with the government.

The Chinese have a saying about this, as they do most things: "It's better to be the head of a chicken than to be the tail of the dragon." In other words many local authorities wield more authority and live more comfortable lives than their counterparts at the national level in Beijing.

The regulatory and legal landscape is changing, however, because it has been a source of great frustration for the reform-minded President Xi and Premier Li. They have openly criticized local authorities for not carrying out the reform mandates that they consider vital to the country's advancement and the party's survival.

At the Third Plenum of the Communist Party of China's Eighteenth Central Committee, the plenum at which new administrations have typically unveiled their reform agenda, the primary topic was "the rule of law," which some noted could be interpreted as "rule by law." Essentially the party stripped local authorities of some of their ability to influence the local judiciary, making it more difficult for localities to deviate from the national agenda.

I suspect the federalization of power will continue in the years ahead and is in general a good development for China. There will be more legal and regulatory clarity, and the central government will be in a stronger position to advance its progressive reforms.

It won't all be good, however. By definition regulators will have to think more and more in absolute terms. Harmonious solutions reached through negotiation can be good or bad. When you lose the bad solutions, however, you inevitably lose the chance to find the good ones as well.

CHAPTER 45

JING-JIN-JI

Imagine a single metropolis of 130 million people. The Chinese are building it. It is called Jing-Jin-Ji and encompasses the current megacities of Beijing, Tianjin, and the more rural Hebei Province that sits in between.

It is the brainchild of President Xi Jinping and his urban and economic planners who view the supercity as the future of economic reform and environmental protection (absolutely counterintuitive to the deductive thinker, of course).

The key is collaboration where there has previously been little. As noted before, China is not the economic or political monolith that most Westerners perceive. It is a tapestry of cities, regions, and provinces that have operated largely independently and perpetuated income inequities through the strict residency controls of China's hukou system first established in 1958.

That is why when you cross the line between Beijing and Hebei Province today, as I did every day for eight years, you feel like you have stepped back in time. The glass high-rises of the capital give way to the brick warrens of traditional Chinese villages. The people are poorer—much poorer—and the sanitation and general appearance of the people and the place is a stark reminder that in many ways China is still very much a developing country.

Unlike the megacities of Beijing, Shanghai, and Guangzhou, Jing-Jin-Ji ("Jing" for Beijing, "Jin" for Tianjin, and "Ji," the traditional name for Hebei Province, home to smaller cities like Langfang and Baoding), this city will not emerge organically. It will be a planned city at every level, all built around a strategically designed network of high-speed rail lines.

And therein lies the key to its success. In the past urban planners generally agreed that cities could be no larger than the equivalent of a one-hour drive by car. But trains capable of traveling in excess of 300 kilometers per hour change the math dramatically.

Enabled by that enormous increase in commutable reach, Jing-Jin-Ji will be spread over 82,000 square miles, an area roughly the size of Kansas. It will, however, hold a population larger than a third of the population of the United States and twice the size of France.

To relieve its own traffic and environmental congestion, Beijing will shed itself of all businesses and government bureaucracy nonessential to the fulfillment of its civil role as the capital of China. Even hospitals will be moved.

There are hurdles to overcome. How, for example, will tax revenues be distributed between areas that today do not share such income?

Nonetheless, it is an ingenious concept that probably wouldn't be possible in any other country on earth. In the United States, it would surely be wrapped up in the courts for decades.

It shows just how holistic and inductive the Chinese are in their thinking. They know that without more equitable income distribution, there will eventually be social unrest. But they can't just dismantle the hukou system, or cities like Beijing will be crushed by the inflow of people looking for higher incomes and a better way of life. So instead of eliminating the system, they will expand its footprint, but they will do so in a way that minimizes the environmental impact of such high population density.

And, of course, the transformation itself will provide plenty of jobs during the economically challenging years of China's pivot away from an industrial export economy to a service-led consumption economy.

It is a classically inductive solution that is symbolic of why the West finds it so difficult to decipher China in a deductive way. How can building a city of 130 million people possibly relieve the pressure of environmental degradation and congestion? But it can.

In the West we think of it as thinking outside the box, or circular thinking, if we're inclined to be pejorative. And it's both, in a sense. But isn't that what innovation is all about? Isn't that exactly the kind of thinking we need to solve the problems of the world, most of which, by the way, have been created by deductive thinking and a resulting obsession with cause and effect and the process mentality that such a relationship stands on.

CHAPTER 46

AIIB

Taking its growing status and influence to a new level, China is promoting a new financial institution called the Asian Infrastructure Investment Bank (AIIB) to fund infrastructure projects throughout Asia, in direct competition with the Western-dominated World Bank and the International Monetary Fund. The AIIB will be based in Beijing.

To date, fifty-seven countries, including four of the five UN Security Council members and half of the European Union members—France, Germany, and Italy among them—have committed to joining the AIIB. The United States has not, although it has not closed the door to future participation. For now, however, the United States has been actively campaigning against the new institution and attempting to coerce its allies not to play ball.

Their efforts have been consistently unsuccessful. Great Britain, Canada, Australia, South Korea, and New Zealand have all signed on. Only Japan has heeded the United States plea for noninvolvement, but even it is expected to ultimately join.

It is yet another sign of the United States' loss of global leadership and declining influence. But the loss is more than symbolic. I dare say it is hastening the decline.

After all, what possible argument can be made against the funding of much needed infrastructure projects in Asia's developing countries? If the World Bank is a worthwhile institution, how can the AIIB not be?

The only difference will be that the AIIB will operate more democratically, and the United States will not have the veto power it enjoys at the

World Bank. By declining to play, the United States has shown not only ignorance of the new world order but also has clearly exposed its often-denied concern over the rise of China.

In fairness, it is a reflection of political reality in Washington. It is doubtful that a vote to join an institution sponsored by China and of which both Russia and Iran are founding members would stand any chance of getting through Congress.

But nothing gets through Congress. As a political system, the United States has become entirely dysfunctional, precluding action on any issue of such global significance.

But it is perspective, I believe, that is America's greatest failing on the matter.

The American Century came about not so much by its victory in two world wars as by its actions in the wake of World War II. We didn't punish our former enemies. We helped them to rebuild. And that brought us both new allies and a thriving global economy in which those allies helped pave the way to America's economic supremacy.

China is merely following the same script and will, I suspect, enjoy the same success. By helping its neighbors develop, it will deepen its ties that might otherwise be inclined to heighten the tension over disputed atolls or promote separatist objectives within China.

For America it is more than unfortunate. Why would a country of its stature and international experience take on a battle it could not win? Or does it think it can? That, perhaps, is the scariest scenario of all. Can the power-brokers within the Beltway be so uninformed as to think the United States can thwart China's efforts to do what the West has already done? Wars have been started over far less significant errors in judgment.

I believe part of the problem is that too many politicians view global power as a zero-sum game. If China gets stronger, the logic goes, the United States must get weaker.

But history does not support this logic. China and the United States can both get stronger. There is more than enough of a leadership vacuum in the world today for both to play a significant role in shaping the future world order. Together they would be a global political force that could not easily be denied or overlooked. In competition, however, they only provoke rogue leaders to play one against the other.

To present a united front, both countries must redefine their relationship to eliminate distrust and build consensus wherever it can be built.

It strikes me that the AIIB would be a good starting point. What is the downside?

The only downside I can see flows from a unilateral decision to stay on the sidelines. That can only result in isolation and virtually precludes any opportunity to influence the evolution of the institution.

As a university student, I had an economics professor who sat on the board of directors of the local power utility. He once told our class that he was often taken to task by his fellow professors for supporting such a crassly commercial enterprise that many believed negatively impacted the environment of an otherwise pristine and sparsely populated state.

He said, "I do it because to refuse to participate is a one-time protest that would soon be forgotten. At least now I have a seat at the table and can attempt to influence the company in a way my fellow professors would be proud of."

I suspect, however, that none of our country's current foreign policy decision-makers sat in on that lecture.

CHAPTER 47

PRESIDENT & CHAIRMAN XI JINPING & THE FIGHT ON CORRUPTION

In October of 2012, Xi Jinping, a member of the Han ethnic group, became general secretary of the Eighteenth CPC Central Committee, the first member of the Standing Committee of the Politburo, and chairman of the CPC Central Military Commission. In March 2013, at the annual meeting of the National's People Congress, he was elected president of China and chairman of the PRC Central Military Commission.

The reality is that all leaders, great and otherwise, both shape their times and are shaped by them. Every once in a while, however, the conditions for change are particularly ripe, posing the opportunity for truly great leaders to change the world for the better in profound and far-reaching ways. Abraham Lincoln was such a leader at such a time, as was Franklin D. Roosevelt and Nelson Mandela. Each led a nation through profound and ultimately positive change.

And Xi Jinping? Only history can answer that question, but there is little doubt in my mind that the time is ripe in China for great and world-changing leadership to leave its mark on history.

If, as Henry Kissinger noted, President Hu Jintao, Xi's predecessor, led China on to the world stage, President Xi Jinping is surely the first Chinese president to lead from the established position of world power. So while it is undoubtedly true that President Obama remains the most powerful man in the world, President Xi is undoubtedly the man with the opportunity to change the world to the greatest degree—one way or the other—during the lives of today's children.

So what can we expect from the man who now leads one-fifth of the world's population and oversees the world's second largest economy, or the first, according to the IMF, when measured in terms of purchasing power parity.

President Xi was born in Shaanxi Province, currently sixteenth in gross domestic product (GDP) of the twenty-two provinces in China. He is the son of Xi Zhongxun, a former revolutionary hero and one of the first generation of Communist Chinese leaders. As a senior provincial leader of Guangdong Province, China's most prosperous province, the elder Xi helped to bring about the development of the special economic development zones that were the cornerstone of Deng Xiaoping's efforts to redefine socialism with Chinese characteristics. He subsequently moved on to Beijing, where he was elected to the politburo and the party secretariat, retiring from government service in 1988.

From the accounts I've read, Xi Zhongxun was a man of moderation and tolerance, seeking political solutions whenever possible and displaying sincere accommodation of religious and ethnic diversity. And without question he was a man of both idealism and conviction, having been purged and imprisoned on several occasions throughout his career.

This included imprisonment during the Cultural Revolution, a time during which Xi Jinping, at age of sixteen, was "sent down" to work and study at an agricultural commune in Yanchuan County, part of a widespread program developed by Mao Zedong to allow urban youth to learn from the simple ways of Chinese farmers.

After six years on the commune and at the end of the Cultural Revolution, the young Mr. Xi went on to earn a university degree in chemical engineering and later a doctorate in law, both from Tsinghua University, widely considered the MIT of China and one of the best and most competitive universities in China today.

Having joined the Communist Party of China (CPC) while still in Yanchuan County, President Xi's first job after graduating from university was personal secretary to Geng Biao, the minister of defense, eventually moving on to a variety of county and provincial level posts before becoming party secretary of Shanghai and emerging on the national political scene.

Beyond those basic facts, of course, neither we as Westerners nor the average Chinese know all that much about Xi Jinping the man. Chinese leaders are notoriously private, although his wife, Peng Liyuan, a famous folk singer, is widely adored by the Chinese and unlike political wives of the past, is frequently seen accompanying her husband on official state visits. Still, no Chinese person that I've talked with is even certain where the couple lives, so the idea that the first family might invite television cameras into their home to share a holiday celebration, as is the custom in the United States, is virtually unthinkable.

From watching President Xi on Chinese television, however, I must say that he strikes me as a man comfortable in his own skin. He seems quite relaxed in front of an audience and often displays a sense of disarming humor and self-deprecation seldom seen publicly in any senior government official here in the decorous Middle Kingdom.

His father, as all fathers inevitably do, undoubtedly shaped Xi Jinping's thinking in many ways. And, I suspect, he was likewise greatly influenced by his time on the agricultural commune in Yanchuan County.

But before my fellow Western readers jump to any conclusions, I mean "influenced" in the most positive way. While Westerners tend to think of being "sent down" as akin to an old Soviet political dissident being sent off to a gulag, I don't believe that is in any way a valid analogy.

My first assistant in China was a retired professor who herself, with several of her classmates, was "sent down" during the Cultural Revolution to work on a similar agricultural commune. And while the living conditions were austere, food was not always plentiful, and the work was long and grueling, I never once heard her utter anything close to anger or resentment about the experience.

She spoke about it very matter-of-factly. While her own family suffered at the hands of the Red Guard for allegedly being *bourgeois*, she always talked about her time on the commune in terms of the friendships she made and the lessons she learned about life. To this day she and her classmates visit the village from time to time, and she holds a heartfelt reverence for the poor farmers, who like farmers the world over, feed the rest of us in relative obscurity, enjoying faint praise for their hard labor.

But this woman, who was always referred to by the simple but highly respectful term *lao shi*, meaning teacher, had two notable qualities beyond her general reverence for the poor that I believe she would attribute to her time in the country. One was the complete and total lack of fear. The other was perspective.

President Xi, I suspect, shares all three of these qualities—respect for all people, invincible courage, and balanced perspective. If you can read a man from his eyes, this is a man who has complete and total respect for people—all people. This is a man who genuinely shares the hopes and dreams of the Chinese people for a harmonious and comfortable life—the Chinese Dream that he so often references in his public speeches.

And the achievement of that dream, I believe, will ultimately define the agenda for the decade he will serve as the president of China. Which is to say that the first Chinese president to lead China as an established world power will spend more time and energy focused on China itself than on its influence over the rest of the world.

He faces many daunting domestic challenges: environmental degradation, the polarization of wealth, corruption—both public and private—and regional unrest and the violence it has spawned. I believe these are the challenges that will occupy his time and attention.

That is not to say that he will simply defer to the rest of the world in defining China's role in the new world order. He is the son of a soldier, is married to a major general in the People's Liberation Army, and himself served in the military. From what we've seen so far, he is a man who is both cool under pressure and not intimidated by either saber rattling or bellicose rhetoric. His father risked it all and willingly paid the price for what he believed; the son, I strongly suspect, is cut from the same cloth.

I believe the quality that will ultimately come to define President Xi Jinping in history, however, is the same quality that so prominently defined my assistant—perspective. He has seen it all and experienced it all, and he, unlike so many of today's valueless leaders intoxicated by their own power, knows exactly how it all fits together.

And for that reason I am willing to bet, without hesitation, that this, more than anything else, is a man who simply deplores hypocrisy. I don't think he expects to agree with the world leaders he will meet and work with in his duties. I don't think he even cares if they share his perspective or his world view.

But God help them if he concludes that they are hypocrites. More than anything else, it is the perceived hypocrisy of their enemies that gave Mao and his fellow revolutionaries, including Xi Zhongxun, the strength to win despite unimaginable suffering and against the longest of odds.

I believe it is hypocrisy that the Chinese Dream ultimately seeks to destroy, and it is the battle against hypocrisy, both here in China and the world over, that I believe will ultimately define the leadership of President Xi Jinping.

In no way has he tackled hypocrisy more intently than in the area of corruption—both public and private. President Xi's anti-corruption credentials are beyond challenge. In July Zhou Yongkang, a former member of the powerful Politburo Standing Committee and chief of China's internal security apparatus, was placed under official investigation for "serious disciplinary violations," the first time an official at this level has *ever* been disciplined by the party. On December 5 the Political Bureau of the CPC Central Committee expelled Zhou from the party and handed his case over to the judiciary for prosecution.

Ling Jihua, fifty-eight, the former head of the General Office of the CPC Central Committee, is being investigated for "suspected disciplinary violations," along with a former vice governor of Anhui Province and a former police chief of Licang District in Qingdao, Shandong Province.

And the list goes on…and on.

Even senior officers of the People Liberation's Army have not been spared investigative scrutiny. Officers ensnared in the crackdown include Xu Caihou, seventy-one, retired general and former vice-chairman of the Central Military Commission, and Yang Jinshan, sixty, lieutenant general of the PLA ground forces and former deputy commander of the Chengdu Military Command. Gu Junshan, former deputy head of the PLA General Logistics Department, and Gao Xiaoyan, deputy political commissar and chief of discipline inspection at PLA Information Engineering University, were also caught in the net.

Shortly after coming to power in October 2012, the government of President Xi Jinping and Premier Li Keqiang issued what came to be known as "the eight rules," the beginning of a long and ardent campaign to alter government behavior.

The rules specifically addressed the elimination of government privilege and urged a dramatic reduction in the pomp and circumstance that accompanied official behavior at the time.

One of the rules states: "All government meetings shall be short, clear in focus, and all empty and courteous comments should be eliminated." Another specifically forbids the organization of Chinese students studying abroad to "welcome" visiting Chinese officials at the airport.

And the application of the eight rules has been expanded and more broadly interpreted since. Prior to this past Spring Festival, a time of traditionally generous gift giving within families, from companies to their employees and customers, and from subordinates to their superiors, the government specifically forbade the use of public funds for the purchase of printed materials to be used as gifts, a move that had a devastating impact on the calendar industry, once a beneficiary of the government's annual largesse.

For the most part, the Western media has interpreted all this to be part of a broader program to curb corruption and graft, a perspective reinforced by the vigorous and well-documented campaign the administration has conducted to expose and punish corrupt officials at every level of government. It is a campaign unprecedented in its scope and scale, bringing down officials considered off-limits in previous campaigns.

I believe, however, that the Western media is missing the real story here. While Westerners tend to think of corruption in the context of Judeo-Christian morality, the real storyline here is Xi Jinping's desire to reinvigorate the party's commitment to Marxist ideology.

President Xi is not in any way attempting to remake China in a Western image. He has specifically warned his party faithful not to ape Western morality and behavior. The implication is that Western ideology and morality, with its emphasis on material and financial achievement, is the root cause of government corruption and the polarization of wealth and income that plagues most capitalist democracies.

As the head of the Communist Party of China, President Xi, of course, is a Marxist. As with most ideologies, however, there are Marxists and there are Marxists. There are, to put it another way, Marxists who buy into the mechanics of Marxist politics (ie, technocrats). And there are idealists who truly believe in the utopian community Marxist ideology seeks to achieve. President Xi, I believe, falls decidedly into this latter camp.

It is true, as some analysts have correctly maintained, that President Xi and Premier Li took office at a time of growing concern within the party about its grip on power. Mao Zedong was a revolutionary. But he was a populist revolutionary. He was, even at the height of his power, a man of the people and continues to be revered as such today, even among those who suffered during the Cultural Revolution.

As China has prospered economically, however, many members of the Communist Party have prospered far more than the average Chinese citizen whose hard work and sacrifice were the engine that raised 300 million people out of poverty in a single generation. In fact, some senior government officials and their families became obscenely wealthy and enjoy a life of luxury and privilege that the average Chinese cannot comprehend, much less abide.

President Xi, simply put, understood that the party was losing touch with the citizenry from which it rose. And, in the end, he understood all too well that this would ultimately lead to a loss of legitimacy and jeopardize the very existence of the party and its singular grip on power in China.

I believe, however, that President Xi is motivated by more than mere self-preservation. After all, once enriched, which the president is clearly in a position to do, the loss of legitimacy and power would have little impact on the families of "naked officials" whose families are living comfortably abroad. (The term "naked official" is commonly used here to describe a government official whose spouse and child live abroad in one of the Western democracies such as the United States, Canada, and Australia. And there are thousands of them.)

On July 21 of this year, a statement from the Organization Department of the Communist Party of China (ODCPC) announced a sweeping plan to reeducate government officials in basic Marxist principles, noting a loss of faith and a moral decline among their ranks.

This is not, however, a sign that the CPC has any desire to adopt a Western model of morality and virtue. In its announcement the ODCPC specifically and meaningfully noted, "Chinese officials should safeguard the spiritual independence of the nation and avoid becoming an echo of western moral values."

The official government-run Chinese news agency, Xinhua, later noted that authorities would "work to improve officials' morals, calling on them to be noble, pure and virtuous persons who have relinquished vulgar tastes."

The government officials are not alone. Chinese journalists, who must be certified to have access to government spokespeople and official government announcements, are likewise undergoing remedial education in Marxist ideology and the Marxist view that journalism be both objective and supportive of party ideology.

Westerners will naturally interpret this as a move to silence dissent. And that is, by definition, true to a degree. Journalism, however, is no more immune to corruption than government service, and several leading Chinese journalists have recently been investigated for taking bribes.

To paraphrase Freud, all of life is personal. And journalists are no exception. We all have an agenda, whether it is consciously articulated or not. True objectivity, even when it comes to journalism, is a journey, not a destination.

And social change, more than anything else, is a political enabler. Once the genie is out of the bottle, anyone can use the cover of change to pursue his or her own political and social agenda, no matter what it may be.

And at few points in history will a single country of such size and significance go through more change than China as it pivots away from the export manufacturing model that allowed it to become the second largest economy in the world to the consumption-based economy that will be necessary to improve the quality of life for all Chinese and to relieve the pressure that being the factory to the world has put on the environment.

In other words, the government knows that the gut-wrenching changes necessary to complete such a grand economic pivot will open the door to competing political agendas that might have some intrinsic merit, but might nonetheless derail the whole process and plunge the country into social and political chaos. Which is which will depend on your perspective. But neither truth makes the other any less true.

President Xi frequently refers to the Chinese Dream. It is the cornerstone of his administration. And it is, I believe, a dream defined by proud perseverance, national and ethnic pride, and shared community.

It is not a Western dream. It is a Marxist dream. And on balance I believe that is very good news for the West.

Part of the challenge in figuring out how an inductive-reasoning, holistic-thinking society works is understanding the simple fact that there is nothing to figure out from the Western perspective. Definitive and finite answers belong to the world of deductive, linear thinking, where there are beginnings and ends and discernible steps in between. The holistic, inductive world is both seamless and without borders. Logic is a continuum extending infinitely in all directions.

Which is why I believe it is fortunate that China has chosen the path of socialism with Chinese characteristics. While the Chinese excel at business and making money, I don't believe their world view would work in a capitalist, democratic context. The result, I fear, would be sheer and utter chaos and anarchy.

Not a single Chinese person that I have ever met has voiced the desire to vote in a popular political election. Not one. And that reticence is not a function of fear that Big Brother is listening. People here complain about their government in much the same way people everywhere do. Whatever

275

the political process employed, governing is tricky business. You're never going to keep everyone happy.

The difference here is that the governed do not expect to be happy. They accept some degree of political and personal suffering to be inevitable. What they want more than anything else is a government that is going to make every citizen's life equally inconvenient. (How much value do you suppose the Greeks feel about their own democracy today?)

Part of the reason, of course, comes back to their yin-yang world view. Happiness cannot exist without suffering any more than suffering can exist without happiness. (Most major religions, it may be noted, share the same perspective. How else could a benevolent God allow bad things to happen?)

Chinese culture is a village culture, turning as it does on the obligation of personal relationship. It promotes harmony in small settings where there is substantial social interaction (eg, within families and small towns) and mutual obligation.

But China is no longer a village. It is the most populous nation on the planet, and an increasing number of its citizens live in the uber-urban jungle. Personal space is nonexistent. There is so much personal interaction that it couldn't possibly be personal. There simply isn't time. Were China to function as a village, it would quickly grind to a halt.

I have lived on both the East Coast and the Midwest of the United States, and I can tell you that they are very different places with very different cultures. Both have their pros and cons. The one thing I did learn with certainty, however, was that neither culture would work in the other place. Each is ideally suited to its setting and neither is universally applicable.

Which, in a way, explains what happened during the Cultural Revolution. In many ways, China was trying to return an urbanizing China to its pastoral rural roots. A worthy ideal, perhaps, but a challenge comparable to putting the now square peg back in its historically round hole.

The current government has no such agenda. In fact, it has embraced urbanization as the surest and quickest way to improve the quality of life for all Chinese. Social infrastructure such as water, electricity, and medical care is easily leveraged by scale. One big pipe is relatively cheaper and quicker to lay than thousands of smaller ones.

The culture, however, retains many of the characteristics of a traditional village society. Obligation is personal, not institutional. Face is important. And where you are from is an important ingredient of your personal identity.

One of the inherent drawbacks of the village culture, however, is that the villages tend to fight, or at least treat one another with suspicion, like the Hatfields and the McCoys of Appalachian legend. When your personal identity is closely aligned with your village, the people from other villages are, by definition, strangers (ie, foreigners).

Chinese history is certainly testament to that. The founding emperor of the first Chinese dynasty (221–206 BC), Qin Shi Huang, did not unify China at the ballot box. He did so through the conquest of six other states. China, as we know it today, was born on the battlefield. In other words, China did not come to be in the same way that the thirteen colonies of the United States did. (The United States, of course, was born through the War of Independence, but the thirteen colonies did not unite through conflict. Virginia was not conquered by Pennsylvania.)

And despite the shared Chinese culture and national identity that has emerged in the centuries that followed, China remains a largely regional entity. Everything from the food they eat, the alcohol they consume, and even the dialect they speak varies greatly from one region to the next.

Which is precisely why every Chinese person I've ever discussed the topic with has shared the opinion that China must have a strong central government, even if that means the sacrifice of some personal liberties and choices. As one colleague put it, "If we had the American political system, nothing would get done. We would just fight" (perhaps in this regard, it is America that is becoming more like China than the other way around).

I grew up at the height of the Cold War when American schoolchildren were taught to huddle under their desks in the likely event of a Soviet nuclear attack. They learned that liberal democracy was the only path to both economic advancement and social enlightenment. Whether or not that was true in a different time and place, I am certain it is no longer true today—in part, ironically, because the world is smaller. It's a different version of the long tail of culture that I've referred to in the past. Simply put, people are in a much stronger position to decide for themselves.

I believe, therefore, that the biggest risk facing China today is not socialism with Chinese characteristics. It is the potential loss of political legitimacy. Which is precisely why the current government is going to such great lengths to maintain it. It fully appreciates it is a matter of survival.

We live in a diverse world. China is not Denmark, or Croatia, or even Germany. China is China. Massive. Dynamic. A village culture trying to cope with a level of urbanization the world has never experienced before, where cities are expected to exceed 130 million people in population in the lifetime of today's children.

The days of the developed world leading the way for the developing world are over. Nor is the reverse true either, of course.

But the truth remains that we live in a shrinking but diversifying world with an extremely long tail of culture and ethnic identity. And perhaps it is the holistic, inductive world view, rather than the deductive, linear Western world view, that is ideally suited to the increasingly urban landscape that is modern China (and will be the future of many developing nations).

As Westerners we needn't—nor should we—mimic the Chinese solution. Nor, however, should we condemn it. That is ultimately for the Chinese to decide. I can tell you for now, however, what the government already knows. All political unrest in China is social, not political. And all social unrest, in the end, is economic.

The pivot to consumption, and its success or failure, will determine China's political future, not the West or the ballot box,

President Xi Jinping, I believe, understands this better than anyone.

CHAPTER 48

THE ONE-PARTY SYSTEM

The political leaders of all liberal democracies uniformly denounce one-party political systems as hotbeds for oppression, self-indulgence, and political behavior counter to the interests of society at large.

I used to believe that as well. I have, however, changed my tune.

First of all there is no organization on earth that is one of anything. A baseball team is not a single-minded baseball team. An army is not a single-minded army. A terrorist organization is not a single-minded terror machine. Even a family is not a single-minded family.

So too it is with the Communist Party of China. Only the nomenclature is different. They call them factions rather than parties, but inductively speaking, the result is the same.

In America we have the Democratic and Republican Parties. In theory this compels each to compete for the vote, a process of competition that insinuates that the man or woman who represents the best interests of the citizenry will win the seat of power.

But is that theory or reality? When a different party occupies the White House or the Congress, how much does life really change for the average American, other than the Beltway Realtors who prosper as a result of the change?

The fact is that we do have two political parties in the United States, but they are not the Republicans and the Democrats; they are the incumbents and the wannabes. And in reality, how much incentive do the incumbents have to serve the citizenry that elected them?

Gary Moreau

If one party is elected out of power, the reality is that it can reacquire power in two to four years, depending on the election cycle. It is, in other words, a temporary setback for men and women who easily have the financial means—often the largesse of special interest groups—to weather the storm.

For the Communist Party of China, however, it's an all-or-nothing contest. If they lose the legitimacy of their governance, they are gone for good. Many may be killed in the process. History is littered with the bodies of "single party" leaders, however they achieved their monopoly on power.

Competition is a deductive concept that often exists in theory more than reality. Outcome, the focus of all inductive logic, is all that really matters when it comes to things political.

So long as the people of China have food, shelter, safety, and hope, in my opinion the CPC will maintain its position of extreme legitimacy (remember, as noted earlier, even a Harvard survey found that President Xi Jinping enjoys a 95 percent approval rating among the Chinese population).

THE CHINESE CENTURY

CHAPTER 49

CHINA'S GEOPOLITICAL AMBITIONS

In the August 23, 2014, edition of *The Economist*, there was an article entitled "What China wants—After a bad couple of centuries China is itching to regain its place in the world. How should America respond?"

The article basically argues that the United States must give China a seat at the table of power in Asia, pick its fights carefully and with an eye toward materiality, and avoid the temptation of Western hawks to see China as a global threat at every turn. As the article points out, there is little evidence that China has any ambition to upend the current world order.

I personally think the points made in the article are valid, as far as they go. The nineteenth and early twentieth centuries, for obvious reasons, did not endear the Chinese to the notion of foreign colonialism. Virtually nothing good came out of it all if you look at what happened from their perspective. There was, indeed, a great loss of face and an even greater amount of human suffering. Of course China wants to make sure it doesn't happen again. Who wouldn't?

As much as anything else, however, I wonder if the Chinese weren't— and still are—simply bewildered by the whole chain of events. After all, they didn't go looking for trouble. It came to them.

And now, of course, the geopolitical headlines are filled with talk of America's pivot to Asia. The United States, of course, has repeatedly said that its pivot is not intended to blunt the emergence of China. Such reassurances, however, assume that both parties communicate in a similar fashion and that words carry the same weight and meaning in both cultures. On both counts they don't.

And that's where I believe *The Economist* didn't go far enough.

Let's be real. The United States is not going to go to war over a nine-dash red line around some uninhabited atolls in the South China Sea. Nor is China, for that matter. Deductively or inductively, it's just not a rational move.

The Economist notes correctly, however, that Taiwan is not an uninhabited atoll and advises the United States that it must be clear in its intention to come to the aid of Taiwan in the event of a Chinese threat. There are treaties involved, and if other countries can't trust you to live up to your treaties, you might as well not bother with them.

But here's the thing. China is not going to threaten, much less invade, Taiwan. *Taiwan has already invaded China.* Whatever the Western media says, Taiwan is a de facto autonomous region of China, much like Hong Kong and Macau.

Do you know which "foreign" country is the source of the greatest amount of foreign direct investment in Mainland China? I will give you a hint; it's not the United States and it's not Germany. The top two sources of foreign direct investment in Mainland China are Hong Kong and Taiwan, in that order.

Taiwan, as a country, has fewer people (23 million or so) than the single city of Chongqing, a city few people outside of China have ever even heard of. Taiwan's total GDP is less than the GDP of Guangdong Province, only one of twenty-two provinces in Mainland China.

The "threat" is over.

And what about Hong Kong? In the summer of 2014 the Standing Committee of the National People's Congress of China issued rules for the democratic election scheduled to be held in the special administrative region of Hong Kong in 2017, as agreed by all parties when the SAR was returned to Chinese control in 1997. Judging by the reaction from much of the Western media, however, you might conclude that Beijing has driven a stake through the heart of democracy itself.

But this is simply not true. The committee, in fact, reaffirmed its commitment to universal suffrage. It merely clarified the rules by which candidates could be nominated to participate in the election.

And Beijing's logic, for those willing to listen with an open mind, is both sound and well laid out. Democracy is like science. People tend to talk about science as if it is an independent body of absolute knowledge. It isn't. It is merely a way for understanding and explaining reality in the most deductively logical way.

And so it goes with democracy. We tend to speak of democracy as an absolute that requires no interpretation or rules of governance to be effective. But the founding fathers of the United States itself went to great lengths to protect individual freedoms and to ensure that a numerical majority or plurality could not invoke injustice in the name of simple democracy "by the numbers." That is why there are three branches of government rather than one and even the Congress itself is divided into two houses, one of which is not in any way proportionately representative of the population.

Beijing has a legitimate right to be concerned with the democratic process becoming hijacked by a clever minority using the rules of "democracy" to somehow subvert the will of the majority. We need look no further than the United States, or any other Western "democracy," for that matter, to find a reasonable basis for Beijing's concern. It would be difficult to plausibly argue that the Washington Beltway version of democracy has not become the de facto lever by which special interests leverage their power to force an agenda that may not align with the will of the majority of citizens.

If history has taught us anything, it is that political legitimacy, not the machinery of political choice, ultimately determines a government's place in history. Good people make good decisions. Democratically elected politicians may or may not. History is filled with examples of elected politicians who abused their power or otherwise ultimately hurt the people they were elected to protect.

It is commonly accepted in the deductively minded West today that political pluralism and democracy is the only way to hold governments accountable to govern in the best interests of the governed. In the United States, you therefore have two political parties who in theory vie for votes, thus ensuring collective representation of the populace.

But why can't a third political party ever get real traction in the United States? Why does the electorate, over time, inevitably vote the incumbent party out and the other party in? And why does that never seem to lead to meaningful change?

The reality, as noted in the preceding chapter, is that there are two political parties in the United States, but they are the incumbents and the wannabes, not the Democrats and the Republicans. That's why gerrymandering is tolerated.

In fact, there are parties within China as well. They are just all Communists. But there are parties, perhaps to a greater degree than there are in the United States and other Western democracies.

Here they are called factions. Remember the emphasis on personal relationships. The culture turns on it.

In the political and business arena, therefore, one of the most important choices you make early in your career is who you are going to pledge your allegiance to—not in some special salute or verbal declaration, but in your actions. You look after the person you have demonstrated allegiance to, and that person will look after you.

When Westerners look at the Chinese political system, they see Communists. Not the Chinese. If I mention a specific government official to a Chinese colleague, they will immediately associate that official with another. Everybody knows the connections.

If you are a foreigner doing business in China, it is essential that you understand the reality of the local political structure. You must know who is loyal to whom.

If you have a problem in China—such as the need for a special certification or some kind of relief from a regulation that doesn't apply in your situation—it is almost never effective to tackle the problem head on. That's dangerous territory. Instead, you must find out who has the ultimate authority to make the decision you need to be made in your favor and then find someone he trusts. Sometimes he or she will tell you. Not in the Western sense. He or she is not going to call you and say, "Hey, talk to this person and present your case."

Instead, you may be invited to tea, and there will be someone present whom you have not met before and who has an official capacity completely unrelated to the issue at hand. Don't pursue the question of why that person is there. He or she is there simply because the person you are truly interested in trusts him or her.

I'm not talking about bribery. This isn't a scheme for fleecing you as a foreign investor. Most Chinese officials are far too savvy to ever openly make such a request to a foreigner. They know you don't get it. It's inductively logical.

That person is there simply as an advisor. Understand that. Use the opportunity. Don't ask too many questions. Not because that person is there for any illegal or immoral purpose but because questions demonstrate a lack of trust, the foundation of Chinese society.

I believe this relational ecosystem is why the Chinese have no interest in world domination. They, better than anyone else, understand that the Chinese political and social system will not work outside of China. Nor do they want it to. It is what it is. They are the Middle Kingdom. We are foreigners. And throughout history we have brought nothing but trouble to their doorstep.

They want to be respected. They don't want to lose face. That much is completely logical.

In 1793 Great Britain sent its first envoy to China. George Macartney, the British diplomat, was to convince the Qianlong emperor to ease restrictions on trade between China and Great Britain, which at the time was importing massive amounts of tea and silk, and exporting little, creating a massive trade imbalance. Sound familiar?

There is great debate about what happened during the visit, and a lot of Western portrayals focus on Macartney's unwillingness to kowtow before the emperor, which at the time was the accepted protocol in China. (Kowtow is an act of deep respect shown by prostration before the emperor, kneeling and bowing so low as to have your head touch the ground, and obviously leaving you entirely vulnerable to an imperial sword.)

In the end, however, the two sides reached a compromise, and Macartney met the emperor, who, however it is interpreted by scholars today, said, "You can go home now. Your country has nothing that we desire."

There might have been a different outcome if the visit occurred today and the envoy had been from France rather than England. There is much in the way of luxury French products that the Chinese buy in enormous quantities, and in recent years Paris has been one of the top destinations for outgoing Chinese tourism.

There is a great difference, however, between wanting something, even coveting it, and being unable to live without it. The Chinese, I believe, like foreign luxury brands because they have confidence in the quality and because it is an obvious statement that they are one of the ones who, as Deng Xiaoping prophesied, got rich first.

There are few rich Chinese, however, who I believe would give up being Chinese for all the LV bags and Hermes scarves France could ever produce. These are mere things, and I don't believe it is possible for inductive thinkers to personalize inanimate objects to the extent that deductive thinkers can and do.

For all these reasons, I do not believe there is any ideal that would cause China to ever desire to upend the world order. The only property they covet is that which they believe is of strategic importance to their defense and independence or which has otherwise been a part of their historic identity.

When they do emigrate abroad, for reasons of education or quality of life, they seldom do so out of a desire to assimilate. And seldom do they. They remain Chinese, preserving their language and their traditions and core beliefs.

Even Chinese university students, whom one might logically predict to be the most likely to seek assimilation, only assimilate at a superficial level. Their most meaningful friendships and affiliations often remain other Chinese.

———

But what about the South China Sea? Does China's island-building and refusal to negotiate competing territorial claims suggest a new era of imperialism rather than self-defense?

The South China Sea is an important international shipping lane. More oil flows through it than the Suez or Panama canals. And China lays territorial claim to 80% of it, many of those claims overlapping with similar territorial claims by its neighbors. China has been reinforcing those claims, moreover, by building islands on top of low-lying shoals. Such islands, of course, could be used for navigational, rescue, or military purposes.

In anticipation of the annual United States–China Strategic and Economic Dialogue held in Washington in June 2015, the Chinese government announced it had pretty much wrapped up work on its island creation in the South China Sea. The Western media generallhy interpreted this to be a pre-Dialogue attempt by the Chinese to reassure the United States that it had no further territorial ambitions in the area, an interpretation that implies some level of Chinese deference.

I have a different interpretation. I believe the Chinese were clearly stating, as a matter of fact, that the new islands are there—live with it. They don't want to waste any time at the Dialogue negotiating over what they consider to be nonnegotiable.

The Western article I read on the topic quoted several "experts" on the topic, all attempting to decipher the Chinese smoke signals and all pontificating about what the Chinese may or may not do in the future. While much of the conjecture has to do with whether or not China will use the newly created islands for military installations, the gravest conjecture of all appeared to be whether or not China would eventually declare the entire area an air defense identification zone, essentially preventing the military aircraft of other nations—including spy planes—from using the air space.

But of course it will. There is absolutely no sense in debating that. I can only hope that the US government doesn't waste a lot of taxpayer money hiring professors, think tanks, and consultants in an attempt to decipher China's intent. They need only put the comments in the context of the Chinese receiver-oriented, indirect communication style, and even an ordinary citizen can figure it out in mere minutes. From the Chinese perspective, there is nothing to talk about.

The debate over who owns what land has always struck me as a bit disingenuous. History is not a postcard. It's a motion picture. Who owns what is a matter of where you pause the movie.

The Americans clearly don't "own" the United States. Sure, the claim would easily hold up in a court of law, but fairness and truth are not the stock-in-trade of the legal system in the United States. Pragmatism is.

And did the Dutch really buy Manhattan for trinkets worth $24? Maybe. But even if they did, any contemporary judge in the United States would invalidate the sale for some technical reason, I'm sure.

And what about Europe? Who really owns Europe? Again, it depends where you pause the movie of history. The Greeks, rather than begging for handouts from the EU, might be smarter to simply lay legal claims to its former empire. That would surely solve their cash flow issues, and who is to argue at which point the movie should be paused? Indigenous people all over the world are clearly and effectively making that point.

Like it or not, pragmatism, when it comes to matters of territorial claims, is a matter of will—or lack of will, when it comes to those in a position to change the reality. Does Russia have a right to annex Crimea? Who knows? Who cares? They did and nobody, including NATO, is going to drive them out. Fait accompli.

Will the United States return San Diego to Mexico? San Antonio? Of course not.

Our children's children will think of the Spratley Islands and the South China Sea in much the same way. Of course they are part of China. Who is going to rewrite that history?

I honestly don't understand the political aversion to pragmatism. Well, actually, I do. At the end of the day, politicians have no incentive to change. On the contrary, their importance is firmly cemented in the status quo. It is only the threat of being voted out of office—or revolution—that will cause a politician to consider foundational change. That is not a derogatory accusation. It is merely a mirror on the incentives that shape their thoughts and actions.

All of which creates a bit of a conundrum for the United States. It made a lot of commitments at a time when the balance of power was decidedly different in the world. China was a mere shadow of its current presence and might. Russia was strong, but Europe was stronger. Both realities have changed.

Would the United States really commit to all-out war if China invaded Japan? Could it? With its resources already tied up in the deserts of Iraq and Afghanistan, how much of a fight is it prepared to wage? Don't get me wrong. The American military is the mightiest in the world without a doubt. But even it has limits as to how many fronts it can engage on—short of blowing up the planet, of course.

Which brings me to Taiwan. Here is the stickiest wicket of all for the Americans. I don't have to predict whether or not Taiwan will eventually be part of China. It already is. Eventually it will be formally incorporated on a similar foundation that Hong Kong has. In the meantime independence is merely a matter of semantics—and the Taiwanese, in the end, both accept and welcome that reality. It's a nation of twenty-five million people, roughly the size of Shanghai. What possible reason could there be for them to lunge at that windmill? And they don't want to anyway.

Imagine how much taxes could be reduced if we elected our political representatives on the basis of pragmatism instead of ideology. Don't get me wrong; ideology is great, as far as it goes. But that's not very far. Geopolitics is governed by the laws of nature. And nature doesn't stray far from pragmatism. Nature lives by the laws of the food chain.

So does geopolitics. Only the politicians don't get it. Or maybe they do. Perhaps they are merely living in their own pragmatism. There's money, after all, to be made in pontification. Plenty of money.

As one who helps foot the bill, I'm not bitter about that. Such is the way things work. I just hope that ultimately we keep it all in perspective.

As I said before, the islands are there. And there will be military installations there—visible or not. Let's move on.

CHAPTER 50

HOLISTIC POLITICS

Holistic (adjective of the noun *holism*) is a word no one used as I was growing up. And, unfortunately, like a lot of our language, it has been usurped by the world of corporate jargon where companies are centric-this and centric-that when a mere "this is important to us" would do. To many of us, that in itself gives the word holistic the feeling of a word that has no application in real life.

But if used correctly, it does, and you can't avoid it when talking about China, particularly Chinese politics. It goes further than any other word in explaining why Chinese politicians baffle their counterparts in the West and why every move the Chinese government makes is predictable, consistent, and generally, a total surprise to the West.

Merriam-Webster, an Encyclopedia Britannica company, defines holistic as "relating to or concerned with complete systems rather than individual parts." In the past it has primarily been associated with alternative approaches to contemporary Western medicine. In addition to the example of holistic medicine, Merriam-Webster uses the example of the more contemporary concept of holistic ecology, which "views humans and the environment as a single system."

For a Chinese definition, I would say that the Chinese view "the body, society, and the universe, both visible and not, past and present, as a single system." It's a broad view, but in a way, a more holistic view than the Western definition (sorry for the pun).

The opposite of holistic, I would suggest, would be individualism. Things exist individually but can become something else when combined.

It implies discreet steps in logic and behavior that move only in one direction, typically left to right, much like deductive logic. If you want to get someplace, you start walking, one step at a time. These steps (cause) take you in the direction you want to go (effect) in an orderly and predictable process, the preoccupation of the deductive Western world view.

It is true that many Westerners, particularly in business and sports, are fond of saying, "The whole is greater than the sum of its parts." But this is often more of a motivational imploration than a world view. Why else would US corporations continue to give individual performance reviews or would professional sports teams apply such disparate values to individual players?

The American political system has become incremental in the extreme. The electorate often votes on a single issue of particular importance to them, and the emergence of the powerful special interest group is itself the ultimate testament to the trend. A single interest is, by definition, incremental and individual in its focus.

Political party affiliation, while still meaningful, is becoming far less so, a fact reinforced by the number of successful politicians who have declared their official independence. Even the president cannot count on the support of all members of his own political party despite the far-reaching importance of reaching any settlement at all.

The fifth estate and voters alike now insist that political candidates talk only about the issues and take stands on specific issues that they have no reason to have any expertise in. One result of this, of course, is that our government policy is really determined by a tapestry of unelected experts who do have experience in the many specific issues that an incremental electorate is totally focused on.

One has to believe that during the colonial era in America, voters were more focused on the individual and his character, standing, and past behavior than his current position on any specific issue. It's hard to imagine a public political debate in which George Washington or Thomas Jefferson was grilled about their positions on foreign policy relating to specific nations or the individual rights of specific social subgroups whose behaviors or beliefs posed no threat to the community but merely fell outside the norm.

Slavery, of course, did become an incremental issue, as well it should have. But that was an issue of extraordinary proportion that had implications for the future of society itself. It clearly rose to the level of moral imperative, a bar reached by relatively few of the special interests today (eg, special subsidies for the sugar industry).

Chinese politicians, by contrast, remain completely holistic in their world view. While individual Chinese are following their Western cousins along a path of individualism, the Communist Party of China (CPC) is not. It remains completely holistic in both its decision-making and its public posture.

Fewer than 6 percent of the Chinese population belongs to the CPC, although it alone controls all things political in China. This in itself is evidence of the holistic Chinese world view. As Confucius himself noted, a government cannot rule by the sword alone. The power of rule requires the voluntary acceptance of the ruled if it is to survive the sixty-plus years that the CPC has.

And is it even plausible that each member of the CPC shares the same perspective on all issues? It's unthinkable. I'm sure there is as much division within the party as there is within any governing body, be it the UN or the local school board in the United States.

The difference is the holistic world view that holds the government of China together and has allowed it to do things that few other developing countries, including India and Brazil, have been able to replicate.

A current example.

At the end of August 2015, Beijing hosted the World Track and Field Championships and celebrated the seventieth anniversary of the end of World War II, culminating in a giant military parade on September 3 to commemorate the specific surrender of Japan, its adversary during the war.

Starting in early August, the government set up security checkpoints on all roads leading into Beijing. Every car and truck was stopped. Licenses and registrations were carefully checked. The contents of the vehicle were carefully scrutinized.

Anyone mailing a letter or parcel to a Beijing address had to present identification to the receiving postal authority or carrier, and all delivery companies were given strict security protocols to follow.

And, of course, the government promised "APEC blue" skies, so factories and construction sites were closed down throughout Beijing and its neighboring provinces. The steel mills of Tianjin and Hebei Province were ordered to cease production during most of August and September (the government apparently wanted to ensure blue skies for the Mid-Autumn Festival, which falls at the end of September, and the important National Day Golden Week that begins October 1 and is a popular time for Chinese to visit their capital).

For the same reason, from August 20 until September 3, cars were allowed to drive in Beijing only every other day on an even/odd plate system similar to the one employed during the Summer Olympics of 2008. Cars not registered in Beijing were not allowed in the capital at all.

Security bureaus in the areas surrounding Beijing were also put on alert and took strong measures to limit the access of potential terrorists to industrial materials that could be used to disrupt the festivities, closing even more factories and limiting the transportation of critical industrial raw materials.

Even the subways were swarming for most of August with police who used handheld electronic devices to check the ID cards of Chinese nationals they chose randomly and/or profiled and pulled out of the crowds.

Inconvenient? Yes. Acceptable? To the Chinese, yes.

———

Imagine that you are a political analyst on either side of the Pacific. For the Chinese analyst predicting American political intent, the process is fairly straightforward. You merely watch the nightly news and the Sunday morning talk shows. The politicians are happy to tell us what they think and what they are doing to achieve that result.

And public opinion polls keep us continuously informed of what the populace is thinking, at least that portion of the populace who is willing to participate in such polls and provide honest answers that have enough conviction to stand over time.

If you want to know how a US politician feels about China's island-building in the South China Sea, you need just to ask. They will be happy to tell you. And depending on who they are and what political office they hold, it is relatively easy to conclude with some certainty how much influence that opinion will have on America's ultimate behavior on the topic.

The question then becomes only one of capability. Even if the United States is unhappy with China's growing influence in the South China Sea, what will it do about it? Or, more appropriately, what can it do about it? This, I assure you, is the real discussion going on behind closed doors in Beijing.

And the obvious answer is that the United States will, or can, do nothing, despite pressure from its allies, Japan and the Philippines, to play the big brother in this schoolyard dispute. The United States is without question the most powerful military force in the world. It is not about to turn that force against China, however, over sovereignty over a group of uninhabited atolls that pose no offensive threat to the US mainland.

China, for its part, will never back down, despite exhaustive attempts at diplomacy from the West. And, I have no doubt, it would not hesitate to engage militarily to back up its claim.

And the reason is simple. To the Chinese, this is not about the South China Sea. This is only part of a much larger holism having to do with national pride and China's role in the future of Southeast Asia. It's about assuring its people that the horrors of World War II will never again occur on Chinese soil and that the face of those who built America's railroads and did its laundry will be restored.

But the real difference here is that the individualist West believes in narrative. It believes in the power of diplomacy and that there is always a path (an incremental geometry) to the solution it desires—a win-win.

The Chinese, on the other hand, believe, as Confucius famously said, "Wherever you go, there you are." The holistic narrative isn't a narrative at all. It is merely what is and what is not. While this can change over time, such change results not from linear diplomacy but from changes, for whatever reason, in the balance of power.

This is, in part, why the speeches of Chinese politicians, even to the Chinese, are frightfully boring and void of any real actionable meaning. US political analysts painstakingly attempt to interpret the "meaning" of key political addresses, an exercise largely useless in reality.

Instead, American political analysts should focus solely on the holistic Chinese objective. Everything they do is subordinate to, and supportive of, that objective.

CONCLUSION

In the preceding chapters, I have feebly attempted to share just a small sliver of what the Chinese have taught me in my years living and working here. At the very least, I hope I have provided a glimmer of insight into the why behind the what.

There is the linear versus the circular, the deductive versus the inductive. There is the long rich history, the years of colonization, the plundering at the hands of foreign governments. There have been the decades of suffering and doing without. There has been the hukou system, the Cultural Revolution, and the current purge of corruption at the highest levels.

So many explanations. And yet, in the end I'm not convinced that the Chinese care about explanations, at least not in the way that we as Westerners do. They want solutions. They relish advancement.

They write beautiful poetry. Their artwork is full of creativity and symbolism. But these are art forms. These are crafts that are themselves beautiful and timeless and born of tradition.

But I am not convinced that they have any real desire to contemplate the universe, to understand the meaning of life. Why are we here? What is our purpose? Isn't that what we in the West spend our lives attempting to understand?

But we never quite get there. There have been noble attempts. And the monotheistic religions appear to provide the road map to an answer. But even those maps assume that we are journeying to somewhere—a place that can be defined.

But perhaps there is no such destination. Perhaps the question is the answer.

In the Robin Williams movie *Awakenings*, Williams played British neurologist Oliver Sacks, who in 1969 discovered the beneficial effects of the drug L-dopa when administered to catatonic patients who survived the 1917–1928 epidemic of encephalitis lethargic. In this true story, the neurologist begins to theorize that the brain of these patients is operating relatively normally, but its output is contained by the physical catatonia.

So he poses the theory to his then-retired predecessor who spent years working with these patients and who replied quite adamantly that the young doctor's theory was pure folly; that these patients have no thought or feeling, expressed or otherwise. And when the young doctor asked why that was such a farfetched theory, the elder doctor replied simply, "Because the alternative is simply unthinkable."

And so, perhaps, it is with the Chinese. "Wherever you go, there you are." It can either be the most complex philosophy or the simplest observation. Or perhaps both.

And why should we care which it is? Perhaps there is only family and obligation. Perhaps everything else is just a futile attempt to explain that which, in the end, doesn't really matter anyway.

It gives me a certain serenity to think about life in those terms. And perhaps in the end, that is the greatest gift of all that I have received from the Chinese.

I am intensely proud of my American heritage. To me it will always be the shining city on the hill that the ever-optimistic Ronald Reagan so powerfully referred to.

China, as I've so feebly attempted to articulate, is a very different place at every level. The people look and behave differently; they speak a different and difficult language; their world view is in many ways the polar opposite of the one I held for more than half of a century prior to moving here.

And at first, like most Western expatriates living in China, I found that to be the source of great stress. There was never a break. As soon as you walk out the door or even turn on the television, there it is. The difference.

The difference, as I often note, between the straight line and the circle; the difference between deductive and inductive logic; the difference between Aristotle and Confucius.

After all this time, however, I must admit that I now find the opposite to be true. When I return to the United States, I relish the clean air, the ability to drink water straight from the tap, the ease with which I can communicate with other people in my native tongue. At the same time, however, I find myself increasingly out of place. America has lost its feel of familiarity. But more than that, it has lost its—what to call it—simplicity, innocence, predictability?

That's it. Predictability. America, for me, the land of my birth, has lost its predictability.

But why?

Part of the reason, of course, is simple familiarity itself. Much of my firsthand knowledge of day-to-day America is outdated. Culturally speaking, the years I have lived in China is a lifetime in this day and age. I seldom even turn on the television when I go to the United States now, despite the seemingly infinite choice of channels, simply because the faces and the drama I find there are completely unknown to me. (Television is highly regulated here. Satellites and foreign-streaming TV are not available.)

Part of the reason, however, I think gets down to the fundamental issue of predictability. It's the other side of the coin of stress, which psychologists tell us is not a function of pressure, but our sense of control, or lack thereof. People in high-pressure jobs who nonetheless feel that the task at hand is within their abilities and the tools at their disposal may feel relatively little stress. People performing simple and repetitive jobs, on the other hand, are often overwhelmed with stress due to their total lack of control over the work they do.

Western behavior used to be equally predictable for me. Westerners are linear and absolute in their world view, so they tend to be idealists in the sense that they project ideal behavior in the face of uncertainty. They give people the benefit of the doubt. Predictability, as a result, was less urgent, less necessary.

If someone approached you in a crowd, you didn't need to give it much thought. You could generally assume that person meant you no harm. He or she probably wasn't about to cheat you out of your spot in line. Heck, the person was probably friendly.

At least that used to be the cultural norm. I wonder, however, if America isn't losing some of that idealism, and, in the process, some of the predictability that goes with it.

If I'm waiting in a line in the United States today, I can't be at all sure that someone won't attempt to cut. But more importantly, when that happens, I'm not at all confident how to react. If I stand my ground, will the person react in the same way that a Chinese person would, or will there be a confrontation or conflict? And will the people around me support my move to enforce justice, or will they look the other way?

Part of the change is simply a reflection of added mobility and the anonymity that enables. I grew up in a small town of a few thousand people, where people left their car keys in the ignition and many homeowners had long forgotten where they left the keys to the house, even if they were inclined to lock the door while away on a trip. (What if a neighbor needed to borrow some eggs?)

Those days are gone, of course, and I don't lament them per se. The world is smaller.

The Internet, of course, has made it smaller still. You may well be reading these words at the same time as someone you've never met on the other side of the planet. Such is the wired world.

One of the by-products of that connectivity is the ability for relatively small groups of people to bond over some shared passion or interest—good or evil. Marketers refer to it as selling to the long tail. The customers for your product or service may be relatively small in number and scattered across the globe. And you can, due to connectivity, create a viable commercial market that would have been financially unsustainable when connectivity was largely limited to the physical movement of goods and information.

But connectivity has also created another long tail—the tail of microcultures. One of America's great strengths always has been its melting-pot structure, with the ability to assimilate diverse ethnicities and cultures. America's extreme connectivity now enables sustainable diversity of every kind. Your physical neighbors no longer represent the community in which you live and with which you identify. They are merely people who share the same day for garbage collection.

Time magazine recently republished an article by Sierra Mannie entitled "Dear White Gays: Stop Stealing Black Female Culture." The point of the article was powerful and well articulated, but I was horrified nonetheless. I had no idea that black women or gay white men had their own cultures. Affiliations, yes; interests, yes; shared political agendas, yes; but cultures?

When I was growing up in America, your culture was generally defined by your ethnic heritage or the region of your birth. There was French culture and New England culture, and so on. But even they generally shared a common world view. The reason people came to America, for the most part, was to share in that world view of cause and effect, hard work and success, talent and opportunity.

China, as I've noted many times, is home to fifty-six officially recognized ethnic groups. And it is, in my experience, a people and a country that truly embraces diversity. They accept differences as a simple fact of life. I am a foreigner with a big nose and always will be. But that's OK.

There is, nonetheless, a homogeneity to the Chinese world view and the inductive, holistic logic on which it is based, which is genuinely reassuring in its predictability. I get it. I understand the circular cause and effect that creates logic that is, dare I say it, deductively logical.

Cause and effect. "Wherever you go, there you are."

It makes sense. It's predictable. And that is quite comforting to me. It took me many years to accept the logic of inductive thinking, but now that I have, it is the source of great calm, great insight, and great respect for the people who tutored me.

Xie Xie!

APPENDIX

I've covered a lot of ground, so I thought it might be helpful to boil it all down to my own top ten—the ten most important things the Chinese have taught me in my time here. Here they are:

1. To look at problems holistically.

As a Westerner I was taught to solve problems by uncovering the root cause(s). And such deductive analysis can be helpful in understanding cause and effect. Such granular reasoning, however, can cause you to miss the universe for the atom.

Instead of stepping into a problem, sometimes you need to step back to fully understand the context within which a problem exists. It is this context that often defines a problem and gives it shape. It may not amount to cause and effect, but it is the context that often gives a problem sustenance, so it is context that often holds the key to definitive resolution.

Side note: In the West we sometimes call this the big picture, but it's not a picture at all, and "seeing" it is not just a function of enlarging the frame of your vision. Context is more like an autostereogram. It's always there. And you can't discover it one section at a time. It's the picture behind the picture. Once you make the right adjustment, the original vision changes completely.

2. To have hope.

An Indian writer noted that when she spoke to a man cleaning a public toilet in China, the man expressed great confidence that he would some day own his own business. The man doing the same job in India, she noted, surely has no such expectation. For the moment, the Chinese people are full of hope, and it's contagious. A better life is just around the corner. How can you not buy into that?

3. To appreciate the importance of flow.

If you've visited China more than once, you have surely marveled at the pace of change that is evident here. As they used to say about the weather in my native New England, "If it doesn't suit you, wait a minute. It will change."

Change, however, is only the superficial manifestation of flow. To understand China, and, I am coming to believe, life itself, you must understand flow. The Chinese, who understand the importance of flow and apply it to every aspect of life, from traditional Chinese medicine (the flow of *qi*), to the notions of good and bad luck (*yun qi*), to the weather (*tian qi*), recognize that life is not static.

Nor is it linear. Beginning and end can occupy the same logical place on the continuum of reason (eg, in the death of an era comes the birth of another). "White" lies and "black" lies are but lies told in different contexts. Success and failure exist only against a backdrop of time.

This must be why water plays such an important metaphorical role in Chinese culture. As we all learned in elementary school, the oceans cover three-quarters of the planet's surface. To understand the oceans, however, we must understand the currents that define them. It is the currents, not the water itself, that give the oceans their sustenance and define the mutable patterns within which the life therein transpires.

4. To value clean air and water.

The next time you drink water from the tap or swim in a clear lake with a blue sky above, be thankful for what you have. Clean water and clean air are priceless. Truly priceless. I've come to believe that everyone is entitled to priceless things, such as love and safety. The rest is just logistics and financing.

We get too hung up on who is to blame and who should pay (linear issues of cause and effect, in the end) and lose sight of the fact that we, collectively, allowed cause and effect to play out. Either through our direct actions, our buying behaviors, or simply through our collective refusal to act, we've all contributed in a way. Pollution is a global issue, and we must all be part of the solution.

5. To appreciate the power of suffering.

Driving to work each day, I left the cosmopolitan comfort of world-class Beijing and entered the rural China that remains home to hundreds of millions of the poorest Chinese. As I watched them live and work in the harshest and most unforgiving of conditions, I was forced to marvel again and again at the Chinese people's capacity for suffering.

If the West needs to fear anything about the Chinese, in my humble opinion, this is the one thing to be feared most—their capacity for suffering. Whatever the contest—war or commerce—the ability to endure suffering is a weapon that, in the most literal sense, has no defense.

6. To realize what really matters.

In Maslow's hierarchy of needs, the need for connection is number three. We cannot feel fulfilled or realize our full potential until we feel a sense of connection to the people and world around us. I am a foreigner here and will forever remain one, but I have learned from observation what true personal commitment and obligation really looks like.

7. To put process in perspective.

The violation of process is the root cause of a lot of stress in the West. I know. I was the quintessential rule-follower when I moved here. It annoyed me to no end when someone cut in line or otherwise disrupted the orderly flow of everyday life as my deductively molded mind came to define order and the need for it.

The Chinese have helped me to realize what a slave to process I had become and how much of my daily stress and angst flowed from that one simple obsession.

In the West we talk yearningly of the innocence of youth. But it is not the innocence of youth we've lost at all. I have come to believe that innocence never leaves us. We just learn to confine it in a prison of adult-minded process.

8. To have pragmatism.

In the 1980s an American TV show called *MacGyver* featured an everyday guy who could accomplish anything with everyday things. He could build a 1,000-kilowatt power station out of discarded avocado pits or craft a working computer out of used paper towels.

Well, MacGyver is alive and well and living in China. When you free your thinking from the burden of cause and effect and focus exclusively on outcome rather than deductive theory, anything is possible. Things that can't be done are. *To do* is but another tense of *done*.

(Yes, I know, MacGyver relied on the physical sciences to accomplish his feats of wonder. But that is but explanation. What held our fascination was what he did, not how he did it.)

9. To smile.

Most Westerners consider the Chinese to be inscrutable in their facial expressions. And that, I believe, is a byproduct of the Chinese aversion to wasted effort.

When the Westerners aren't looking, however—remember, we are foreigners, so more than a little inexplicable and worthy of caution, at the very least—what the Chinese do best is smile. I have endless images in my mind of Chinese peasants working in the fields, smiling ear to ear under an oppressive sun. It's an effortless smile, full of abandonment and devoid of restraint or structure.

It is a smile born of hardship and the wisdom to put it all in perspective. The wisdom to know that this, whatever this is, either bad *or good*, shall pass. And wherever we go in this life, there shall we be.

10. To know how to communicate.

Language is but simple symbolism designed to promote efficient communication. And it is notoriously poor at the job.

Or is it our reliance on language, not language itself, which is at the heart of the problem? Is it our inability or unwillingness to listen that is the root cause of our universal failure to communicate?

I live in a country of 1.3 billion people whose language I speak no more proficiently than a two-year-old. And yet in all of my years, I have never felt more capable of real communication.

I believe the reason is that my ability to rely on language has been stripped away, forcing me—appropriately so, given my location—into a more holistic, less process-driven approach to communication. You might say that because I cannot communicate, I have been forced to listen.

And in the act of listening, really listening, with my eyes, my ears, and my mind, I have learned the greatest lesson of all—an understanding of self. It took more than 1.3 billion tutors to get me there, but I think I'm finally starting to understand me—a foreigner in Beijing.

My sincerest and humblest thanks to each and every one of you for reading my musings. May the coming year bring you closer to the world and the people around *you*.